Developmental Ruptures

This book questions the diagnostic categories applied to adolescents from a developmental viewpoint, putting forth an alternative perspective for assessment that considers prognostic and risk indicators.

Going beyond the classification of adult psychopathology, Anna Maria Nicolò presents a multidimensional approach to the adolescent mind that explores its complexities through a clinical lens and accompanying theoretical prism. Often, crises in adolescence might well mark the onset of a psychotic process that does not respect phase-specific tasks. Yet in other cases, such developmental ruptures are the opportunity for a positive reorganisation of personality. In this way, adolescence may highlight latent childhood functioning or allow for new integrations. Therefore, accurate diagnosis and early intervention are necessary to enable the developmental reorganisation of both the patient and the family. Drawing on clinical case material, this book provides readers with the practical and theoretical tools to intervene in developmental ruptures.

Developmental Ruptures will appeal to psychoanalysts, psychiatrists, and developmental psychologists, as well as to people working with psychotic onset and crises emerging particularly at the outset of puberty or young adulthood.

Anna Maria Nicolò, MD, child neuropsychiatrist, Training Analyst and Full Member of the Società Psicoanalitica Italiana (SPI) and International Psychoanalytical Association (IPA), expert in child and adolescent psychoanalysis. Past President of the SPI. President of the International Association of Couple and Family Psychoanalysis (IACFP). She is a member of the Forum for Adolescence of the European Psychoanalytical Federation (FEP) Committee, of which she was Chair. Director of the *Journal Interazioni*.

THE NEW LIBRARY OF PSYCHOANALYSIS
General Editor: Anne Patterson

The *New Library of Psychoanalysis* is published by Routledge Mental Health in association with the *Institute of Psychoanalysis*, London. The purpose of the book series is:

- to advance and disseminate ideas in psychoanalysis amongst those working in psychoanalysis, psychotherapy and related fields
- to facilitate a greater and more widespread appreciation of psychoanalysis in the general book-reading public
- to provide a forum for increasing mutual understanding between psychoanalysts and those in other disciplines
- to facilitate communication between different traditions and cultures within psychoanalysis, making some of the work of continental and other non-English speaking analysts more readily available to English-speaking readers, and increasing the interchange of ideas between British and American analysts.

The *New Library of Psychoanalysis* published its first book in 1987 under the editorship of David Tuckett, who was followed by Elizabeth Bott Spillius, Susan Budd, Dana Birksted-Breen and Alessandra Lemma. The Editors, including the current Editor, Anne Patterson, have been assisted by a considerable number of Associate Editors and readers from a range of countries and psychoanalytic traditions. The present Associate Editors are Susanne Calice, Katalin Lanczi and Anna Streeruwitz.

Under the guidance of Foreign Rights Editors, a considerable number of the *New Library* books have been published abroad, particularly in Brazil, Germany, France, Italy, Peru, Spain and Japan. The *New Library of Psychoanalysis* has also translated and published several books by continental psychoanalysts and plans to continue the policy of publishing books that express as clearly as possible a variety of psychoanalytic points of view. The *New Library of Psychoanalysis* has published books representing all three schools of thought in British psychoanalysis, including a particularly important

"In this fascinating volume, Anna Nicolò masterfully combines her long and in-depth international experience with the innovative creativity of Italian psychoanalysis, of which she is today one of the most authoritative and appreciated exponents. The result is a free and wide-ranging - though rigorous - capacity for theoretical articulation, with special effectiveness in the in-depth clinical reading of adolescent situations and their kaleidoscopic evolutionary complexity."

Stefano Bolognini, *IPA past president*

"In her excellent book *Developmental Ruptures*, Anna Maria Nicolò gives a vivid and subtle representation of adolescent psychic turmoil. She goes beyond the classification of adult psychopathology, to detect the evolutive power most often hidden in adolescent ruptures and collapses. Due to her exceptional clinical and theoretical competences, she opens broadly the field of observation and of listening of adolescent patients, and she proves that 'adolescence is not only a temporal phase, but also an enzyme that permeates the mind and forces to confront oneself with the life cycle' – as she writes. Every practitioner in the field of psychic disease will benefit from reading this outstanding book."

Florence Guignard, *Founder of the Société Européenne pour la Psychanalyse de l'Enfant et de l'Adolescent (Sepea), Honorary full member of the Paris Psychoanalytical Society (SPP)*

"This book is an important contribution to the psychoanalysis of young people. The author shares her vast clinical experience and also her approach to theory from a pluralistic and open approach. We have long been used to thinking in terms of processes and continuities. The concept of ruptures is very timely in the context of the times we have been living in, where uncertainty and disruption predominate. Children and adolescents are the most vulnerable and prone to break-ups in this context. This book is essential reading for those who work with these patients."

Virginia Ungar, *M.D., Buenos Aires Psychoanalytic Association; IPA Past President*

work edited by Pearl King and Riccardo Steiner, "*The Freud-Klein Controversies 1941–45,*" expounding the intellectual and organisational controversies that developed in the British psychoanalytical Society between Kleinian, Viennese and "middle group" analysts during the Second World War.

The *New Library of Psychoanalysis* aims for excellence in psychoanalytic publishing. Submitted manuscripts are rigorously peer-reviewed in order to ensure high standards of scholarship, clinical communications, and writing.

For a full list of all the titles in the New Library of Psychoanalysis main series as well as both the New Library of Psychoanalysis "Teaching Series" and "Beyond the Couch" subseries, please visit the Routledge website.

Developmental Ruptures

The Psychoanalysis of Breakdown and Defensive Solutions

First Edition

Anna Maria Nicolò
Translated by Olivia Marchese

Routledge
Taylor & Francis Group

LONDON AND NEW YORK

First English edition published 2024
by Routledge
4 Park Square, Milton Park, Abingdon, Oxon, OX14 4RN

and by Routledge
605 Third Avenue, New York, NY 10158

Routledge is an imprint of the Taylor & Francis Group, an informa business

Translated by Olivia Marchese

First published in Italian by Raffaello Cortina Editore 2021

ISBN: 978-1-032-66335-7 (hbk)
ISBN: 978-1-032-66334-0 (pbk)
ISBN: 978-1-032-66337-1 (ebk)

DOI: 10.4324/9781032663371
Typeset in Bembo
by MPS Limited, Dehradun

Contents

Preface to the English edition   xi

Introduction   1

PART 1
The adolescent and developmental ruptures   15

1 The adolescent mind   17

2 The problem of assessment in adolescence   29

3 Breakdown and developmental ruptures   48

4 The negated, repudiated, persecutory body   72

5 Sensoriality and developmental ruptures   91

6 Fear of breakdown and beyond   102

7 Developmental ruptures: A transformative pathway   115

8 Pathological transpersonal links and adolescent
breakdown   135

PART 2
The defence against developmental breakdown   153

9   Perverse solutions and perversion   155

10   Daydreams and their evolutions   176

11   Martina: Alienation in the other   191

12   Violence as a defence against breakdown   201

13   Delusion, secrets and reciprocity   214

14   The transgender enigma   234

15   Self-harm and cutting   255

Preface to the English edition

Anna Maria Nicolò

In my practice as adolescent psychiatrist and psychoanalyst, I have encountered patients who at various times, from puberty to young adulthood, displayed severe symptoms that could point to psychotic functioning. A number of them, after careful intervention, both individual and environmental, resumed life and development. However, others worsened, as their disorder grew permanently chronic. The assessment of these situations is highly complex, also considering that in adolescence, due to the typical features of this age, certain signs may mimic psychotic symptomatology. The preconscious is not yet fully organised, impulsivity and acting are inherently present, thereby clouding processing and thinking abilities, as I discuss in the chapter on assessment, and as we are also told by numerous neuroscientists who study the peculiarities of the adolescent brain (Siegel, 2013; Monniello, 2019).

Moreover, in adolescence, the true challenge is the re-founding of identity, using and transforming the past we all carry with us.

The central focus of this book is therefore the distinction between developmental rupture, a crisis that can evolve in different directions depending on various factors that I discuss in the book, and psychotic onset, which can be variously compensated for, yet whose structure may remain throughout life. Upon emergence of this crisis, it is necessary to intervene early on and effectively, to catch the young person in time, as Bollas (2013) tells us in a fine volume whose title is significant: *Catch Them Before They Fall.*

These cases have greatly challenged me and I have sought help, questioning experienced psychoanalysts and of course benefiting from my clinical work with patients, who always remain the analyst's "best colleagues," as Bion put it.

Moses and Eglé Laufer's findings on breakdown (1984) proved enlightening for me, for a number of reasons, but particularly due to the developmental viewpoint put forth.

They have enriched us by allowing us to view the evolving diagnosis with the relativity that comes with growth over time. They have marked and distinguished psychotic manifestations, differentiating structure from psychotic organisation and crisis. I am particularly grateful to Eglé Laufer (2002) for her pioneering attention to the centrality of the body at this age and to its vicissitudes, and I have always admired her extraordinary clinical intuition.

However, many other colleagues have clarified issues that remained obscure and enigmatic to me, first and foremost one of my Italian supervisors, Arnaldo Novelletto, with his insights into the adolescent Self (2009), and his support in attendance to the Italian seminars that Raymond Cahn repeatedly held in Rome. Nonetheless, this long-standing research has been complex and diverse.

Threads of various colours weave the canvas

In January 1924, Paul Klee held a talk at the Kunstverein in Jena on the occasion of one of his exhibitions. The conference was published more than two decades later, in 1945, under the title *On Modern Art*, and in it, which is perhaps the summation of Klee's reflections on art, he illustrates the growth of a painter's work of art by resorting to an interesting comparison. The work of art is like a tree whose roots sink into the ground and constitute a dawn of the visible through which the invisible sap penetrates the artist's person and then flows to the artist; the latter is therefore the trunk that passes on what he or she has seen while the artist's work is the crown of the tree. Klee then adds that "nobody would affirm that the tree grows its crown in the image of its root," therefore, "between above and below can be no mirrored reflection" (1945, p. 13).

In this case, the artist is merely a mediator, occupying a rather modest position in that the beauty of the crown has passed through him or her. Yet in the midst of this operation, "the artist [is] at times denied those departures from nature which his art demands. He has even been charged with incompetence and deliberate distortion" (p. 13). Anyone who produces scientific or artistic work, no matter how small, no matter how far from the magnitude of a work of art such as Paul Klee's, will be in the same position of bringing into their work, as roots, the thought of others who have preceded them, but to then transform it by giving, if capable, a new development, an original shape and innovative thoughts.

In our field, this happens to all psychoanalysts who draw on Freud as a core framework, continuously transforming it and revitalising it. How faithful are you, or to what extent do you betray the work of your masters? How faithful are you to Freud, or to what extent do you believe you are following the thought of a master, but are actually using it to communicate your beliefs? I confess this is a question I no longer ask myself, as it simply might not be possible to answer. Many threads converge into weaving the canvas of an analyst's thoughts, theories, and technique at work. The final product will encompass experiences that have been internalised and transformed into a new fabric.

The roots of this book are therefore numerous, and in the course of my professional life I have found several teachers, as mentioned in the introduction, using their teaching and sometimes readjusting it according to my subjectivity and the patient's need.

Early in my profession, I undertook Kleinian psychoanalysis and then continued with a Winnicottian-oriented training. At the same time, prompted by political interests in anti-psychiatry, I trained in systems therapy and studied the relationship model in the therapeutic approach to the family and couple. The study of pathology in these settings allowed me to learn about very diverse theoretical models in psychotherapy and to work with leading clinicians in the field. Through the one-way mirror, I had the chance to observe the work of remarkable family therapists. It was a markedly intense period of criticism to psychoanalysis in many fields of the cultural world and in psychiatry, also on the spur of Franco Basaglia's anti-psychiatric movement as it spread in Italy and parts of Europe; yet in other countries, there was correspondence in the clinical experiences and theories of Ronald Laing.

Studies such as these allowed me to discover different psychoanalytic models by contrast, which were far more open to the study of the relational world surrounding the individual, and to question the nature of the unconscious.

Furthermore, at the *Istituto di Neuropsichiatria Infantile dell'Università degli Studi di Roma* [Institute of Child Neuropsychiatry of the University of Rome, translator's note], where I specialised (as I write in the introduction to the Italian edition), I was developing a strong interest in Winnicott's approach: his discoveries on the specific nature of the mother-child relationship, the transitional space that is neither completely subjective nor completely objective, an illusion yet also real, in a creative paradox that we can merely accept, without being able to resolve. To date, I believe this approach to be the best explanatory theory we might use in clinical and observational work.

Moreover, working with severe patients and in particular adolescents has inevitably prompted me to observe the patient in his or her internal world, in his or her interactions with the other, as well as in his or her concrete, acted-out manifestations.

Speaking of *Interactions* refers not only to the phantasmatic relations on which psychoanalysis has long reflected upon, but also to the actions between individuals, the acted out behaviours, and thus to the person as a whole, through body and psyche, inevitably modified by the other and capable of modifying them. Indeed, two paradigms are counterposed, one that is well represented by Green, who while discussing an interactionist work by the American psychoanalyst T. Jacobs at the 1993 IPA Congress in Amsterdam, authoritatively and polemically asserted that in psychoanalysis "there is no place in an analytic session for acts, either by the analysand or by the analyst" and that "models based on a reference to action-'interaction,' 'trans-action' – thus represent not so much a step forward as a dangerous sidetrack" (Green, 1993, p. 1135). On the contrary, another paradigm asserts that interactions are phantasmatic and may contain content, experiences and communications that are acted out rather than represented (Nicolaus & Raineri, 1997). However, in the last two decades, a major revolution has taken place in the very field of psychoanalysis and psychology with a gradual and inevitable slow shift in focus from a unipersonal to an intersubjective perspective, a shift that we might call "a quiet revolution." We thus use a term otherwise employed by many psychoanalysts, from Ogden to Fonagy, to indicate the quiet but revolutionary operation induced by Sandler, through the production of ever-evolving convergences between psychology, object relations theory, Kleinian theory, and interpersonal psychology (Fonagy, 2005). Indeed, we might say that the findings of the last three decades point in this direction, beginning with Winnicott's (1989) assertion: there is no such thing as an infant without his or her environment.

In various parts of the world, in parallel, the topics of group, institution, couple, family, and extensions of the setting in psychoanalysis have been explored.

Only recently have such studies and research seemed to find some coordination and reciprocal articulation: the Argentinian school with Pichon Riviere, Bleger, the Barangers, Berenstein, Puget and Losso, and the French with Anzieu and Racamier, have proposed significant studies on the matter.

More recently, Kaës (2015) has sought to structure an articulated theory around these topics, with a strictly Freudian framework and references mainly to French psychoanalysis, particularly to Piera Aulagnier (1985). His work has the merit of bringing to light doubts and unresolved issues, albeit providing answers to long-standing questions.

According to Kaës, there are three dimensions to the space of psychic reality: the intrapsychic dimension, where the logics of the unconscious have been extensively illustrated; the interpsychic dimension, which concerns the psychic space between subjects within the link – couple, group, family – and the trans-psychic dimension, which characterises the psychic reality that is passed on through subjects, their links and the groups they are members of.

Central here is the reference to the theory of linking, which, moreover, bears ancient origins and has been re-declined by various authors in differing ways. Following Kaës, the link is "the specific unconscious psychic reality constructed by the encounter between two or more subjects" [tr. by O.M.] (Kaës, 2008, pp. 770–771).

What follows, as advanced by the French psychoanalyst, is the idea that a third topography must or can be founded, that is based on the articulation between the common and shared psychic reality, the internal world of the individual subject, and the space of the link between subjects (Cahn, 2010; Kaës, 2001).

It thus appears inevitable to foresee an approach that considers the multidimensionality of reality.

A multidimensional approach (Morin, in Nicolaus & Raineri, 1997) and the theory of linking allow us to understand new disorders – or rather, to shed new light on old disorders – yet more importantly, they provide us with new tools to tackle them.

What use do we make of the other? How is the other implicated in the origin and maintenance of severe disorders? To what extent, particularly, are severe disorders an expression of the overall functioning of the group, of the quality and type of links between members within the group? These are but some of the questions this approach allows us to ask. This is not to replace the logic of the intrapsychic with that of the intersubjective, but to observe the coexistence of the two levels. As is now agreed upon by many, I believe that when dealing with severe disorders, we must work not only with the individual patient, but also with the group to which they belong, with the family where they were born and shaped, (as I attempt to discuss in Chapter 8). A fruitful aspect of clinical work at this level is the study of and intervention in the connection between the intrapsychic and the interpersonal, the oppositions, confusions, and misunderstandings between these two levels (Nicolò, 1992; 1996; 2009; 2014).

Clearly, reasoning along these lines also entails changes in the dual setting.

In considering the aspect of link, the object of observation will therefore be not only the other, but also the analytic pair itself. A perspective we had already been accustomed to through the theories of the Barangers (1961–1962), of Ferro (2009) and of many others. Ogden (1997) himself speaks of the "analytic third" as a "third subject, a subject that is neither analyst nor analysand but a third subjectivity unconsciously generated by the analytic pair" (p. 9).

In my opinion, following this viewpoint imposes not only the observation of the links within the subject's mind and the intervention in the geography of internal relations, but also the observation of the analyst's participation as an active co-constructor of the relationship with the patient. This also entails working on the processes of splitting, dissociation, denial, and negation, given that patients often do not bring certain parts of themselves to the session, as they are externalised in everyday life, immobilised in the other and in his or her relational life outside analysis. This is an inevitable consequence of the fact that we are all bearers not only of our own psychic space, but also of another space that we share with other subjects. Among the psychoanalytic discoveries of the past decades, a particularly fortunate theory affirmed the existence within the subject of phenomena such as the repository (Bleger, 1966), the crypt (Abraham & Torok, 1978), alienating identifications (Cahn, 1991), and maddening objects (Garcia Badaracco, 1986). These discoveries stand in natural continuity with classic theories, although in truth they refer to mechanisms of operation that somewhat differ.

This way of thinking about the individual has proved to be a tailor-made suit for a particular type of patient, the adolescent, who only a few decades ago was considered unanalyzable, to the point that Anna Freud had complained that this age of life was the Cinderella of psychoanalysis.

For many analysts, intervention in the developmental age and with severe patients has acted as propelling force for the very change in psychoanalytic theory and technique.

This is due to the features themselves of adolescence and young adulthood, which look to the past while at the same time facing the future, mobile and flexible, as they challenge us in psychoanalytic technique.

On this and other issues, an important debate was opened a couple of decades ago, thereby triggering significant discussions among scholars: Moses and Eglé Laufer, numerous English analysts and a number of important French-speaking analysts such as Raymond Cahn, François Ladame, as well as Italian analysts such as Novelletto and some of his students, among which myself.

The Laufers reiterated the importance of going back to proposing the classical four- or five-session psychoanalysis with the adolescent, where the dynamics are to focus on the young person's inner world, particularly on the Oedipal vicissitudes.

In near contraposition, according to Cahn (1991), adolescence itself constitutes a juncture of the biological, the psychic and the social. Consistently, he asserted that the treatment of adolescent crises requires the following: an appropriate environment for the adolescent and his or her system of relationships, an organisation allowing him or her to resume school activities, the need to modify family inter-relationships, and a sufficient duration for psychoanalytic treatment.

Famous for his research on subjectivisation through his work at Mont Souris Hospital with psychotic, pre-psychotic, and borderline adolescents, in his latest book *La Fin du Divan?* [The End of the Couch?; translator's note] (2002), Raymond Cahn reiterates the importance of maintaining the typical treatment as a reference, yet in the footsteps of Winnicott's thought, he suggests renewed modalities regarding the setting and listening, especially for borderline state patients or for those with impaired symbolisation. In these situations, the *vis à vis* setting with an analyst who is sensitive to the patient's every variation is to be preferred, an analyst who must tolerate great levels of tension, patiently reconstructing the functioning of the preconscious. According to Cahn, the intersubjective dimension is prevalent here, and countertransference plays a key role.

As we can see, these are pivotal statements that have moved through and still move through the psychoanalytic world. Personally, I believe the process of adolescent subjectivisation is articulated along two axes: on one hand, the psychic work that leads the patient to a symbolic reorganisation of the body, to a process of narcissistic re-founding of Self in order to cope with the potentially traumatic impact of the adolescent big bang; and on the other hand, the debate and new experiences with the other, with the new and subjectualising object that can be represented by the analyst in the setting.

Conclusions

Of course, these reflections concern psychoanalysis in general and not only developmental psychoanalysis. Many psychoanalysts invite us to welcome changes for psychoanalysis to continue to exist. Specifically, we are called to accept the disillusionment of analytic ideals to evaluate the effects of treatment and healing, on which judgment is subjective (Cahn, 2002).

Psychoanalysis and its understanding of the mind, the discovery of the unconscious with the realisation that *the ego is not master in its own house* have been revolutionary, challenging many of our certainties. Psychoanalysts have persevered down this road. Today, we see a favourable coexistence of models that are opposed and lack dialogue, yet coexist. At times, we witness prejudicial clashes over the search for "truth," as if one model rather than the other were the bearer of it. This represents one aspect of the crisis of psychoanalysis within itself. Yet I strongly believe that "the wisdom of psychoanalysis lies not in its diverse theories of mind or of psychic development, but in the process that it provides" (Bollas, 2013, p. 108).

References

Abraham, N. and M. Torok (1978). *The shell and the kernel: Renewals of psychoanalysis*, Vol. 1. University of Chicago Press. 1994.

Baranger, W. and M. Baranger (1961–1962). The analytic situation as a dynamic field. *International Journal of Psychoanalysis, 89*, 795-826. 2008.

Bleger, J. (1966). *Symbiosis and ambiguity. A psychoanalytic study*. London: Routledge. 2013.

Bollas, Ch. (2013). *Catch them before they fall: The psychoanalysis of breakdown*. London: Routledge.

Bollas, Ch. (2013). *China on the mind*. London: Routledge.

Cahn, R. (1991). *Adolescence et Folie. Les Déliaisons Dangereuses*. Paris: P.U.F.

Cahn, R. (2002). *La Fin du Divan?* Paris: Odile Jacob.

Cahn, R. (2010). Una terza topica per l'adolescenza? *Adolescenza e Psicoanalisi, 2010*(1), 19–35.

Ferro, A. and R. Basile (Eds.) (2009). *The analytic field: A clinical concept*. London: Routledge.

Fonagy, P. (2005). An overview of Joseph Sandler's key contributions to theoretical and clinical psychoanalysis. *Psychoanalytic Inquiry, 25*, 120–147.

García Badaracco, J.E. (1986). Identification and its vicissitudes in the psychoses. The importance of the concept of the 'Maddening Object'. *International Journal of Psychoanalysis, 67*, 133–146.

Green, A. (1993). Two discussions of 'The inner experiences of the analyst' and a response from Theodore Jacobs. *International Journal of Psychoanalysis, 740*, 1131–1136.

Kaës, R. (2001). Il concetto di legame. *Ricerca Psicoanalitica, XII*(2), 161–184.

Kaës, R. (2008). Définitions et approches du concept du lien. *Adolescence, 26*(3), 763–780.

Kaës, R. (2014). The psychical reality of linking. In A.M. Nicolò, P. Benghozi and D. Lucarelli (Eds.), *Families in transformation: A psychoanalytic approach*. London: Karnac.

Kaës, R. (2015). *L'Extension de la Psychanalyse. Pour une Métapsychologie de Troisième Type*. Paris: Dunod.

Kaës, R. (2015). Topique, dynamique et économie de troisième type. In *L'Extension de la Psychanalyse. Pour une Métapsychologie de Troisième Type*. Paris: Dunod.

Klee, P. (1945). *On modern art*. London: Faber. 1966.

Laufer, M.E. (2002). Il corpo come oggetto interno (talk presented at the *Centro di Psicoanalisi Romano* in November 2022). In A.M. Nicolò and I. Ruggiero (Eds.), *La Mente Adolescente e il Corpo Ripudiato*. Milano: Franco Angeli.

Laufer, M. and M.E. Laufer (1984). *Adolescence and developmental breakdown: A psychoanalytic view*. Yale University Press.

Monniello, G. (2019). Psicoanalisi dell'adolescente e neurosoggettivazione. In A.M. Nicolò and I. Ruggiero (Eds.), *La Mente Adolescente e il Corpo Ripudiato*. Milano: Franco Angeli.

Nicolaus, O. and A. Raineri (1997). Dialogo con Edgar Morin. *Interazioni, 1997*(2), 15–20.

Nicolò, A.M. (Ed.) (1996). *Curare la Relazione: Saggi sulla Psicoanalisi e la Coppia*. Milano: Franco Angeli.

Nicolò, A.M. (2009). Subjectual links and transpersonal pathologies. *International Review of Psychoanalysis of Couple and Family*, 6, 2. www.aipcf.net.

Nicolò, A.M. (2014). Where is the unconscious located? Reflections on links in families and couple. In A.M. Nicolò, P. Benghozi and D. Lucarelli (Eds.), *Families in transformation: A psychoanalytic approach*. London: Karnac.

Nicolò, A.M. and G.C. Zavattini (1992). *L'Adolescente e il suo Mondo Relazionale*. Roma: Carrocci.

Novelletto, A. (2009). *L'Adolescente. Una Prospettiva Psicoanalitica*. Roma: Astrolabio.

Ogden, Th. (1997). On the art of psychoanalysis. In *Reverie and interpretation: Sensing something human*. London: Routledge. 1999.

Siegel, D.J. (2013). *Brainstorm: The power and purpose of the teenage brain*. New York: Penguin Putnam.

Winnicott, D.W. (1989). *Psychoanalytic explorations*. Cambridge, MA: Harvard University Press.

INTRODUCTION

Throughout my specialisation in child neuropsychiatry, I began to work with adolescents or young adults who presented developmental ruptures.

At the time, a specialisation course in child and adolescent psychoanalytic psychotherapy was being organised at the *Istituto di Neuropsichiatria Infantile della Facoltà di Medicina* [Child Neuropsychiatry Institute of the Faculty of Medicine, translator's note] of the Sapienza University of Rome. Some of the world's most prestigious psychoanalysts would periodically hold lectures or seminars. For many months and on several occasions, Christopher Bollas and Frances Tustin, Moses and Eglé Laufer came, and many others were invited for conferences or seminars, which I myself organised over time, once I had obtained my specialisation as Child Neuropsychiatrist and my diploma as Psychotherapist. Particularly, among the French-speaking psychoanalysts, Raymond Cahn, François Ladame, and Philippe Jeammet held seminars and supervisions, and important congresses on adolescent psychoanalysis were organised. I was therefore extraordinarily fortunate to participate in events hosting some of the greatest child and adolescent psychoanalysts, to attend their scientific discussions, sometimes even their direct debates; I was also able to present my cases for direct supervision, and all this taught me enormously. Unfortunately, unlike the present state of affairs, in those years child and adolescent psychoanalysis around the world found no place within psychoanalytic societies and training institutes, perhaps due to ill-concealed fears. Psychoanalysts therefore came together outside the formal institutions, in many nations and in Italy, forming various psychoanalytic child and adolescent psychotherapy societies.

DOI: 10.4324/9781032663371-1

In the past fifteen years I have contributed from the start to the organisation of the Forum for Adolescent Psychoanalysis of the European Psychoanalytical Federation, first as member and later as Chair of the Committee, which expert colleagues from various European countries attended: Eglé Laufer, Cathy Bronstein, Enrico De Vito, Patricia Grieve, François Ladame, François Richard, Teresa Olmos, Sarah Flanders, to name a few. This gave me the unparalleled opportunity to engage with a number of colleagues from all parts of Europe.

Furthermore, my supervision in numerous public institutions and centres for young psychotic patients has broadened my vision, allowing me to work on clinical cases which, due to their severity, hardly reach psychoanalysts' offices in favour of psychotherapy that follows a more complex institutional path.

For the reasons I have mentioned, this book is permeated by references to different psychoanalytic models that eventually found a dialogue and composition within me, in my clinical work, in my model for understanding the patient and the analytic pair.

The roots of this work

In the course of my specialisation, I treated my first case of psychotherapy of an adolescent under the supervision of one of the most experienced Italian analysts in the field: Arnaldo Novelletto.

This was a boy who presented a very peculiar defence: he insistently claimed to be stupid and opposed this resistance to any intervention I would offer him. In truth, he was a very sensitive boy who had begun to present this fixed idea with which he defended himself against any kind of communication. He had interrupted ties with the peer group and was rather visibly distressed. One year into therapy, our work came to a halt and I learned that his father had decided to have him discontinue treatment, and sent him to a psychiatrist who had him admitted shortly after. To my great sorrow, I thus lost all contact with the boy. A year after the discontinuation, his father telephoned me and asked me to take him back into treatment because Carlo had requested it and refused any other intervention. In fact, in the meantime, his situation had grown far more complex. After being admitted to a major hospital in Rome, he had been diagnosed with schizophrenic onset. I reflected on that case at length, especially on the possible underestimation of the disorder he had presented, and it had then struck me that the boy had asked to see me after some time.

In revisiting the article I wrote together with my supervisor, Professor Novelletto, and presented with Professor Giannotti as Chair at *the IX Congresso Nazionale della Società Italiana di Neuropsichiatria Infantile* [IX National Congress of the Italian Society for Child Neuropsychiatry, translator's note] (Giannotti et al., 1980), I reflected in hindsight on the history of the patient and the evolution of therapy. In light of what we know today about these patients, some things would have changed.

I summarise the article we published at the time:

I receive a phone call from Carlo's father, a nineteen-year-old adolescent, announcing that his son needs treatment.

At the appointment, a boy shows up looking younger than his age, intellectually and culturally well-rounded. He has had repeated failures in school and obsessively repeats that he has evidence of his absolute, organic stupidity, which he particularly notices in his relationships with others. Despite claiming that no one can help him, Carlo does not want to give up.

He is the second of two children and lives with his mother and sister, his parents separated when he was six years old. His disorder is long-standing, given he has sensed the difficulty in relating to peers and the urge to be complacent with adults from a very young age.

Carlo acknowledges that his preoccupation with stupidity has replaced the intense concern about discovering himself to be gay. From the earliest sessions, he is worried that he is not being entirely truthful and is pretending. He feels empty, fragile, vulnerable, and had periods of intense regression in the past, to the point of no longer eating or drinking, and limiting himself to bed and being alone. *In his first dream, he recounts being in the water-filled therapy room with many bunk beds, where a twirling white whale bites the legs of anyone who jumps into the water to fish out artistically forged gold ingots, deposited on the bottom.* He recounts his anguishes, and particularly those pertaining to sexuality. He was at the theatre and saw a young actor waking up on the floor, relaxed and laughing. He then imagined that the young man was having sex with a girl, and he felt stupid, empty, and obnoxious.

The article we published at the time highlighted Carlo's difficulties in achieving a more defined identity and coping with homosexual anxieties, some of which also emerged around his voice, which he felt was ridiculous. The defences he used attempted to deny and split his emotions. From the beginning, it seemed clear to me that he used the defence of stupidity to push away the other and give himself the advantage of being unique, as I interpreted to him. But Carlo did not accept working to build an identity for himself and felt it was dangerous "for [him] to turn to positive things by constructing a building with a fragile foundation," as he told me.

Regarding his parents, he claimed to have suffered great trauma due to their separation. At times, he described his father as brilliant and intelligent, but also considered him a weak man, with the need to perform and centralize attention while actually lacking vitality, as he had appeared to me on the phone the numerous times he had called me, appearing unable to accommodate his son's limitations and needs. Carlo described his mother as depressed and passive, with no affective relationship with him, but he was particularly struck by "the woman's stupidity."

A turning point in therapy was marked by the earthquake dream he had after a year's work. Carlo *dreams of the earthquake as something from which he is born through dying. Hence, he approaches a girl standing next to him and hugs her, and as she cries, he exclaims "let's hope there is a God."* From that moment on, this earthquake in the dream appeared to me as the fear of the sudden collapse of defences in the face of which, despite the support of the sessions, only trust in a magical and omnipotent intervention was foreseeable. Subsequent work sought to bring him to reconsider aspects of his identity and his choice of object. During the sessions, Carlo reached the point of talking about his fear of homosexuality, and about the emotional bond he had with the analyst.

Carlo's therapy went on through small steps forward and conspicuous steps backward, with the activation of powerful resistances. At that time I proposed he lie on the couch, given my belief that a classic technique was necessary for him. However, a defiant silence gradually crept in, and he often skipped sessions.

On the occasion of a one-week suspension due to a bereavement of mine, the patient interrupted the sessions permanently. At the first meeting after this unforeseen break, he communicated his decision not to continue, strongly motivated in this by his father who, as I mentioned above, had decided to send him to a psychiatrist. Shortly thereafter, he sent me a letter of thanks, promising to return as soon as he "succeeded in having a more constructive and confident attitude," as he himself wrote.

Reflections in retrospect

Over the course of many years, I have long wondered about this clinical case, consciously or unconsciously, perhaps because it was one of the first cases of adolescent breakdown that I followed in treatment. At that time, we had just begun to think about these modes of functioning, and in retrospect, I wish to make a few points that seem important to me in light of my decades of experience.

First, these patients require a modified psychoanalytic technique, as Kernberg (1975) strongly argued at the time. The most important thing is for the analyst to be concerned with treating the patient, with helping the patient survive. This means, in Winnicott's (1963) words, that we must carry out analysis if analysis is necessary, otherwise we will do something else. In such cases, Winnicott points out the importance of *management* (*Ibid.*).

I now realise the importance of adapting the rules to the patient, and not vice versa (Balint, 1959). Freud himself (1928), in a letter to Ferenczi, wrote: "[...] the obedient [analysts] didn't take notice of the elasticity of these dissuasions and subjected themselves to them as if they were taboos. That had to be revised at some time, without, of course, revoking the obligations." I believe the rules of the setting are hardly tolerable for patients with these disorders, instead, it can be very useful to understand these difficulties with tact and sensitivity, and work towards the construction of the setting. The latter therefore becomes a point of arrival rather than a starting one, a progressive process that allows the patient to accept the principles of the therapeutic space whilst also internalising it. This is an operation that cures precisely because of the characteristics implicit in the mute part of the setting, where, as Bleger (1966a) says, the psychotic part of the patient's and analyst's personality is deposited. In this process of construction, which may last months or even years as we will see in the chapter on Gaia's case, the patient learns to distinguish reality from fantasy, the internal world from the external world and, in the case of the adolescent and young adult, his or her personal world from that of the parents. Through the internalisation of the setting, he or she creates that boundary, that psychic skin that in these patients is fragile and lacking.

It is doubtless that the treatment of these patients imposes modifications of technique, for example, on the use of the couch or frequency, and this is possible given that psychoanalysis is a method, a science that must be applied to the reality it considers.

In Carlo's case therefore, the first mistake I made was to ask the patient to lie down on the couch, which in him evoked extraordinary anguishes of loss of control. Fortunately, Carlo resisted my invitation, yet the couch is a metaphor for a type of analytic work that emphasises the importance of regression, which these patients fear, and which must in any case be evaluated on a case-by-case basis. It is not something that can be immediately achieved, but rather modulated and supported by both the environment and a solid analytic relationship.

It is extremely important, in the treatment of these cases, to set up an "integrated psychotherapy," a term I proposed a few years later in a book I published on adolescence (Nicolò & Zavattini, 1992). It refers to a third setting made up of a team of colleagues with different skills, for example, an analyst, a good pharmacologist willing to agree on appropriate drug treatment, a psychotherapist capable of working with the family or parental couple, possibly a therapeutic community willing to admit the patient, and, in some cases, even an "adult companion."[1] In Carlo's case, drug treatment and therapeutic work with the parents were lacking above all. Although I had repeatedly urged the father and mother to turn to a colleague and work on the parental couple, they refused. Particularly, the father underestimated his son's condition and was quite accusatory toward him. Generally, the impossibility of treating the phantasmatic world pertaining to the family, of the environment where the severe patient lives, is, in my experience, one of the most negative prognostic elements that undermine treatment. The work with the family or parents, which I discuss in Chapter 8, should be envisaged as an essential and necessary condition to begin the work. Unfortunately, in that situation it was not possible to carry it out, also due to the widespread belief at the time that borderline, psychotic, or breakdown situations were solely a matter of the patient's internal world.

Carlo's struggle between two parts of his personality were apparent from the start. His bond with me expressed his intention, in spite of everything, to overcome his problems, yet the anguish of dealing with them was too strong for him, also because of the environmental pressure that his father exerted.

Both Freud and Bion distinguish two parts within personality. Freud (1938, p. 203) speaks of the existence of two psychic organisations: the normal one that takes reality into account, and the one led by drives, which detaches the ego from reality. Freud describes the struggle between these two parts by asserting that the outcome depends on their relative strength: "the two exist alongside of each other. [...] If the second is or becomes the stronger, the necessary precondition for a psychosis is present" (Freud, 1938, p. 202). Bion also argues something similar by distinguishing the functioning of the neurotic part that is capable of introjecting, elaborating and differentiating, from the psychotic part, which instead implements violent projections to get rid of the accumulated indigestible elements of reality (Bion, 1957).

As I have ascertained in most cases of developmental ruptures in adolescence, anguishes related to gender identity and sexual orientation are in the foreground. This is due to the processes of identity restructuring and Oedipal renegotiation that are typical of this period, terrifying the young person and oftentimes parents as well, and creating a massive emotional storm. It seems to me that Carlo's fear of homosexuality is paradigmatic of this, a fear that had become the representation and defence of his fragility.

The stupidity we had equated with his homosexual anguishes actually showed a fear of being fragile in relation to paternal intrusions or, on the intrapsychic level, to the intrusions that the phase-specific tasks of adolescence could effect in a personality like his. As occurred in many cases I dealt with after him, Carlo warned me of what was happening. The earthquake dream showed the extent to which his whole self was undergoing a sort of earthquake, a drastic upheaval of his personality. What was lacking in this case was mainly time, because of the sudden and unexpected decision to hospitalise him, and the ward doctors' decision to medicate him heavily. In actual fact, these patients require a great length of time to be able to reassure themselves within the therapeutic relationship and wait, just as we are working to support them. We must catch them before they fall, as Bollas (2013) tells us, but we must also hold them at length by modulating the intensity of emotions, of tensions that can result in dangerous defences, such as a drastic retreat into isolation, a refuge, a sensory dismantling of which, in Carlo's case, the hatred of his voice was a sign.

The hatred of his voice, which he perceived as feeble, weak and childish or feminine, also showed the primary lack of sensory integration at the body level.

From this viewpoint, integrated psychotherapy can prove to be most useful if it succeeds at an early stage in modulating the terror of the conflict between the psychotic and neurotic parts of the personality, which, if excessive, could produce further slippage toward more radical defences, such as the negation of emotions, dissociation or splitting and emptying of the self.

We must also consider that in this period of life, the psychotic aspects of personality are inherently in the foreground, potentially inducing diagnostic confusions. Moreover, there exists a continuity between the neurotic and psychotic aspects in each of us, and particularly in adolescence, where slippages between one functioning and the other are frequent. Hence, in the course of time and depending on various factors that I address in the book, we may witness varied developments. These depend on intrapsychic, interpersonal, family-related factors, or on a fortunate therapeutic encounter. The clinician's task is therefore complex and twofold: on the one hand, to attempt to understand the extent to which these emerging aspects refer back to an organisation that is in fact psychotic, or only appear to be so; on the other hand, to recognise them in their initial manifestation, as the first gusts of a hurricane approaching.

In any case, it is always necessary to consider the battle between the two sides in the field, thus consistently working toward strengthening the self and the ego, never losing hope that we can indeed change things. Furthermore, it is paramount to bear in mind that precisely the most severe patients tend to attack the trust we may place in our work and make us feel their despair, as is palpable in the clinical account of Laura, the patient reported in the chapter on self-harm and cutting.

As the Laufers (1984) taught us, the *fil rouge* of all developmental breakdowns is the body. Today we have learned to recognise it, and I will address this in Chapter 3, but the new pathologies of adolescents also show us this, considering that in most of them the body is at issue, as in self-harm – which I discuss in Chapter 14 – or in the epidemics of anorexia. Image today has become crucial, and at the expense of the more profound identity, a fragile aesthetic identity has replaced it.

We might advance several criticisms of the Laufers' theories, foremost among these the centrality attributed to the Oedipal conflict as the cause of breakdown, the disavowal of the importance of the early stages of development, the strictly Freudian framework of their clinical theory and technique, the massive interpretations they report without realising that the patient cannot even comprehend them and therefore experiences them as attacks on the fragile self, or even the refusal to consider the interpersonal environment surrounding the adolescent. Some of their findings, however, remain important and valid, such as the concept of developmental breakdown itself, which, however debatable, as I point out in Chapter 3, has accustomed us to consider such an event as potentially movable and transformable. Equally valuable still today is the developmental point of view, which they inherited from Anna Freud's school, and that allows us to assess pathology according to the young person's ability to cope with specific life stages and tasks, as well as the attention they give to the body, and the distinction they propose between structure, crisis, and psychotic functioning.

Often, as is the case with many great analysts of the past, they have been robbed and unrecognised, which in certain scientific disciplines constitutes a substantial problem that creates great confusion and prevents coherent growth. However, I believe it is of the utmost importance to bear in mind that on the surface and in the early stages, a psychotic onset may be confused with a developmental rupture, and that at times one might overlap with the other, or evolve into the other. We must also be well aware that it is possible to intervene in both cases, and that adolescence is a second chance offered to the person to re-found oneself, following Evelyne Kestemberg's aphorism "everything is prepared in childhood, [...] but everything is played out in adolescence" [tr. by O.M.] (Kestemberg, 1984, p. 18).

In order to face an arduous struggle, the person will quite often make use of defensive solutions (as I illustrate in Chapter 8) that do not solve the problem, but short-circuit it, bury it, or hide it. In such cases, the problem remains intact or hardly changed. Thus, in a breakdown that has not manifested itself, or that no one has seen, defensive solutions may become structural. The personality reorganises itself around these conflicts and defences, remaining mutilated. In some instances, this reorganisation may use the body by attacking it in destructive ways, as happens in some forms of anorexia that are in fact ways of avoiding breakdown, or in forms of transgender as negation and dissociation of the sexed body (as I elaborate in Chapter 13). In other cases, as in Martina's (illustrated in Chapter 10), alienation into the other succeeds in compensating these patients.

In the most severe situations then, which could have resulted in a frank psychotic organisation, if the patient defensively proceeds to empty the self of emotions and thoughts, the personality will be impoverished and will at best live a life based on a false self.

In conclusion

Paraphrasing Winnicott, modern psychoanalysis has taught us, that there is no such thing as an infant, rather, the infant must be considered in his or her relationship with the environment and the mother, and, might we add, with the father and the whole family. The last decades have seen the radical shift from unipersonal to multi-personal psychology. Over the last thirty years, I have progressively deepened the study of interpersonal ties and realised that, especially in certain disorders, we cannot disregard the other, the co-constructor of the relationship – both in assessment and treatment – and that certain dimensions of the unconscious itself, in general, are ectopic, extra-topic, interpersonal.

For the pathologies discussed in this book, the analyst cannot resort to a merely reconstructive view, and the unconscious involved is not the repressed unconscious of classic psychoanalysis, but rather the emotional unconscious. The avenues of understanding toward the non-repressed unconscious are acting out, bodily sensations, enactments, and communications, eluding consciousness and passing from one individual to another, as Freud alluded to in *The Uncanny* (1919). These modes of functioning are present at multiple simultaneous levels, and the analyst is immersed in them and participates in them by his or her presence. Even without explicitly theorising it, psychoanalysts working with children and adolescents have always taken these levels into account by making significant interventions around them. We can therefore acknowledge that psychoanalysis of the developmental age and of severe patients has taught much to adult psychoanalysis, indeed bringing considerable stimulus for change in technique and beyond. With his great lucidity, Novelletto noted that "if psychoanalysis has been able to move from a theory of psychopathology to a theory of development, much of the merit goes to child and adolescent psychoanalysts" [tr. by O.M.] (Novelletto, 2009, p. 184).

In this book, I have decided to collect my reflections over the years on this topic, to reiterate the importance of intervening in the developmental ruptures that occur at a young age. Because it is a crisis that bears great potential and, if treated well, may evolve positively, allowing the personality to resume its interrupted path, and make fruitful use of the opportunity that has opened to question an organisation that limits the person and his or her future.

Ronald Laing, in his book *The Politics of Experience* (1967), re-ported the words of one of his patients who had managed to overcome a schizophrenic crisis, communicating his sudden feeling: "everything was so much more real than it had been before. The grass was greener, the sun was shining brighter, and people were more alive, I could see them clearer. I could see the bad things and the good things and all that. I was much more aware" (p. 136). Certainly, Laing's romanticised and idealising view of mental illness exudes here, which, contrary to the author's own assertions, gen-erally leaves the patient mortified and frightened. Yet, there is a seed of truth to Laing's words: the patient acknowledges that having worked through his or her crisis and overcome it has enabled him or her to see true aspects of reality, without the need for a false and condescending self.

My frequently turbulent encounters with these patients, their vicissitudes and the alternating roller-coaster phases of their treatment have taught me a great deal. Above all, it has prompted me to reflect on what is meant by the word 'healing'. This word inevitably evokes the concept of 'normality', a term reminiscent of the other, decidedly uncanny term 'norm', a predetermined ideal. The pathological state occurs when the individual fails to adapt to the environment in which he or she lives and to the cultural and historically defined norms that characterise it. The inability to adapt should sometimes be seen as proposing a model of functioning that follows different – or at least alternative – patterns of reference to adaptation. Instead, it is stigma-tised as 'pathological state' and 'abnormality'.

Norm and adaptation are words that may evoke conflicting meanings. Even in biological medicine, one thing is health, and another is the absence of illness. In fact, none of us can consider ourselves healthy, even in the absence of illnesses – at least apparent ones. However, each of us has learned to live with our own disorder. The problem rather lies in the quantity and quality of it.

Some of the cases presented in the book I treated personally, while others are cases I supervised.

The reader will find some new chapters and others that have instead been reworked in light of my current reflections.

I am unsure whether this might burden the text, however, to me it is an expression of the ongoing reflection that these patients have stimulated in me. Changing others begins with changing ourselves.

I wish to thank the colleagues with whom I have shared these exciting emotional and cognitive experiences, and a thank you to the patients, who have taught me so much.

Note

1 The term was coined among a group of colleagues, including Novelletto and myself, to refer to a support figure, generally a young psychologist in training, who accompanies young patients in the day-to-day.

References

Balint, M. and E. Balint (1959). *Thrills and regressions*. London: Routledge, 1987.

Bion, W.R. (1957). The differentiation of the psychotic from the non-psychotic personalities, *International Journal of Psychoanalysis, 38*. Reprinted in *Second Thoughts*. London: Karnac Books, 1984.

Bleger, J. (1966a). Psycho-analysis of the psycho-analytic frame. In C. Moguillansky and H.B. Levine (Eds.), *Psychoanalysis of the psychoanalytic frame revisited: A new look at José Bleger's classic work*. London: Routledge, 2022.

Bollas, C. (2013). *Catch them before they fall: The psychoanalysis of breakdown*. London: Routledge.

Freud, S. (1919). The uncanny. *S.E.* 17: 218–256, London: Hogarth Press.

Freud, S. (1928). Letter to Ferenczi (4 January 1928). In E. Jones (Ed.), *The life and works of Sigmund Freud* (1953–57). London: Hogarth Press, 1953.

Freud, S. (1938). An outline of psychoanalysis. *S.E.* 23: 139–208, London: Hogarth Press.

Giannotti, A., Nicolò A.M., Novelletto A. (1980). *La stupidità come difesa dal crollo*. Talk presented at the 9th National Congress of the Italian Society for Child Neuropsychiatry: *Attualità di neuropsicopatologia dell'età adolescenziale*, Repubblica di San Marino, 17–19 October 1980.

Kernberg, O. (1975). *Borderline conditions and pathological narcissism*. New York: Jason Aronson.

Kestemberg, E. (1984). La pathologie de l'adolescence: prémices, passage ou catastrophe? In F. Ladame and Ph. Jeammet (Eds.), *La Psychiatrie de l'Adolescence Aujourd'hui: Quels Adolescents Soigner et Comment?* Paris: PUF, 1986.

Laing, R.D. (1967). *The politics of experience*. New York: Knopf Doubleday Publishing Group.

Laufer, M. and M.E. Laufer (1984). *Adolescence and developmental breakdown: A psychoanalytic view*. New Haven: Yale UP.

Nicolò, A.M. and G.C. Zavattini (1992). *L'Adolescente e il suo Mondo Relazionale. Teoria e Tecnica Psicoanalitica*. Roma: La Nuova Italia Scientifica.

Novelletto, A. (2009). *L'Adolescente. Una Prospettiva Psicoanalitica*. Roma: Astrolabio.

Winnicott, D.W. (1963). Psychiatric disorder in terms of infantile maturational processes. In (1965) *The maturational processes and the facilitating environment: Studies in the theory of emotional development*. London: Routledge, 1990.

PART 1

THE ADOLESCENT AND DEVELOPMENTAL RUPTURES

1

THE ADOLESCENT MIND

In order to discuss the specificity of developmental ruptures in adolescence and young adulthood, it is necessary to illustrate, albeit in general terms, the physiological features of adolescence which, I believe more than others, underlie and characterise these pathologies. Although widely known, I will briefly outline them.

Adolescence is not only a temporal phase of transition, but an organising agent of the mind allowing access to adulthod and the restructuring of identity.

This definition, which we owe to Raymond Cahn (1986) and indirectly to the contributions of Laufer and Laufer (1984) as well, allows us to view adolescence as an enzyme that permeates the mind and forces to confront oneself with the life cycle. In the background of this proposition is the debate between advocates of continuity versus discontinuity, namely, between those who view the growth of the individual in a continuous progression, though mainly considering adolescence a recapitulation of childhood, and others who instead point to the emergence in adolescence of new processes, problems, developmental and biological challenges that permeate and determine new paths. The consequence of these positions is the conclusion, to quote Novelletto (2002, p. 26), that "adult psychopathology is not a direct consequence of the re-emergence of childhood neurosis" [tr. by O.M.].

If we consider adolescence an activating enzyme of phase-specific functioning, we will be attentive to the assessment of such functioning in personality, and able to recognise adolescent mental functioning (what the French colleagues call 'the adolescent position') in each of us and in each patient. This will allow us to accept or encourage its reactivation when needed in the analysis of the adult. The rediscovery

DOI: 10.4324/9781032663371-3

of the importance of observing and working on the reactivation of adolescence in the psychoanalytic process of the adult patient (Nicolò, 2001; Novelletto, 2009; Tonnesmann, 1980) certainly still deserves further study and bears numerous potential perspectives.

What challenges must the adolescent face?

Let us now ask ourselves which challenges the adolescent faces in his or her growth, which he or she must overcome in order to become an adult, and what characterises the specificity of the adolescent mind.

The developmental tasks that this age of life entails have often been mentioned by many authors, starting from Freud, and can be summarised in the following: the integration of sexuality and of new bodily transformations; separation-individuation from the childhood past, the childhood body and childhood parental objects, with the consequent developmental mourning; the integration of aggression and that transformation from action to thinking–dreaming that is also one of the goals of analysis. All this is summarised in the process that analysts such as Blos (1979) and Jacobson (1954) describe as *identity restructuring*.

Nowadays, it is more appropriately referred to as the process of subjectivization, which defines – according to Cahn – a continuous process from birth to death of subjective appropriation and self-creation through which the subject feels he or she owns his or her thoughts, acts, desires, feelings, and conflicts (Cahn, 1991, pp. 1431–1432). This process is both the result of the subject's invention of self and offered by the other in the dynamic that Winnicott described as "found/created", to recall the mother's operation of letting the child find the object she creates.

The subject is constructed within the bonds that he or she helps to build. Kaës (2007) calls it a "plural singular": on the one hand, it is the fruit of the inter- and transgenerational links in which it is embedded, and on the other, thanks to the subjective appropriation and trans-formation it operates, it reconquers and comes to own what it has inherited, following Goethe's aphorism quoted by Freud "What thou hast inherited from thy fathers, acquire it to make it thine" (1913, p. 158). In this regard, Raymond Cahn affirms the importance of a third topography for understanding the adolescent mind, hence em-phasising the function of the other, of others, of culture and society, of

18

what he calls "the subjectualizing object" (Cahn, 2010, p. 31) as contribution to the creation of the subject. He himself reminds us of the extent to which the analyst is called upon to fulfil that subjectualizing function that parents were not able to fulfil, particularly in today's world.

Thanks to recent neuroscientific advancements, today we know that there is not only a restructuring of the psyche but also of the brain. Indeed, adolescence is also a process of neuro-subjectivisation (Monniello, 2016), an important time that sees stimulations from the internal world and the environment influencing brain growth and remodelling.

Brain growth in adolescents is characterised by an excess of brain synapses and nerve ramifications, as well as by their simultaneous regression.

The adolescent brain thus transforms and constructs itself based on the stimulation it receives, the most important of which is the pubertal event. As Mark Solms tells us, the environment in which the brain finds itself at critical moments determines which connections will be used (activated), that is, which will survive, and which will not. Insufficiently activated connections will be "pruned" from the evolving structure. During these critical periods, therefore, the structures of the forming brain are particularly sensitive to environmental influences. In the first thirteen years of life, roughly from infancy to puberty, these critical periods occur with great frequency (Solms, 2016). All this bears significant consequences for the clinician.

In adolescence, the process of brain growth occurs continuously throughout several areas of the cortex, including the parietal lobes, the regions associated with logical and spatial reasoning, and the temporal lobes, linked to language (Giedd et al., 1999). The frontal lobes develop as well, with a peak around age eleven for girls and twelve for boys, although their development does not end until after age twenty (*ibid.*). The prefrontal cortex is not fully tuned (*ibid.*). For emotion recognition, adolescents use the amygdala instead of the frontal cortex, as young adults. They are therefore predisposed to instinctive behavioural responses (Yurgelun-Todd and Killgore, 2006).

What occurs in this period of life is progressive specification: while some neural connections decrease, others suddenly and abruptly increase. This confirms the clinical observation according to which the healthy adolescent has a physiological tendency to act, even impulsively, rather than to reflect, which will be a later acquisition.

The assessing clinician must take this into great consideration, given that action at this age is a way of experiencing reality by trial and error. Unless it exhibits destructive characteristics, acting should be considered physiological. Yet the adolescent mind shows other specific modes of functioning: massive projective identifications, the re-actualisation of the Oedipus complex, the misuse of aggression, and finally, the use of daydream that may sometimes result in actual refuges of the mind.

The irruption of the sexed body and sensoriality

A central event in adolescence is the irruption of the sexed body, which imposes the need to integrate a new body image and reinvest it with a new narcissistic libido.

We owe it to Eglé and Moses Laufer (1984) who drew our attention to the importance of the body in adolescent pathology.

Following Stoller's (1975) distinction between body and body image, Eglé Laufer (2002) highlights that the body, considered an internal object, represents the integration between the libidinal body, subjectively experienced and resulting from the interaction between mother and child, and the body image based on sensory experience endowed with an identity that is separate from the mother's body. As Eglé Laufer points out, these two aspects integrate in healthy situations, while in dysfunctional ones there is a split in such integration, a source of perverse solutions or hatred for one's body or aspects of it. A hunger for sensations to be integrated, or conversely, a terror of them, may then characterise the later stages of growth and particularly adolescence. If the adolescent has not been able to internalise the body as an intact internal object and loved by the mother, even based on healthy sensory integration, he or she will approach the new experiences of adolescence problematically.

It is a time of new sensations that were never experienced before and relating to the advent of changes in the body: hormonal changes, shape, height, sexual maturation, as well as sensations related to new experiences associated with menarche, pubarche, and sexual initiation. In briefly returning to the debate between continuity and discontinuity in adolescence, we might consider there to be both a novel sensoriality and sensuality that emerge at this age, yet they are embedded within old experiences, within the archaic "sensual sensory" that Gutton (2003) illustrates.

The integration of new and primary sensations therefore enables the secure experience of having an intact body, the foundation of the self. The end point of this highly complex process is also to achieve a healthy sexual relationship, although to get there, the adolescent must travel through numerous stages. One of these is sexual initiation, which allows the emergence, particularly in girls, of new sensations associated with experiencing the internal organs (Laufer, 2005; Nicolò, 1992). New sensations are also offered at this age by masturbation.

Hence, the sensuality that emerges in adolescence and is embedded in old experiences bears endless aspects of novelty. It is of great importance that these processes be modulated and balanced, given that a surplus of arousal may also carry a traumatic value due to the difficulty in mentalizing. All this might generate dangerous defences and especially lead to a split between sensoriality and sensuality. The great challenge of this time is therefore this sensory and sensual storm that characterises adolescence, and which the analyst himself or herself perceives in session while treating some of these patients. The analyst may indeed be disturbed by it in his or her countertransference, or in personal experiences in general regarding such patients.

These kinds of experiences are also supported and complicated by an otherwise normal phenomenon in adolescence: the reactivation of polymorphous-perverse dispositions, which are also related to the reactivation of the Oedipus complex and riddled with bisexual confusions. What Meltzer (1973a) calls zonal confusions (mouth-vagina-anus combination and then nipple-tongue-faeces combination), which the child had already learned to distinguish, erupt in puberty and are sometimes accompanied by an idealisation of the confusion. We might therefore find acting out or fantasies that refer to transient perversions in this period of life, as an expression of a difficulty in the process of subjectivization and identity achievement. On the other hand, from Freud on, and through McDougall and Kernberg, we know that a share of perversion is present in common adult sexual relationships. Nonetheless, such phenomena may be attempts at exploration, or a turbulence in the definition of identity, or may represent a test, a way of experiencing oneself and ultimately understanding what the definitive configuration will be.

In addition, we might hypothesise that just as the mother was a source of arousal for the child, but also a source of integration of sensoriality and sensuality, so a new object in adolescence will allow for new sensory and sensual experiences, implanted on archaic sensations, whilst also containing new, never-before-experienced features. If the adolescent progressively acquires rewarding and affective love and sexual experiences, this will contribute to self-acceptance. Through the experience with the other and the awareness of a differentiated body that is different from that of the parent, a further step will be the integration of a new sensuality and smooth functioning of the sexed body. Clearly, this is but one of the many tasks and challenges the adolescent must face, yet it is one of the crossroads towards adulthood upon which many adolescents stumble.

Central here is the acceptance of the limit to the fantasy of bisexual omnipotence. At the end of this process, the adolescent will accept the mourning of renunciation by choosing to be male or female, thereby renouncing the possibility of being everything. But he or she will also operate the renunciation of incest, which in the Oedipal elaboration will involve the acknowledgement of the difference between generations. In this process, also the vicissitudes of the reworked superego are embedded, and, as the Laufer and Laufer (1984, p. 90) note, through the modification of the superego as it becomes less strict and persecutory, one has the measure of this adolescent's ability to elaborate the Oedipus complex and separate from the parents.

Another important process concerns the activity/passivity dialectic, which is yet another of the themes in adolescence, particularly in male adolescence. This is also due to the pubertal changes potentially being experienced as changes in the body as it subjugates the mind, subdues it, or makes it passive. The adolescent may be amazed as well as ashamed by the appearance of menstruation, or the change in voice, or the first facial hair, which appears seemingly unexpectedly and out of control.

Developmental mourning

A crucial aspect of identity construction is closely linked to the ability to operate sufficient separation-individuation from parents, from the infant world, and from the prepubescent body, yet this also gives reason for the inevitable mourning that accompanies it.

Indeed, these vicissitudes are at the crossroads of individual, family, and group functioning. The difficulties that some adolescents present are the litmus test of parents' and the family environment's ability to in turn separate and operate their own counter-individuation. Parents are accessing a later phase of the life cycle that may come with experiences of loss of their youth, mourning over their own changing bodies such as with menopause, or mourning over the death of grandparents. Processes of confusion between self and other, fleeting boundaries of the self, as well as specific family functioning, may complicate this evolution, a topic I address in later chapters. Oedipal vicissitudes lie at the heart of this process, present in both the adolescent and his or her parents, given that Oedipal reviviscency characterises both the adolescent and the parents who counter-identify with him or her. In this situation, parents may sometimes enact an adolescence they never experienced before.

The increasing frequency of parental separations during adolescence reveals the deep disturbances that the re-actualisation of the Oedipus complex brings about. Some parents will allow themselves a new partner or new explorations in sexuality, propelled by the massive magmatic unconscious movement determined by their children's adolescence.

Integrating and directing aggression

Working with adolescents, I have had the chance to observe and reflect upon the specific use of aggression at this stage of life. While observing a number of passive, torpid or depressed adolescents, inhibited both in school and in their relationships with the peer group, I often wondered to what extent the fear of aggression had thwarted them in their development. In treating these adolescents, work on the conflicts around aggression and on the fear it arouses often led to improvement, after which, at first, emerged temporary aggressive behaviours, sometimes characterised by aggressive or even violent acting out. Although it could frighten parents and appear to them as a worsening of the situation, such shifts could in fact be helpful. Through a positive use of aggression, the patients could thus resume the path they had interrupted or momentarily blocked, define themselves and mark boundaries with their parents and the childhood world. In other, far more severe situations, violent or aggressive acting out could bear multiple defensive meanings, yet I believe it is important for the analyst to consider that the process of subjectivization itself, which culminates in this age of life, comes with specific vicissitudes of aggression.

As I have mentioned in other works (Nicolò, 2009), the manifestation of aggression in adolescence is also more significantly apparent because the body itself has greater strength and capacity than in childhood. Its strength is decisive for phase-specific developmental tasks. In fact, aggression is useful for processes of separation from childhood and parents. The integration of the sexed body and the exercise of sexuality itself are organised around a modulated use of aggression that can also have a defensive function against pregenital or perverse fantasies, or even against incestuous or parricidal desires. Through emotional and libidinal investment in a new object, the adolescent preserves the parent from his or her attacks.

Toward the experience of sexuality

Because this book focuses specifically on developmental ruptures in late adolescence or young adulthood, I will give special attention to adolescent sexual intercourse, to the first initiation. Indeed, in certain situations with certain patients they may occasionally represent the trigger of developmental rupture.

Certainly, rather than conceiving of the first sexual encounter as a unique event, we must consider it a true process of initiation that is favoured, at least in the most classic versions, by the love state that lies at the apex of the idealisation processes that are typical of this phase.

The initiation process is made possible by the coagulation of numerous factors, such as the need to transcend the limits of the self and merge with an external other representing good aspects of the self, split and projected. In the first sexual encounter, the possibility of experiencing the phantasmatic union of the Oedipal parents in a new object relation is enacted, allowing not only identification with the same-sex parent, but also temporary identification with the partner and confirmation of one's separate and autonomous identity (Nicolò, 1992). Finally, the first sexual encounter can take place thanks to the ability to overcome masturbation, understood until then as an act of testing and experimenting with one's own body, moving now toward mutual pleasure-giving with the other's body.

In adolescence, the new sexual investment of the body can be put to the test through the use of the sexed body in relation to the other. If it is not a form of acting out aimed at evacuating anxiety, or being accepted in the group, sexual initiation is a turning point, one that unfortunately frequently gives rise in some problematic adolescents to developmental breakdown.

All these vicissitudes are not only intrapsychic. On the inter-personal level, adolescents are grappling with the group. As Meltzer tells us in a landmark article, as they begin to change in body and mind, they begin to move away from the monosexual pubertal community (Meltzer, 1973b), that is, the group of same-sex girls or boys on which they leaned and mirrored, to move toward the adult community based on couple functioning. While the monosexual pubertal community was riddled with confusing experiences, slowly there emerges in it an active stimulus toward differentiation between self and other, between male and female, leading to the active choice of the other as partner in the couple. Group processes are therefore highly significant, given that they are able to promote growth or multiply arousing stimuli.

In any case, mirroring processes that are useful for the definition of the self are activated within the group, yet every so often these groups carry a destructive potential that drags the immature ado-lescent down. An assessment of these and of how the adolescent uses them is essential.

Adolescence today

We are currently observing a significant change in adolescents' be-haviour, at least in the Western world, and the emergence of new phenomena. Anything social nowadays is largely represented by the internet. The internet, chats, Instagram or TikTok are all means through which adolescents keep informed and present themselves, perform and spectacularize themselves.

Aesthetic identity has become of great importance, sometimes at the expense of a real identity. "I am my image, and if my image is not accepted, I am not", this seems to be what some adolescents are saying, as they constantly change their image in search of an unknown self.

This transpires, by contrast, in the tendency to cling to the body, which unfortunately characterises some of the new pathologies we see in adolescents: epidemics of anorexia, self-harm and cutting, or the multiplication of tattoos and piercings, in an attempt to find a solid rock, a last bastion.

We are therefore witnessing various forms of externalisation that ultimately speak of compensations for impaired internalisation.

Moreover, sexuality as well manifests itself in multiple, variously declined ways. We might ask ourselves how valid the Laufers' gender identity claims remain today, while, on the contrary, we see an unfolding of plentiful declinations, in a world where sexual experience has almost become an obligation imposed by social rules or a pass to join the group. Homosexuality, too, has been rightly declassified by the WHO from the list of disorders and is a normal object choice on par with the heterosexual one. Yet, this sometimes risks becoming, because of "political correctness" and the current trend, an alternative type of choice that conceals marked distress, as a true fragility of identity, as can be inferred from the words of Kurt Cobain, a grunge singer who in an interview stated: "In high school I became best friends with a well-known gay guy. Hanging out with him made me look gay too, and I was proud of that, proud to be gay even though I wasn't! I had almost found an identity: ultimately, I was an outcast, but an average outcast (average, geek), I was an outcast unlike others" [tr. by O.M.] (Corcos, 2015, p. 18).

Hence, in the world of youth today, we are witnessing rampant pornography, internet addiction with exhibitionist or voyeuristic phenomena, the rise of spontaneous child prostitution run through the internet by very young adolescents, and the staggering surge of true or alleged sexual dysfunctions, especially in boys, as many andrologists report to us.

In some cases, adolescent sexuality, especially in its early stages, has become more precocious but also ephemeral and transient, based on acting and experiencing sensations rather than building romantic relationships. The love connection and sexual experience can be split and in some cases pursued on their own, one detached from the other. Oftentimes, sexual relationships precede acquaintance, they are not expressions of psychic intimacy, and they are a space where one can have experiences and sensations, albeit rarely alluding to a preliminary period of a meaningful romantic relationship. It is often an activity around which friends, or the group, are pivotal.

Adolescents who seemingly acknowledge no psychological distress whatsoever recount their sexual experiences, sometimes experienced in the class group and managed within dynamics where intimacy and secrecy fail to find a place. As an illustration, a boy recalls his school trip during which, following the orders of the class leader and under his classmates' apparently amused gaze, one or more girls would take turns in sexual intercourse with their classmates, and this was portrayed as the usual possible bravado. My patient, a borderline adolescent who told me about the event, recalled feeling perturbed as he remained on the sidelines.

These transformations are of great interest to us, and it would be meaningless to make value judgments about them. In fact, they are so widespread that ruling on normality/pathology or normality/perversion might prove to be faulty and out of context.

Notwithstanding, this does not exempt us from attempting to understand the challenges facing the adolescent today, also because the greater freedom adolescents have in their expressions perhaps allows us to delve deeper into personality functioning *tout court*. Yet, it remains doubtless that these new forms and styles of adolescents and young adults challenge psychoanalysis by posing questions pertaining to sexuality, identity, object choice, gender, and parenting. Furthermore, they call into question the foundations of psychoanalysis, such as the Oedipal vicissitudes and the significance of the primal scene in the construction of adult sexuality.

References

Blos, P. (1979). *The adolescent passage: Developmental issues*. New York: International UP.

Cahn, R. (1986). *Psychanalyse, Adolescence et Psychose*. Paris: Payot.

Cahn, R. (1991). Du sujet. *Revue Française de Psychanalyse 55*: 1354–1490.

Cahn, R. (2010). Una terza topica per l'adolescenza? In *Adolescenza e Psicoanalisi*, V, 1, pp. 19–35.

Corcos, M. (2015). La costruzione dell'identità (sessuata) in adolescenza. In *Adolescenza e Psicoanalisi*, X, 2, pp. 15–34.

Freud, S. (1913). Totem and taboo. *S.E.* 13: VII-162, London: Hogarth Press.

Giedd, J., Blumenthal, J., Jefries, O. (1999). Brain development during childhood and adolescence: A longitudinal MRI study. *Nature Neuroscience, 2* (10): 861–863.

Gutton, P. H. (2003). Esquisse d'une théorie de la génitalité. *Adolescence, 21* (2): 217–248.

Jacobson, E. (1954). *The self and the object world*. New York: International University Press.

Kaës, R. (2007). *Un Singulier Pluriel: La Psychanalyse à l'Epreuve du Groupe*. Paris: Dunod.

Laufer, E. (2005). Le corps comme objet interne. *Adolescence 23*: 363–379.

Laufer, M. and Laufer, M. E. (1984). *Adolescence and developmental break-down: A psychoanalytic view.* London: Routledge, 2018.

Meltzer, D. (1973a). *Sexual states of mind.* Pertshire: Clunie Press.

Meltzer, D. (1973b). Adolescent psychoanalytical theory. In D. Meltzer, M. Harris and M.H. Williams (Eds.), *Adolescence: Talks and papers by Donald Meltzer and Martha Harris* (2011). London: Karnac.

Monniello, G. (2016). Psicoanalisi dell'adolescente e processo di neuro-soggettivazione. In A.M. Nicolò and I. Ruggiero (Eds.), *La Mente Adolescente e il Corpo Ripudiato.* Milano: Franco Angeli.

Nicolò, A. M. (1992). Maria e Ludovica, ovvero iniziazione sessualità e illusione amorosa in adolescenza. In A. Novelletto (Ed.), *Adolescenza Amore Accoppiamento: la Prima Relazione Sessuale.* Roma: Borla.

Nicolò, A. M. (Ed.) (2001). *Analisi Terminabile e Interminabile in Adolescenza.* Milano: Franco Angeli.

Nicolò, A. M. (Ed.) (2009). *Adolescenza e Violenza.* Roma: Il Pensiero Scientifico.

Novelletto, A. (2002). Adolescenza e psicoanalisi. Modelli teorici e strategie cliniche a confronto. In *Quaderni di Psicoterapia Infantile,* 43, "Adolescenza e psicoanalisi", pp. 15–34.

Novelletto, A. (2009). *L'Adolescente. Una Prospettiva Psicoanalitica.* Roma: Astrolabio.

Solms, M. (2016). The biological foundations of gender: A delicate balance. In G. Schreiber (Ed.), *Transsexualität in Theologie und Neurowissenschaften.* Berlin: De Gruyter.

Stoller, R. J. (1975). *Perversion: The erotic form of hatred.* New York: Pantheon.

Tonnesman, M. (1980). Adolescent re-enactment, trauma and reconstruction. *Journal of Child Psychotherapy, 6* (1): 23–44.

Yurgelun-Todd, D. and Killgore, D. (2006). Fear-related activity in the prefrontal cortex increases with age during adolescence. A preliminary FMRI study. *Neuroscience Letters, 406* (3): 194–199.

2

THE PROBLEM OF ASSESSMENT IN ADOLESCENCE

Introduction

I have been reflecting for many years on the topic of diagnosis and particularly of assessment in adolescence. Diagnosis is first and foremost, as the word itself says, "*diágnōsis*," beginning to know through time and through the relationship between the analysand and those who diagnose. *Diágnōsis* is also constructing a diagnostic pathway that is not a punctual moment, and it is a sometimes highly variable and inherently complicated process. It is inevitable for any clinician to initially organise his or her impression, and most of the time, even as psychoanalysts or psychotherapists, we use psychiatric categories to do so.

This starting point, however, can be dangerous because it risks turning into a label or stigma, especially on a social level, and this is particularly true in the age of development. In this regard, Modell (1984), commented that the "facts" of the encounter with the patient may be placed within two different categories, depending on the relationship between the observer and the object of observation. There can be an I–You relationship configuration or an I–It relationship configuration. Both aspects are important, both the I–It relationship, namely, the objectified phenomenon, and the I–You relationship, or the relationship between two subjects. The presence of the observer, and his or her relationship, is therefore extremely important and can orient diagnosis. Psychoanalytic diagnosis must then be a point of arrival that ultimately proves to be uncertain or surprising. Freud (1933) told an amusing story relating to this matter, recalling how this procedure is somewhat similar to the Scottish king's test. This test was designed to assess whether a woman was a witch or not, and essentially consisted

DOI: 10.4324/9781032663371-4

(as Victor Hugo recalls in one of his novels) of taking the woman and putting her into boiling water. After this immersion, the broth was tasted and it could then be decided whether the woman was a witch or not. In the end, in any case, the woman was dead.

The central feature of psychoanalytic diagnosis is a special kind of listening, as containment of anguish and attentive to the other. All this makes any diagnosis, provided it is well conducted, therapeutic. A diagnostic interview is transformative, and indeed, if the patient shows the ability to access a moment of contact and thinkability, we have important information on his or her mental functioning. Particularly in the developmental age, the ability to access an understanding of the unconscious, be it only for a moment, provides information about how the patient functions and might move.

Diagnostic specificity in adolescence

Adolescence requires specific parameters, firstly due to the fact that our assessment may change over time: at this age, there is great mobility of a personality that is being restructured, and because primitive mechanisms may appear on the surface and mimic quite severe pathologies. The fact is that in adolescence, as Florence Guignard (1997) tells us in her book *The Infantile in Psychoanalytic Practice Today*, the preconscious – the buffer area that regulates exchanges between the inner world and external reality – becomes "more transparent and more fragile" until the adolescent has grown. It is precisely this transparency that allows us to see, without pretence, what is happening in the adolescent's inner world. In addition, the inherent tendency to act, the phase-specific processes described in Chapter 1, such as, for example, the inherent difficulties in reflective thinking, can be confusing in the assessment phase.

At the onset of adolescence, which by accepted convention coincides with puberty, we present ourselves with a basic equipment whose most important element is personalisation, that is, the localisation of the self in the body, born – as Winnicott (1949) states – from the settlement of the psyche in the body, thanks to complex processes of integration with its alternating phases of non-integration. Such processes do not end once and for all in childhood, but instead unfold along a continuum, even if there are ages of life such as adolescence in which they take on unique significance. For some, in other terms, adolescence is a crucial period in the process of subjectivization that begins with birth and spans a lifetime. Much can then be played out in those moments as if it were, in the most fortunate cases, the beginning of a new story. But alas, the opposite happens as well. Disorders, problems, difficulties in this first phase can condition new experiences, and the adolescent will then be faced with a two-fold problem: he or she will have to manage the new developmental challenges with more lacking resources.

All this has imposed specific criteria for assessment. Interest has shifted from the diagnosis of structure to another type of assessment that concerns the functioning of the mind rather than the patient's produced material, and relates to the observation of the analytic pair, rather than the repetition in the singular history in *après coup* of old traumas. The study of the workings of the mind and its transformations, how they play out in the analysis room and what promotes the development of thinking instead of acting, the ability to dream and metaphorization processes, have become the central challenge of such a way of conceiving both assessment and treatment of adolescents.

Pre-empted by the positions of Anna Freud, to whom we certainly originally owe the fine-tuning of a developmental model (Freud, 1965), this perspective has found increasing articulation, enriched in various strands of both practice and research. Still today, however, analysts' prejudice and ambivalence around a number of its characteristics remains. This ambivalence was originally due to Anna Freud herself who, as Edgcumbe (1995) argues, believed that developmental help did not constitute a correct analysis, since it could combine the educational and interpretative aspects; conversely, in keeping with the ideas of the time, the aim of analysis should remain the widening of awareness and a greater control of the ego (Hurry, 1997, p. 27). Instead, the aim of this model is rather to remove obstacles that thwart a developmental process, and in this sense, the analyst is also an evocative object that stimulates growth.

From this perspective, one imagines maturity as a path that may be resumed if it is interrupted, and one thinks of the analyst not only as an interpreting object, but as a new object favouring new identifications (Nicolò & Zavattini, 1992).

The central element is no longer the assessment in economic terms, but the assessment of the patient according to his or her ability to cope with the tasks associated with the life cycle phase. If trauma has been re-actualised in *après coup*, there are also new energies and new tasks connected with adolescence that can question the past by re-founding an identity.

Liaisons, déliaisons, reliaisons ["linking," "unlinking" and "re-linking," translator's note] (Cahn, 1991, p. 21; Green, 2002), both in the internal economy and in interpersonal relations, are a dynamic and evolving weave within this tension-filled dialectical movement. As I often like to repeat, what interests us is not so much how the adolescent has been, but what kind of person he or she will be in the future. We are interested in his or her movements, in the risk indicators, negative or positive prognostic elements that can be determined in that person, with that history, living in that environment, and who encounters that analyst. Assessment is thus something that not only implies the consideration of trauma, but above all the patient's resources, as well as the analyst's ability, the work in the analytic pair and the relational world surrounding the adolescent. These positions evoke Laufers' (1984a) admonition to ask ourselves, in assessing the adolescent, whether he or she has tackled the developmental task of puberty or has regressed, or even skipped it altogether.

One of the complications of assessment stems from the fact that the symptom developed by an adolescent before puberty, in childhood, or during adolescence, may have arrested or may arrest the complexity of growth, the processes of subjectivization, or as other analysts have stated (Blos, 1979; Jacobson, 1954), the definition of identity.

If an adolescent withdraws into voluntary seclusion, we must assess not only the withdrawal itself, but the extent to which that symptom deprives him or her of growth, of relationships with peers, deprives him or her of sexual experiences, slows down or blocks cognitive growth, thereby possibly compromising his or her being an adult in the future. Moreover, the symptom in adolescence tends to substitute object relations, and can thus induce a movement of de-objectualisation (Jeammet, 1992, p. 102). We are hence faced with the fact that the natural characteristic of the symptom might replace object relations, thereby inducing a further pathological movement.

This movement alters the capability for libidinal investment, impoverishing the adolescent's relational life even in its phantasmatic dimension.

In these situations, conflicts and issues risk shifting from the internal and external parents to several of the individual's dimensions that are connected, depending on the adolescent's personal story, to different realms: sexuality, the body as whole or specific parts of it, thought in its concrete aspects, learning, or socialisation. All this will obscure the complexity of the underlying organisation and tasks associated with growth.

One of the elements to take into consideration will be the adolescent's ability to use the encounter with the other, be it the therapist or the teacher, for growth. Finally, in the assessment, the functioning of the family as a phantasmatic whole will be crucial, particularly in the cases discussed in this book, where the fragile boundaries of the self call for a thorough screening of the family as both an educational and phantasmatic organisation. In broadly summarising the parameters to bear in mind for assessment, the first concerns the adolescent's relationship with himself or herself; the second, the adolescent's relationship with reality and the outside world; and the third, the adolescent's relationship with the psychotherapist.

As far as the relationship with oneself is concerned, it is useful to observe whether the adolescent is able to acknowledge the state of need and request help. The acceptance or bargaining of dependency are indications that the omnipotent defence and negation of the problem are not so massive, and the capability for self-reflection exists. On the other hand, regarding the adolescent's relationship with reality and the outside world, in addition to the family, a significant element is the conservation of ties with the peer group, school and significant adults. Furthermore, needless to mention the centrality of the relationship with sexuality. As far as reality testing is concerned, we must remember that the adolescent's first reality is the body, as a result, negation of the body equates to negation of reality. Let us also bear in mind that, by definition, psychosis breaks with reality.

An indicator of the adolescent's relationship with himself or herself is the presence or absence of conflicts typical of the various sub-phases – early, middle, and late adolescence – which present differing features. The presence of daydream that usurps mental life or withdrawal into daydream must be carefully considered. An interesting manifestation today is the frequency of withdrawal in internet, situations where the adolescent closes himself or herself off in role-plays or chats, only entering relationships with chat partners, sometimes exhibiting false or rehearsed identities. For example, the adolescent may present himself or herself as male but is female, older or younger than his or her actual age. The functioning of the mind and modulation of tension are also ensured by a healthy use of the preconscious, which, as a buffer zone between the unconscious and the conscious, allows to modulate the terrifying impact potentially deriving from internal disturbances, conflicts, and sexuality. All this is called upon to face the severity of judgement and the rigid superego that some adolescents carry.

The process development of the superego is linked to the elaboration of the Oedipus complex, and a welcoming superego shows the adolescent's ability to separate and individuate from his or her parents. In developmental ruptures, the patient often displays the struggle with a persecutory and torturing superego, as Klein had reported for psychotic patients. Upon closer examination, however, we might see in certain severe patients who feel subjected to destructive and persecutory dynamics and reproaches, that rather than the superego, it is a matter of frighteningly dangerous and terrifying internal objects, that are "split off [...] and are relegated to the deeper layers of the unconscious" (Klein, 1958, p. 242).

Finally, acting is one of the adolescent's ways of communicating, and is unfortunately increasingly taking on destructive characteristics in our society.

We must also bear in mind that physiologically, as the adolescent grows, he or she progressively shifts investment from narcissistic to object-oriented functioning. A positive narcissistic reinvestment on oneself is entirely useful at this age, but it must be progressively transformed into a healthy investment on the other. The phenomenon of the double is particularly significant in this regard given that the double of the self, as seen in the best friend, useful at this age to foster mirroring and stabilise identity, can instead become a figure that immobilises or arrests evolution. It can be a psychotic double, a pathogenic figure that impedes the processes of growth and separation. Finally, the presence of perverse solutions must be carefully considered: they may be passing experiments, or immobilise the subject, or be the defensive outcome that protects against psychotic breakdown.

Recently, the publication of the Psychodynamic Diagnostic Manual PDM-2 (Lingiardi and McWilliams, Speranza, 2017) on childhood and adolescence has provided us with useful parameters of great validity in public service for adolescents or for comparing research on the topic. The axes it considers are well-known and relate to the study of personality (P-axis), the profile of mental functioning (M-axis) and the symptom patterns of subjective experience (S-axis). Quite rightly, despite constituting a vast and admirable effort to order the infinite nuances of pathology, this manual implicitly acknowledges that there exist a myriad causes and characteristics. This is clearly noticeable in the last chapter of the book and, although every clinician must be aware of it, when we find ourselves in front of a person, our assessment will inevitably be the result of an encounter that is hardly classifiable.

Diagnosis as a tool to define setting

Rather than labelling the patient, an accurate diagnosis aims to clarify, in the situation, the most suitable setting – individual, parental couple, family, group, psychodrama, integrated psychotherapy – but also, how to get there.

It may happen, in fact, that individual or family or parental couple treatment prove to be preparatory to one another, progressively overcoming the patient's or the family's resistance to treatment.

At times, it may be necessary to initiate preliminary family treatment to allow the patient to accept pharmacological or individual treatment, or vice versa. For example, it may be that parents who are reluctant to treatment are induced and convinced by their child's behaviour when treated in individual therapy.

Clinical work with adolescents prejudicially requires an assessment of the forces at play, which can be identified in the patient, the family, the treatment team, and the new encounter.

Clearly, with the exception of severe deficits, a plausible prediction of treatment effectiveness depends on a number of different factors, including diagnosis, which is not necessarily the main one. These factors concern the individual patient, namely: age, age of symptom onset and thus chronicity, as well as internal functioning as a primary crucial factor. With regard to the family, alongside its phantasmatic organisation, the possibilities of mobilising its resources, the presence of a member with bargaining power – preferably a parent – capable of offering therapeutic alliance or developing an elaborative capacity, are of great importance. Families with elderly parents or families that are more socially closed off, or those that cannot resort to other resources such as those of the extended family, present a worse prognosis. The greater the level of tension and destructive aggression or the greater the tendency to act out, the poorer the possibility for therapeutic mobilisation.

There may therefore be situations in which the patient's symptomatology does not appear to be severe or particularly limiting to life, development, or relational and emotional abilities, yet the family appears rigid or unable to use its resources. Or, on the contrary, there may be severe situations on the individual level alongside the mobilization of environmental resources that prove to be particularly effective and transformative.

Sound assessment of these aspects also has the effect of warning the psychotherapist against exaggerated pessimism around the possibility of change or, on the contrary, against a perilous therapeutic frenzy that would risk pushing the patient or his or her family far beyond their strengths.

Thus, an extended context of therapy may well not be the most suitable when the adolescent is already seeking to develop an autonomous ability to cope with his or her own problems. The family therapy context would then re-propose the making public of what is being built in secret, allowing parental intrusion and interference into a still fragile individual space.

Based on my clinical experience, the setting with parents will be preferred when the parental couple is overly involved or experiences their child's adolescent crisis with exaggerated rejection or involvement, or when it appears unable to cope with it for reasons pertaining to its internal functioning. It will also be advisable in certain counselling situations where, in the presence of educational dysfunction, parents may be asked to modify certain aspects of family functioning or their relationship with their children.

The family therapeutic context is an appropriate choice, allowing for an effective solution, in the following situations:

a   when, for both the adolescent and the family, acting prevails as a concrete mode of communication or tension evacuation;
b   when the problems expressed by the adolescent are transient but exaggeratedly amplified by the family;
c   when the adolescent's problems are a defensive response to problems of the parental couple or of one of the parents;
d   if the adolescent, even severe, refuses necessary individual treatment.

Finally, there are situations where family treatment must be integrated with individual treatment:

1 Severe situations, such as a psychotic breakdown, where the adolescent presents a fragile ego, whose boundaries are ill-defined, with an insufficient distinction between self and object. In these cases, in the family system there is a difficulty of differentiation, as has been pointed out by many authors, including Searles (1965), but also a sort of "ban on thinking" to use Piera Aulagnier's expression (1984), perpetuated and aggravated over time. In these circumstances, several authors now point to the importance of family work, due to the intrusion processes of parental fantasies into the child's psyche, when the type of family functioning finds its spokesperson in the patient;

2 Psychosomatic situations, in which we might, among other signs, observe that the body vehicle is often chosen by several members of the same family as a means of evacuation or symptomatic communication.

In these cases, only the possibility of integrating the split and projected phantasmatic dimensions into the therapist's mind and into the process allows for effective change.

Moreover, they are not situations that occurred once and for all at the beginning of a child's life. In these pathological situations, we are faced with the traumatic permanence of relational modes of functioning which, not finding the possibility for correction through experience, progressively worsen. Let us therefore put forth the last elective parameter of indication for a psychoanalytic family psychotherapy that accompanies or precedes individual work:

3 situations in which, due to the prevalence of specific modes of interpersonal relations within the family, subjectivization is prevented and, in family life, "the interactive register prevails to the detriment of the intrapsychic one" [tr. by O.M.] (Racamier, 1986, p. 143).

Only an accurate diagnosis is able to indicate, based on the specific situation, whether family treatment should precede or accompany individual treatment of the patient, or whether treatment of the parent couple is instead appropriate, or whether a form of support aimed at proving pedagogical indications or tools for coping with the anxieties emerging in these situations is sufficient.

I believe that any clinician, but above all those who work with the developmental age, even in an individual session, must consider integrating the intrapsychic and interpersonal perspectives, and be aware that all our manifestations, and therefore all symptoms, are located at the intersection between these two modes of functioning. This will prove particularly important at this age given the massive projective identifications and counter-identifications that the adolescent uses and that transform his or her world.

As an illustration of this point and to highlight the extent to which a patient's diagnosis not only becomes clearer as encounters proceed, but can also be modified, I will now discuss Barbara's clinical case.

Barbara was a very pretty fifteen-year-old, but when she came to the first consultation, and also to the subsequent ones, absolutely lifeless and unkempt. She was dressed in such a way that she looked like an elderly lady in a bit of financial difficulty. She did not even seem very interested in seeing a psychoanalyst but had been persuaded by her school friend's mother. She came from a wealthy middle-class family with a successful professional father and a mother who was a teacher, had a brother a few years younger and seemed not to complain about anything. She was a very sensible-looking girl, there were occasional flashes inside her but she was calm, which is strange for an adolescent of that age. One might have thought she was full of guilt. She was not particularly good at school, had no particular interest in boys, had no love life. Upon my request, she told me about her family, with whom she lived: she saw very little of her father, who was away from home until late in the evenings, while her mother spent part of her time on engagements outside the home. I then concluded that the girl had a slight depression of which she seemed to be partially aware. In fact, when asked how, for example, she envisaged her future, she replied that she imagined it, to my great surprise, as a good housewife. She was not interested in going to university, neither was she interested in graduating, nor particularly interested in working. Having concluded this first consultation and awaiting the second, I asked Barbara if she had any trouble with me seeing her parents. Barbara told me that I could talk to them about this on the phone and arrange a meeting with the father, and indeed the father phoned me. He told me that both he and his wife were fully trusting, that it seemed to them that their daughter only needed support, but that they had been given very positive information about me and about the work I could do. It was not possible for the mother to come at that time because she was away from Rome, and the father said they would come at a later date if necessary. Which is rather surprising, given that parents usually want to meet the doctor who will see their child.

The second interview with Barbara more or less repeated the first cliché. The girl talked to me about school, about her friends, but always in a lifeless tone. She stirred my sympathy, however, as well as an intense need to protect her. In any case, Barbara was happy to come and talk to me.

She would occasionally visit Luisa, her best friend, or invite her at her home, although this happened less often. Hence, I started to work.

One day, after a few months, she came somewhat sadder than usual. I asked her what had happened, and she replied that unfortunately she had not been able to go to school due to some engagements. She was very sorry because there was an Italian test, a subject in which she usually did well. A few weeks later, the same thing happened, which made me curious. I asked her what engagements she had had that were so pressing as to keep her out of school: she was attending the first classes of high school and this was important for her future. Barbara answered that she had had to spend the morning repotting the terrace plants and that her mother had forced her to do it because, in her opinion, she had done it wrong a few days earlier. This utterly surprised me, prompting me to further investigate Barbara's relationship with her mother. She was generally rather evasive around her relationship with her parents. The only thing she made clear at that time was that she had the impression that her mother treated her younger brother much better than her; in short, there was jealousy towards her younger brother.

Gradually, a rather astonishing picture opened up to me and, without realising it, the girl revealed the frequent maltreatments her mother subjected her to and the fact that she was progressively pulling her away from her schoolwork. I asked Barbara about what she thought of her mother and of the orders, in my opinion abstruse, that she gave her, but the girl continued to accuse herself of the faults that her mother was blaming her for, albeit utterly insubstantial. The faults were, for example, that she had spoken loudly, had not washed her brother's undergarments well and was to wash them again, had not looked at her nicely, had eaten too much cake, or had taken the liberty of talking to the concierge. Progressively, I began to realise that Barbara was unaware of the mortification she was subjected to. I sought to communicate this to Barbara cautiously but encountered strong resistance. As the months went by, the situation worsened. I was constantly tormenting myself about how true my feeling was that this girl was being maltreated, at the mercy of a severely mentally ill mother, or the extent to which, instead, I was underestimating the girl's pathology, and that perhaps Barbara's problems were so severe as to bring her to tell me things that were unrealistic, or her fantasies. My concern gradually increased, and I eventually told Barbara that I believed it was important for me to see her parents and that this was unavoidable.

She eventually agreed, but needed reassurance that I would be tactful, and that I would not tell her parents about the things she told me. Clearly, I reassured her about my discretion.

Hence, the father phoned me and came. The session took place in Barbara's presence, given that she wanted to look over what was going to happen between me and her father. On that occasion, the father told me a secret, seemingly unknown to Barbara: her mother had been under drug treatment because she had been diagnosed with psychosis, but was currently refusing to take the drug and undergo treatment. We worked on this and the father, in that session, seemed to finally realise that that modus vivendi *was no longer sustainable. In the following months, he decided to force his wife to take medication and return to treatment. His wife refused; therefore, he eventually decided to move and take the children with him. The girl recovered rather quickly. After a few years, having accompanied her up to university, our work terminated. She came after a few years because she wanted to talk to me about a boyfriend she had many doubts about and whom she later left. Today she is a professional, she is married with children, she also takes care of her mother, who is schizophrenic but still refuses medication.*

Comment

In a paragraph from *The suppressed madness of sane men* (1987), Marion Milner puts forth a very interesting reflection on what it means for a child to live with a mother who is insane. In this case "simply to be sane (reality adjusted) involves loss of feeling relation with mother. Madness involves a rigid restriction of the personality and therefore of the ability to share "meanings" with other people." In such instances, "effective therapy in this sort of case requires that the analyst struggles to be free of his own clichés of thought" (*ibid.*, p. 296). I believe this aspect to be of the utmost importance: the need for the observer, the treating analyst, the consulting analyst, in the face of certain cases, to rid oneself of clichés of thinking.

The assessment of psychotic onset in adolescence

Most adolescent analysts suspend the diagnosis of psychosis at this age. This diagnostic caution not only has the value of nosographic precaution, but it also testifies to a specificity of adolescent pathology (a much debated topic) that is quite different from that of adults due to its mobility and evolution, to the point that major psychotic symptoms such as paranoid delusions or hallucinations may be a transitory phenomenon linked to the defence put in place against developmental conflicts.

Thus, the development of adolescents with breakdown presents features that are quite different from those of adults, and perhaps our assessment criteria should also be modified.

With considerations on personality structure or symptomatic manifestations in the background, diagnosis based on risk and prognostic indicators within an accurate study of the global situation proves to be more useful and cautious. Among the criteria to be taken into account I would list, modifying Cahn's (1991) suggestions:

1   the adolescent's ability to preserve, below the narcissistic defences, actively invested object relations (Cahn, 1991);
2   the permanence to varying degrees of object relations with the peer group, in whatever form the group is configured for the adolescent, hence even if it is a group that he or she uses in a confusing, mimetic or adhesive way, or that is based on acting for evacuation or destruction;
3   the ability to mobilise the family environment for therapeutic purposes and thus transform the phantasmatic family world wherever possible;
4   the possibility of a developmental encounter in the therapeutic setting.

Numerous authors, such as Cahn and Jeammet, urge us towards the need to distinguish between various types of psychotic pathology. Yet, in my opinion, the distinction made by the Laufers between psychotic episode, psychotic functioning and ongoing psychotic process (Laufer and Laufer, 1984b), depending on the degree of fracture and/or deformation of reality, is very clear albeit schematic.

By the term acute psychotic episode, they refer to the temporary rupture with reality, as for example occurs in a suicide attempt. Hatred in this case concerns the body and internalised parental objects. In this category, we might also include what is called "brief psychotic disorder" in Chapter 7 of the PDM-2, namely, "a sudden onset of positive symptomatology characterised by delusions, hallucinations, formal thought disorders, and grossly disorganised behaviour, including catatonia. In adolescents, these psychotic symptoms are frequently associated with phenomena of depersonalisation and/or derealisation, extreme mood lability, and a dream state of consciousness without proper confusion" (p. 391). The characteristic feature of these episodes is their abruptness and short duration. In certain cases, however, they are the prodromes of a far more complex disorder, such as schizophrenia.

In the case of psychotic functioning, reference is made to pathologies such as anorexia, severe addictive forms that may conceal a true psychotic organisation, or certain pathologies such as severe depression or similar disorders. In these cases, in addition to acting against the body, a denial of reality is established, and sometimes even a delusional or hallucinatory mode of functioning may occur (suffice it to recall the denial of the body or body dysperceptions in some anorexics).

Finally, the ongoing psychotic process, in the course of which, in order to maintain the cohesion of the self, the adolescent constructs a new reality where the internal parents have been destroyed by incestuous or incestual functioning. Anguished doubt around identity, acknowledgement of the possibility of change, or acknowledgement of otherness, is replaced by delusions.

As can be seen, albeit to varying degrees, in the distinction the Laufers propose, we find that common element that is the partial or total loss of connection with reality.

Already in itself, the underlying problem for the psychotic patient is precisely the impossibility of relating to what is real. For the adolescent, then, this aspect takes on further significance, as the challenge in adolescence is the modification in relating to reality.

I believe there is a further type of functioning that temporally originates precisely in adolescence, and that I have called "latent psychosis." By this term, I wish to designate those personalities that maintain themselves, sometimes fortunately, in a precarious equilibrium throughout their lives. A latent psychosis can remain in the balance for years, compensated by the bond with the other, who is parasitised, exploited, and in turn exploits and parasites the patient in the relationship, as we can see in certain parent-child couplings or in certain marital couples. These are patients who sustain themselves even into old age through the use of rigid defences and by mutilating aspects of their lives and personalities. These patients may never decompensate or do so late in life, when traumatic events or emergencies in their life cycle lead to a recurring surge in tension and a reappearance of unresolved conflicts dating back to adolescence.

These individuals have evidently short-circuited or skipped adolescence altogether, and thus the challenge and crossroads of subjectivization that adolescence represents.

Finally, the developmental rupture may have compensatory outcomes that bypass the possible creative and healthy development of personality, but are rather adjustment solutions that sometimes mutilate the individual. I discuss these in Chapters 4 and 9. Particularly, perverse solutions and their future can be difficult to assess considering that at this age we witness the presence of polymorphous-perverse dispositions riddled with bisexual confusions (Meltzer, 1973). We know that the preoccupation that adolescents may have with the definition of gender identity is quite frequent, as are the homosexual anxieties arising from the vicissitudes of identification, as well as frightening and haunting passivity. All this is part of the *development from childhood homoeroticism to puberty* (Gutton, 1991).

Such worries and anxieties must be delicately assessed, as they may also be indications of an incipient and broader regression. Every so often these aspects result in polymorphous-perverse acts, an expression of a difficulty in the process of subjectivization. These phenomena can sometimes be organised in a sort of transitory perversions (Bonnet, 2006; Cahn, 1991; Nicolò, 2009), which are also facilitated by the normal reorganisation of the superego, which in this period of life is not a willing ally (Freud, 1936).

Complexity of diagnosis

Despite the widespread past and current effort in the attempt to understand these phenomena and bring order to their complexity, I believe the outcome has been a multiplication of syndromes, parameters, and groupings.

In my experience and in that of many clinicians with whom I have consulted, particularly in adolescence, the same type of patient can evolve quite differently depending on fortunate encounters or effective therapy. Adolescents whose lives seemed marked by severe and profoundly limiting challenges in their development, first struggle to live with them, to then go on to integrate and function happily. Therefore, given the same symptomatology (if such a claim can be scientifically made!), the way each person responds to it and contains it, the ability to cope with it, and the help received from the environment, can all play a relevant role.

43

The risk factors in the creation and development of mental illness have always been discussed. Assessment of the risks of evolution towards a psychotic disorder in patients with specific features has become a topical issue, to the extent that a new category has been created, that of "clinical high risk status" (Fusar-Poli et al., 2012) in predicting the onset of psychosis. Indeed, establishing risk factors might prove particularly interesting in defining possible preventive interventions. Genetic, environmental, and experiential factors undoubtedly play a role, yet they can be challenged by effective agency or other personality resources.

I must emphasise the fact that psychoanalysis has always posed this problem, albeit indirectly and not specifying it in these words, but the thorough study of early childhood and adolescence indeed informs us in this regard.

Certain patients' diagnoses challenge our need for security, the canons on which we have built our knowledge. I believe that, in the encounter with the patient, a two-fold perspective is needed: the psychiatric point of view, but at the same time – as psychoanalysts and psychotherapists in general – the centre of our relationship with the other must always be the encounter of two subjectivities. What happened in Barbara's case is that the patient's assessment became clearer as the analysis proceeded and changed. As Winnicott says: "a hysteric may reveal underlying schizophrenia, a schizoid person may turn out to be the healthy member of an ill family grouping, an obsessional may turn out to be a depressive. Practicing psychoanalysts would agree that there is a gradation from normality not only into psycho-neurosis but also into psychosis, and the close connection between depression and normality has already been stressed" (Winnicott, 1959, p.131). On the relationship with psychosis, Winnicott adds: "for instance, the artist has an ability and the courage to be in touch with primitive processes which the psycho-neurotic cannot bear to reach, and which healthy people miss to their own impoverishment" (*ibid.*, p. 131).

One mistake we must never make is that of focusing solely on the patient's internal world while failing to assess his or her significant links. In certain situations, if we investigate the family or parental or even work ties that the patient experiences, interesting discoveries can be made, such as the ones I made with Barbara, and this might potentially save the patient, especially in adolescence. In the article *A note on normality and anxiety* (1931), Winnicott speaks of the case of a little girl who was perfectly healthy until the arrival of her little brother. Following this event, she had lost her appetite, lost weight, became withdrawn, did not speak, woke up in the night screaming, bit others and herself, and was afraid, presenting a phobia of animals. After analysing this case, Winnicott's conclusion was that "it can be more normal for a child to be ill than to be well" (*ibid.*, p. 4). In another work, *Symptom tolerance in paediatrics* (1953), Winnicott exposes cases in which a child uses a disorder with a physical or psychic symptom, for example enuresis, to succeed in regaining normality and the fluidity of his or her emotional development, also thanks to the fact that this symptom can stimulate him or her precisely because of the positivity of a crisis, and stimulate the environmental context in which he or she lives. In short, we can fall ill in the other, but also heal ourselves in the other, who can become the bearer of suffering in our place. It is therefore important to give illness its relational meaning as well: it is relative to a time, a phase of life, an environment, and a world of which it is an expression.

Faced with an adolescent presenting a developmental rupture, we cannot lose hope and we must fight for his or her future, as there is always a healthy person in every psychosis, as Freud asserted. Indeed, perhaps the psychotic gaze itself illuminates phenomena and truths that we would not otherwise have known.

Although it may come across as a romantic digression, I would like to recall what Laing wrote: "Madness need not be all breakdown. It may also be break-through [...]. From the alienated starting point of our pseudo-sanity, everything is equivocal. Our sanity is not "true" sanity. Their madness is not "true" madness. The madness of our patients is an artifact of the destruction wreaked on them by us, and by them on themselves. We do not encounter true madness, just as we are not truly sane" (Laing, 1967, p. 129).

References

Aulagnier, P. (1984). Un discours à la place de l' "infans". In *L'Apprenti-Historicien et le Maître-Sorcier: Du Discours Identifiant au Discours Délirant*. Paris: P.U.F.

Blos, P. (1979). *The adolescent passage: Developmental issues*. New York: International University Press.

Bonnet, G. (2006). La perversion transitoire à l'adolescence. *Adolescence*, 24 (3): 555–571.

Cahn, R. (1991). *Adolescence et Folie: Les Déliaisons Dangereuses*. Paris: P.U.F.

Edgcumbe, R. (1995). The history of Anna Freud's thinking on developmental disturbances. *Bulletin of the Anna Freud Centre*, 18 (1): 21–34.

Freud, A. (1936). *The ego and the mechanisms of defence*. London: Karnac Books, 1992.

Freud, A. (1965). *Normality and pathology in childhood*: *Assessments of development*. London: Routledge, 1989.

Freud, S. (1933). New introductory lectures on psycho-analysis. *S.E.* 22: 1–182, London: Hogarth Press.

Fusar-Poli, P., I. Bonoldi et al. (2012). Predicting psychosis: Meta-analysis of transition outcomes in individuals at high clinical risk. *Archives of General Psychiatry*, 69 (3): 220–229.

Green, A. (2002). *Key ideas for a contemporary psychoanalysis: misrecognition and recognition of the unconscious*. London: Routledge, 2005.

Guignard, F. (1997). *The infantile in psychoanalytic practice today*. London: Routledge, 2002.

Gutton, P. H. (1991). L'homonyme et l'anonyme. In *Le Pubertaire*. Paris: PUF.

Hurry, A. (1997). La prospettiva evolutiva nella psicoanalisi contemporanea: implicazioni tecniche per l'analisi infantile. In *Richard e Piggle*, 5 (1): 1997.

Jacobson, E. (1954). *The self and the object world*. New York: International University Press.

Jeammet, P. H. (1992). Sulla specificità della patologia mentale in adolescenza. Conseguenze sugli approcci terapeutici. Tr. it. in *Psicopatologia dell'adolescenza*. Roma: Borla.

Klein, M. (1958). On the development of mental functioning. In *Envy and Gratitude and other works, 1946–1963*. London: Hogarth Press, 1975.

Laing, R. D. (1967). *The politics of experience*. New York: Knopf Doubleday Publishing Group.

Laufer, M. and Laufer, E. M. (1984a). *Adolescence and developmental breakdown: A psychoanalytic view*. London: Routledge, 2018.

Laufer, M. and Laufer, E. M. (1984b). Assessment of psychopathology in adolescence. In *Adolescence and developmental breakdown: A psychoanalytic view*. London: Routledge, 2018.

Lingiardi, V. and McWilliams, N. (Eds.) (2017). *Psychodynamic diagnostic manual: (PDM–2)*. New York: Guilford Press.

Meltzer, D. (1973). *Sexual states of the mind*. London: Karnac Books, 2008.

Milner, M. (1987). *The suppressed madness of sane men: Forty-four years of exploring psychoanalysis*. London: Routledge.

Modell, A. H. (1984). *Psychoanalysis in a new context*. New York: International University Press.

Nicolò, A. M. (2009). Breakdown et solutions défensives chez l'adolescent. Talk presented at the SEPEA Seminar (Paris, 18 September 2009). In S.M. Passone and F. Guignard (Eds.), *Psychanalyse de l'Enfant et de l'Adolescent. Etat des Lieux et Perspectives.* In Press, Collection SEPEA, Paris, 2014.

Nicolò, A. M. and Zavattini, G. C. (1992). *L'Adolescente e il suo Mondo Relazionale.* Roma: La Nuova Italia Scientifica.

Racamier, P. C. (1986). L'intrapsychique, l'interactif et le changement à l'adolescence et dans la psychose. In J.J. Baranes *et al.* (Eds.), *Psychanalyse, Adolescence et Psychose.* Paris: Payot.

Searles, H. F. (1965). *Collected papers on schizophrenia and related subjects.* New York: International University Press.

Winnicott, D. W. (1931). A note on normality and anxiety. In (1958), *Through paediatrics to psycho-analysis.* New York: Basic Books, 1975.

Winnicott, D. W. (1949). Mind and its relation to the psyche-soma. In (1958), *Through paediatrics to psycho-analysis.* New York: Basic Books, 1975.

Winnicott, D. W. (1953). Symptom tolerance in paediatrics: A case history. In (1958), *Through paediatrics to psycho-analysis.* New York: Basic Books, 1975.

Winnicott, D. W. (1959). Classification: Is there a psycho-analytic contribution to psychiatric classification? In (1965) *The maturational processes and the facilitating environment: Studies in the theory of emotional development.* London: Routledge, 1990.

3

BREAKDOWN AND DEVELOPMENTAL RUPTURES

Adolescence is an extraordinary opportunity for growth because it can restructure personality in a new and definitive form by grasping the stimuli that reality offers, even if this transformation always operates based on the childhood past and inter- and trans-generational mandates. It is precisely these characteristics, however, that subject it to potential ruptures, at times impressive breakdowns, which can evolve in a number of ways. In most cases, provided treatment is timely, the outcome can be a positive one. Even in the most severe cases, when well-treated or when reality offers them an opportunity for transformation, the outcome may even not be that of a debilitating or chronic illness.

In *Catch Them Before They Fall*, Bollas speaks of breakdown as "a moment of self-fragmentation [and], at the same time, a moment of coming together inside the self. In the end, it is formative more than fracturing" (Bollas, 2013, p. 69).

In this book, Bollas in fact mentions experiences that may concern the whole course of life, although he refers in particular to young adulthood and speaks mainly of events that may result in growth of the personality and indeed are the occasion of it.

Other authors, such as Eglé and Moses Laufer, limit the diagnosis of developmental breakdown to adolescence, affirming, however, that at this age of life one cannot and should not diagnose a full-blown psychosis. By this term, they refer to a "critical occurrence" that, despite establishing itself in puberty and although it has its antecedent in early childhood – at the time of the resolution of the Oedipus complex, "[exerts] a cumulative effect throughout adolescence, with

DOI: 10.4324/9781032663371-5

serious implications for normality and psychopathology of adulthood" (Laufer & Laufer, 1984, p. 21).

These authors speak of a breakdown that may nevertheless present characteristics of a useful development in the personality. Indeed, Bollas argues that breakdown can be "a necessary crisis" (2013, p. 2) that the therapist, if there is one, must utilise it to prevent it from becoming structural, "as a permanent fault within the self" (*ibid.*).

Along similar lines as the Laufers, Bollas states that "the outcome of a breakdown is not necessarily a descent into psychotic decompensation" (*ibid.*). He argues that people who have had a breakdown, which has not turned into a breakthrough, become a broken self, hence functioning in compromised ways for the rest of their lives.

However, the term breakdown bears different meanings according to different authors. Indeed, other psychoanalysts have underlined the need to distinguish between forms of breakdown that present a rupture, and other more contained forms, where the ego structure remains intact despite a momentary fracture in integration. Cathy Bronstein (2019) reflected upon the elements that distinguish a rupture from a fracture, which in her view is a more contained temporary process in which the ego remains intact. On the contrary, Winnicott, in a psychoanalytic masterpiece (1963a), speaks of breakdown as opposed to psychosis that constitutes a reorganisation against breakdown, as I elaborate in the following chapter.

As much as it is necessary to avoid confusion, I firmly believe the term developmental breakdown has come into such vast use among adolescent psychiatrists and psychoanalysts that one cannot help but use it, except in those cases in which one is able to clearly and definitively distinguish schizophrenic or psychotic onsets, with which breakdown is sometimes confused. In these cases, we are in the presence of a breakdown and not of a developmental rupture.

In this book, I have preferred to use the term "developmental rupture," in alternation to the classic "developmental breakdown," to indicate developmental crises that indeed appear severe to the clinician, but that can also evolve positively. Such ruptures, if not properly treated, progress dangerously: the adolescent's mental functioning is mobile and can be restructured, provided favourable situations occur. Left to its own devices, the psychotic part of these personalities takes over.

It is therefore crucial for the clinician to distinguish between the two modes of functioning, given this distinction indicates different possible working techniques, to distinguish prognosis by intervening with different perspectives. It is then possible to obtain, if the work is effective, recovery in one case, and a significant improvement in the other, albeit with partial healing.

It is important to assess each patient carefully, observing how he or she transforms over time, and with the awareness that the therapeutic process and relationship with reality, with the family, with the peer group, can steer the course in a progressive or regressive direction. In this sense, I wish to lay claim to the importance of a clinical psychoanalysis that is attentive to the efficacy of treatment and able to reflect on prognosis, treatment indicators and patient well-being; a psychoanalysis that adapts to the patient and observes the transformations of the co-constructed pair between patient and analyst, as I have discussed in other works (Nicolò, 2020; 2022).

It is therefore of the utmost importance to be extremely cautious around assessment, in this period of life, with regard to a diagnosis of full-blown psychosis. Firstly, because such a diagnosis functions as a condemnation in the patient's relational world and favours chronicity, but above all, this caution responds to a specificity of adolescent pathology that is quite different from adult pathology.

Specificity in adolescence

It seems to me that developmental ruptures arising in late adolescence somehow repeat, despite their peculiarity, certain common characteristics.

Among these, the most important is the defect or difficulty in subjectivization, understood as the failure of a cognitive-emotional process which, according to Cahn (1986; 1991), allows the subjective appropriation of one's world and the development of a creative ability of the subject that enables him or her to dis-alienate from the parental or transgenerational mandate.

This process finds one of its culminating moments and certainly the most significant, given the developmental tasks these patients face, at the end of adolescence.

Yet the rupture of subjectivization – of which the psychotic symptom represents at its extreme the defensive reorganisation, with its characteristics of omnipotence, negation, massive projection and all the psychotic defensive equipment – is never reducible to the projection of an unconscious fantasy onto a neutral reality. The real situation collides with internal functioning.

Thus, the symptom represents a complex product of the precipitation from an occasional trauma, of a psychotic collusion between the identity conflict, a problem in subjectivization that is typical of adolescence, and primary narcissistic fragility (Cahn, 1991, p. 264).

Occasional causes are reported by patients as triggering events, but in actual fact, they are the prelude to a broader and older problem. Among these we might find, for example, a sentimental abandonment, a momentary distancing from home, contact with the death of a friend or other, a sexual initiation; or even simpler events, such as something a teacher said, or a picture on the internet. These triggering events plunge the personality into a state of massive tension, with a sense of urgency that the adolescent wants to recompose as quickly as possible.

Under these conditions, adolescence will therefore not be able to express its organisational and reorganising capability of mental functioning.

All this takes place on pre-existing and unique grounds, which is the premise of any psychotic breakdown. This is what Aulagnier, one of the most acute scholars of these issues, has called the psychotic potential. It indicates the presence of what the Franco-Italian psychoanalyst calls "an incrusted and unrepressed primary delusional thought" [tr. by O.M.] (Aulagnier, 1975; De Mijolla-Mellor, 1998, pp. 53–85) to signify that peculiar encounter *between the patient's ego and a specific organisation of the out-of-psyche space and the discourse circulating therein* (Aulagnier, 1986). The concept of psychotic potential also expresses the complexity of what takes place in these situations because it speaks of a clash encounter that the patient carries out, the outcome of which cannot be determined from the outset. Indeed, this potential may remain latent even throughout life if the encounter with the other and with life events do not unleash it. It also points to a multifactorial genesis in which the functioning of the environment, of which the patient is an active and integral part, is of great importance, as I illustrate in this chapter.

Precisely this functioning and this encounter carry primal traumatic value, which the subsequent occasional trauma reactivates and evokes. Moreover, this type of functioning will later be echoed in the patient's symptoms. In some ways, the concept of psychotic potential is reminiscent of Cahn's (1991) concept of alienating identifications or Garcia Badaracco's (1986) maddening objects, namely, of an alien introject that derives from the parental phantasmatic world and occupies the patient's self by subjugating it from within. The maddening object is not only pathological, but also pathogenic throughout life, continuing to exert its pathogenic influence even after the onset of symptoms.

When breakdown explodes

We might hypothesise that on the intrapsychic level breakdown explodes when the adolescent is unable to accept the mourning over the childhood past, to integrate aggression and the storm of new sensations generated by the body, subject and object of new sexual and sensual urges. These new sensations in fact threaten a personality that carries an integration of those primitive experiences of the self never fully experienced before. Hence, the threat of being overwhelmed is big, and it is as if the reality of the body itself took on persecutory significance (Laufer, 2002, p. 369). As a result, it is reality itself that is denied.

Despite finding in the body one of its main points of failure, the rupture is the moment in which numerous other vicissitudes coagulate: the impossibility of establishing flexible boundaries of the self and constructing one's own individuation, transgenerational dynamics, the failure of the protective screen, the impossibility of grieving parental objects, in short, all obstacles to subjectivization (Cahn, 1991, p. 103; 1998) and, not least, the elaboration of the renewed Oedipus complex.

Faced with all these distinguishing tasks of adolescence, the clinician will have to assess a number of important factors to define the picture:

1 The organisation and cohesion of the self that the adolescent has achieved, thanks to his or her ability to integrate the sensory and the sensual.
2 The quantity of arousal he or she will encounter at that moment. In this respect, we might pose the interesting question as to whether it is the quantity or rather the quality of arousal that is disruptive.
3 The ability to think these new experiences. The question remains as to whether breakdown represents the failure of this process, or whether there is instead a continuous oscillation between different modes of functioning.

4   The response of the other, currently present and not just the object of the past, will be equally relevant.

The response from the parent, the teacher, the friend, the group, the partner, and therefore also the analyst, may prove crucial. Once again, the other will be implicated, in his or her capacity for containment, mirroring, and *rêverie*. In my experience, then, breakdowns that underlie true psychotic organisations are always located within a traumatic organisation of family links that characterise the subject's origin even before birth.

The psychotic onset as organisation of traumatic links

When we speak of such pathologies, we are faced with real modes of functioning that are sometimes organised over several generations, where the parents were themselves unsuspecting victims of similar functioning, being themselves unsuspecting persecutors of both their children and their parents. Rather, I propose to think of them as real "organisations of traumatic links" that characterise that environment from the very beginning of the child's life, and sometimes precede the child's birth. These organisations influence the subject's future identity because of the maddening objects, the alienating identifications that parents unconsciously operate, colonising the child's mind and impoverishing the self, but also because of the quality of functioning of these families that share specific links within which everyone is imprisoned, usually without realising it. Every member of the family, willingly or unwillingly, is involved in this organisation.

These types of pathologies are rightly to be considered transpersonal, given that they involve not only the intrapsychic and interpersonal level of functioning, but also that area of primitive unconscious communications, acted out or somatized, the site of transgenerational and transpersonal defences characterised by inhibited thought, the inclination to anything concrete and acted, and the site of transmission of unelaborated secrets and traumas. Psychotic relational modes of functioning are above all part of a family lexicon that the child learns from the origins of life and are not only pathogenic at the origin, but persist and perpetuate throughout existence.

Yet, in returning to the explosion that is typical of this period of life, the adolescent will respond differently depending on the resources available to him or her and also depending on the therapeutic encounters he or she will make.

Freud had already presented us with remarkable examples of the extent to which imbalances can lead to different outcomes, and the extent to which it is necessary to follow their evolution over time.

Gradiva and the uncanny

In a rather well-known work, *Delusion and Dreams in Jensen's Gradiva* (1907), Freud brilliantly discusses the psychotic decompensation of a young adult: Norbert.

Ladame (1991) and Ladame and Perret-Catipovic (1998) also compared this case with that of Nathaniel in *The Uncanny*, noting the features that lead to a positive conclusion of the developmental rupture in Norbert's case, and to psychosis, delusions, hallucinations, and finally to a tragic death by suicide in Nathaniel's. To briefly summarise the comparison, I will outline both stories.

In *Delusion and Dreams in Jensen's Gradiva*, Freud tells the story of a young student and his psychological vicissitudes. Norbert and Zoe are two children, inseparable friends in childhood; however, in adolescence Norbert turns away from girls of his age and immerses himself in his studies of archaeology. He meets Zoe, his childhood romance partner, but does not see her. Instead, he develops a vicarious interest in bronze and marble, but also in the foot of a Roman bas-relief depicting a walking maiden. All his energy is absorbed by Gradiva and this foot, to such an extent that he decides to set off for Pompeii. Amidst the excavations, he will meet Zoe without recognising her at first, yet this encounter will ultimately prove to be fortunate. In fact, after a long period, which today we would qualify as withdrawal and confusion, he dreams of the destruction of his beloved Gradiva in the eruption of the volcano that destroyed Pompeii, though this dream is also connected to the beginning of his delusions. He is convinced that he sees Gradiva returned to life and mistakes Zoe, who happens to be in Pompeii, for his idealised heroine. The end of the story, as we all know, is a happy one, as he finally finds in reality his friend from the past, whom he had never ceased to love, and abandons the fantasy/hallucination of meeting the archaeological figure who has returned to life. In this story, we may discern Norbert's fear in approaching the reality of sexuality and the strong defensive intellectualisation used. The hallucinatory phenomena he suffered may sometimes be present in situations of intense stress; nonetheless, despite everything, the young archaeologist maintains a continuity in the structure of the ego and in his ability to think, only momentarily obnubilated.

Different and tragic is the fate of another young man about whom Freud tells us in *The Uncanny* (1919). Nathaniel is the protagonist of a short story, taken from Offenbach's *Tales of Hoffmann*, who cannot rid himself of the memories linked to the mysterious death of his father. One of these memories refers to a sort of ominous fairy tale that a nanny used to tell him before he fell asleep. The Sandman would come find the children who would not fall asleep, he was an evil man who would throw handfuls of sand into their eyes, to the point that these would bleed and pop out of their orbits. One evening, Nathaniel hides in his father's study and believes he recognises the Sandman in a visitor of his father's, the lawyer Coppelius. Later, Nathaniel, who had kept this childhood memory, has the impression that he recognises the figure of Coppelius in an Italian travelling optician, a certain Giuseppe Coppola, from whom he buys a pocket telescope. With this telescope, he begins to watch the house opposite where lives a scientist, Professor Spallanzani, and there he catches a glimpse of his beautiful daughter Olympia, who, however, always appears motionless and silent. The young man falls so madly in love with her that he forgets his wise and prosaic fiancée. In truth, Olympia is an automaton, a mechanical doll into which Spallanzani has inserted a mechanism and Coppola the eyes. It is an argument that he witnesses between Spallanzani and Coppola that will lead to the boy's decompensation. Nathaniel leaps on Professor Spallanzani with the intention of strangling him. After being hospitalised and having recovered from his illness, he intends to marry his fiancée, yet one evening, as he climbs up a tower, he believes he sees Coppelius in the crowd below him, at which point he jumps off the tower and dies.

Freud recounts how, at several moments, Nathaniel seems to have lost touch with reality: as a child when he mistook the lawyer Coppelius for the Sandman; later when he mistakes the mechanical doll for a real maiden and falls in love with her; and finally, when from the tower he believes he can see the lawyer Coppelius below. There have of course been many reflections by psychoanalysts on the analysis of the *Uncanny*. It is well known that Freud develops the relationship between the familiar and the unfamiliar, or in other words the uncanny, yet uncanny is also the body for the adolescent, a body that is both familiar and unfamiliar. This duplicity is another important theme, a harbinger of irremediable uncertainties around identity: the topic of the double is one of the leitmotifs of Nathaniel's story. In fact, we find it represented in several moments by the narcissistic doubling, according to Freud, of the image of the father with a split between opposites, between a bad father, Coppelius, who threatens the son, and a good father who protects him. The double self, the lookalike, is a central figure in the adolescent's development, as it also represents a crucial element in the identification process. In this dynamic, one can observe – says Freud – that "[he] identifies himself with someone else, so that he is in doubt as to which his self is, or substitutes the extraneous self for his own. In other words, there is a doubling, dividing and interchanging of the self" (*ibid.*, p. 234). Olympia, as Freud tells us, is a narcissistic double of Nathaniel, "a materialization of Nathaniel's feminine attitude towards his father in his infancy" (*ibid.*, p. 232). But above all, she is robotic, just as the young man is defensively robotic, and just as these adolescents with a difficult use of their bodies often present themselves as robotic.

Freud's accurate description of Nathaniel's evolution shows us the infantile antecedent of the psychotic onset. From his earliest years, the boy mistakes his father for Coppelius and retains the memory of the Sandman who, by tearing out eyes, prevents him from seeing reality. In a dissociated part of himself, Nathaniel will retain this terrifying secret passed on to him by his nanny, who may represent his mother's evil double, until the psychotic breakdown erupts in adolescence.

Early on in Nathaniel, "two psychical attitudes have been formed instead of a single one – one, the normal one, which takes account of reality, and another which under the influence of the instincts detaches the ego from reality" – as Freud states: "the two exist alongside of each other. The issue depends on their relative strength. If the second is or becomes the stronger, the necessary precondition for a psychosis is present" (Freud, 1938, p. 202).

In keeping with Freud's ideas, De Masi (2011) asserts that the child who will become psychotic in the future has constructed a dissociated part of himself or herself that coexists with a "relational part," from the very beginning. In psychosis, the balance between these two parts progressively shifts in the direction of the former.

According to De Masi, the child who will become psychotic "does not use [his or her] mind to understand the world but to produce pleasurable images-sensations [...] This distortion in the use of the mind is very important to produce, when the psychotic process is advanced, hallucinations that are, in fact, a derivative of the sensory use of the mind that, in this case, produces self-generated perceptions from withdrawal into one's own body" [tr. by O.M.] (*ibid.*, p. 5). A developmental stalemate is thus generated, as the Laufers (1984) described: the adolescent swings between this internal and secret withdrawal, hidden from others and where omnipotence prevails and new sensations are abolished, and the relationship with reality that is dangerous, because it is too intrusive or arousing.

Norbert too had kept secret his love for Gradiva, the dancing figure who had enraptured him, and he too seems to hallucinate a double when he mistakes Zoe for the archaeological figure. Yet Norbert relates with Zoe, a flesh-and-blood person, and the encounter he makes turns out to be salvific. In contrast, Olympia is an automaton, a mechanical doll, a representation of Nathaniel's split and unintegrated body.

Zoe then reveals – as Freud himself states – a therapeutic capability of no small importance. She allows him, through a process in small steps made of ironies and delicate allusions, to recognise reality and replace delusion. Zoe "accepted the role of the ghost awakened to life for a brief hour, a role for which, as she perceived, his delusion had cast her, and [...] she gently hinted in ambiguous words at the possibility of his taking up a new position" (p. 70), "here she was trespassing into the field of archaeology, just as he had trespassed, with his simile of lizard-catching, into the field of zoology" (*ibid.*, p. 83). Freud later continues by commenting on the girl's double meaning speech, where "one meaning of them falls in with the ideas of Hanold's delusion, in order to enable her to penetrate into his conscious comprehension, the other raises itself above the delusion, and, as a rule, gives us the interpretation of it in the unconscious truth which has been represented by it" (*ibid.*, p. 84). Although Freud comments on the obvious impossibility for the therapist to perform the same function as Zoe, we may nevertheless draw some food for thought. Both the Norbert of Gradiva and the Nathaniel of the Uncanny, while having a markedly different outcome – the former in recovery and the latter in full-blown psychosis and suicide – seem at some point to be taking a perverse drift: Norbert becomes interested, albeit transiently, in Gradiva's foot, and Nathaniel is in love with Professor Spallanzani's mechanical doll.

I believe it is now important to observe what happens in clinical practice. Some of the cases I will expose, evaluated based on a criterion in adult psychopathology, would appear very serious. We must not forget, however, that in adolescence some manifestations may mimic psychotic functioning. In fact, without presenting characteristics of severity, there may be temporary confusions between self and other, between reality and fantasy, and between masculine and feminine, momentary refuges in daydream, and an improper use of aggression. All this will be well illustrated by the following case of Giovanni.

Pseudo-delusional fantasies and risk of decompensation

Giovanni,[1] sixteen years old, seeks treatment prompted by his mother who was frightened and feared for her son's sanity after secretly reading some letters he had addressed to a friend. In these letters, Giovanni spoke of his alleged relationship with aliens against whom he was preparing to fight. He was helped every night by a martial arts master who appeared to him in his dreams and thus trained together with two friends. Giovanni comes without any particular resistance to the psychotherapy service of a public facility and accepts the diagnostic consultations proposed. Four years ago, his family moved to a small new town and Giovanni left his old friends behind. He is now alone and, what is more, failed to pass the year in school because of his absences. His life is difficult: he must help his father with work in the fields, pruning trees and chopping wood, because the farmhouse where they live is still being renovated. For example, they are still without hot water in the bathroom and the boy is forced to wash in the swimming pool he goes to. The father is a rough and stubborn man, sacrificing the whole family for the business, without realising the simple needs of the boy, whom he continually debases.

The move has been a real earthquake for Giovanni, which the boy tries to contain as best he can. For example, he keeps up a dense and real correspondence with his two friends, and they sometimes see each other at weekends. They therefore remain for some time the only boys by whom he feels happily accepted, but unfortunately he has no deep acquaintances in the new town or school. Giovanni claims that he and his two friends have a code name taken from cartoon heroes, though he says they are actually special beings with a mission to defend the planet from an alien attack. For now, the three of them must acquire special powers and learn to control the force. Giovanni says that every night a long dream, which he is able to command, unites him with his friends. He recounts, in the second diagnostic session, one of these dreams: *in a grey stone city in the future, scenes of life take place. The master teaches him to concentrate, so as to avoid fighting as he would like. He and one of his friends cook food because they do not like to eat raw. They have a point in the centre of their body that will gradually heat up, and that will be a dangerous moment as they will not be able to distinguish good from evil in that moment.* Giovanni claims that he cannot choose the content of his dreams, even though he can get out of them whenever he wants. For example, if, while falling asleep, he dreams of falling, he is able to wake up.

In subsequent sessions, to the astonished and concerned doctor who is listening to him, Giovanni will tell of other aspects of his life, among which his sudden love for a girl of his age who served him in a bar and to whom he left a note. He then returned to get to know her better and get in touch with her. He comments on his relationship with his parents, whose positive and self-sacrificing aspects he is also able to appreciate. The encounters with the doctor fortunately continue, and as the analytical work unfolds, Giovanni gradually opens up to the new environment and new social relations, while over time the themes he referred to in dreams and daydreams fade away. This case seems paradigmatic in illustrating the confused and confusing boundary we sometimes have between dream, delusion and daydream. The use of daydream is ubiquitous in the age of latency and early adolescence. One wonders in this case if there is not another phenomenon: a defensive refuge that subtracts energy from reality and from the thought process. Perhaps what is interesting in this regard is not only the content of the daydreams, but rather how present they are, to what extent they occupy mental and real life, whether the adolescent manages to escape the compulsion to repeat them, whether they affect aspects of reality, to what extent they blend with dreams, etc.

It is quite legitimate to ponder what we are dealing with in Giovanni.

Is it the persistence beyond early adolescence of daydreams that defensively occupy the whole of mental life? Or are we instead faced with a delusional refuge where perceptions of unpleasant and frustrating reality have been split off, where narcissistic omnipotence reigns supreme, progressively closing the patient to the relationship with the other and reality? What is worrying in this case is the break-in that Giovanni denounces in the space of the dream, in its boundary, that boundary which is the general guarantee of a border existing between reality and fantasy, external world and internal world. Furthermore, Giovanni adds that his dream is shared with other friends, which extends or ends at will, and that daydream seems to implant itself in it without any modification. Yet we would be quite superficial, however, if in the face of all these concerns we did not consider other aspects, such as the patient's ability to ask for help, his need for close friends that he cannot lose, the search for dependency that he fulfils with the fantasy of the master, who in some ways teaches him to concentrate and not be destructive.

Thus, although the master is an expression of Giovanni's omnipotent and megalomaniac fantasy, it is also true that he uses him positively to contain his anger and destructive acts. Friends are doubles who immobilise him by narcissistically preventing new relationships, yet they are also the continuity with his past and the preservation of a meaningful emotional link.

In the dream, we can distinguish a first part characterised by representations in visual images, among which we recognise the grey city of the future and life choices, and a second part structured upon an affective state and related fantasies originating in the body (at the centre of the body there is a point that will gradually heat up). There are therefore visual representations in the dream alongside experiences and fantasies based on aspects of thermal, kinaesthetic, proprioceptive, and interoceptive sensoriality, indicating the presence of different mental states, as well as internalised and non-integrated object relations of a different nature. But what is the developmental significance of these representations and experiences? Dreams show us the coexistence alongside visual images (which precede verbal thought – as Freud states in *The Interpretation of Dreams*, 1900) of primitive body-related experiences consisting of particular sensations.

We might ask ourselves whether these body sensations perhaps represent the "fantasies in the body," some sort of proto-thoughts, of which Gaddini (1982) spoke, pointing out that these fantasies are then followed by the "fantasies on the body," which constitute the first mental image of a separate self; only at a later level of development will the fantasies on the body be followed by the visual fantasies. The latter, replacing and/or joining the previous ones, will further define the image of a separate self that can be elaborated.

Giovanni's dream, following this perspective, with its fantasies in and on the body and with the visual images, shows us the coexistence in his mind of insufficiently integrated experiences of a self that is united with the mother as an omnipotently created object (the experience in the body), and of images of a self in relation to the mother who possesses an autonomous life (the terrifying experience on the body, the visual images).

He therefore expresses not only his own confusion, but also the need for integration that manifests in adolescence, which has originated at the beginning of his existence in his relations with his primary environment. The patient also narrated the dream in session to the analyst whose task it is to welcome him with her *rêverie* and enable his further journey towards representation.

Lastly, the relationship of the daydreams with the dream shows Giovanni's attempt to confine it to an unconscious activity, without allowing it to dominate him, testifying to that passage from acting out to dreaming which characterises the maturation of the adolescent mind.

I will therefore proceed in listing the two-faced attributes of each of these events, that can be interpreted in both a pathological and a transformative sense.

Unlike the adult patient, we are not in the presence here of a delusional refuge organised as a defence against a more dreadful fragmentation.

Even though in the background there is indeed the fear of confusion (Giovanni says: "at the height of the process, I will not distinguish good from evil"), Giovanni nevertheless maintains object investments, albeit hidden (his friends and girlfriend), an environment that is in some ways solicitous to needs (his mother), the permanence of his relationships with his peer group (first with his early friends and later with the new friends he made in the new town).

Similar to Segal's little girl (1990, pp. 16–17) who in a dysperception mistook a discoloration on the wall for an evil and threatening lady by whom she felt persecuted, even with Giovanni cautious interpretations in time called into question his refuge. Working on the needs that had produced the pseudo-delusional fantasy, such as the sense of loneliness, the break in continuity with the past, the paranoid fear of feeling new and rejected, feeling fragile and helpless in the new environment, etc., and the subsequent real change in living conditions, allowed these states of daydream to gradually diminish and fade away. The same cannot be said in the case of a true psychotic onset.

Psychotic onset

The development of Adriana, a young woman in her twenties whom I saw in supervision, seems rather different to me. She has been visibly ill for about two years and comes to a colleague after having tried with various therapists. The family, summoned before the start of treatment, comes without her mother, who lets it be known that she will never come, as she has no faith in these working methods.

Adriana's father and brother are resigned and quite pessimistic about any possible improvement. Only drug treatment seems – according to them – to show some results. They display a markedly formal manner, in contrast to the uncomfortable truths that Adriana denounces about everyone, and particularly the mother's delusional jealousy that she reveals.

Adriana, however, is convinced of this new adventure, not least because of the knowledge of psychology books she made during the university year she attended before eventually dropping out. Bizarrely dressed, at times logorrheic, Adriana seems to rely more on superficial contact and speaking almost in a *falsetto* tone. The analyst's interventions are always accepted on an intellectual level, though they are sometimes criticised and corrected. The pharmacologist with whom the therapist speaks at the beginning of treatment shows great concern: Adriana has already had two admissions for the emergence of paranoid crises that are difficult to manage.

At the beginning of treatment, Adriana displays an enthusiastic attachment which seems rather suspicious to the colleague and which, after six months, abruptly turns into a full-blown paranoid transference.

From the outset, moreover, Adriana presents paranoid ideation which, after an initial phase of idealisation, slowly organises around the transference.

In the sessions, the girl narrates the incessant evolution of her psychotic history; they had not noticed what was happening to her.

She has in fact been ill since the age of six. She imitated her friends in everything, especially in gestures. Her mother is a college-educated and intelligent woman, but always hated her and never realised her daughter's distress. Her teacher would say she was beautiful and her high school friends too would say she was a model, but this caused her great embarrassment because she was extremely shy. The teacher would tell her she was "beautiful, but stupid." In a session before the treatment stopped, Adriana came in and told a dream that she described as horrible: *her father came into her room and had intercourse with her from behind*. During the night, she had to get up to close the door to her room; only then was she able to sleep. Adriana remembers being raped and sodomized by a man when she was a girl. The therapist asks for more information and Adriana says she has the impression that she does not believe her. The situation precipitates and the patient runs away. In the following days she does not come to the sessions, distressed by the idea that the therapist is also a dangerous person and that the therapy may harm her.

Comment

I believe Adriana's case to be quite typical, also because of the precise reconstruction that the patient makes of her onset to the illness, where simultaneously, her difficulty integrating her body, recognised in its novelty by others but not by herself ("the others said I was beautiful, a model. I was very shy") precipitates; her narcissistic fragility barely covered by her false self and the disturbance in her introjective processes ("I imitated my friends in everything"); her hatred for fragility and dependency; the peculiarity of family functioning (her absent mother, paranoid like herself; the family's inability to contain her where, due to the absence of an intermediate space, the slightest anguish turns into terror); the peculiarities of transferential functioning (from the idealised and precipitous attachment to the abrupt transformation into a paranoid transference); the problem of the boundaries between reality and fantasy, self and other, day and night, and the presence of incestuous fantasies (as we see in the dream of paternal incest, which also expresses the paranoid anguishes of being intruded upon by the parent's alienating message, as well as by that of the therapist. Indeed, the patient flees when the psychotherapist asks her questions that she feels are intrusive).

We can then see, in the patient's abrupt estrangement, the rushing into a paranoid transference and thus the confusion of the patient, who experiences the therapist as a rapist father, from whom she must escape.

Psychotic solution or perverse solution: a dilemma in the construction of identity

I will discuss, with regard to Andrea, the risk of a perverse outcome as a solution to a possible breakdown, and its resolution.

Andrea[2] is a sixteen-year-old adolescent. His mother, an addict, leaves him two months before the start of the therapy I supervise, dying elsewhere after having abandoned him countless times throughout his life. His father, also an addict, committed suicide when Andrea was four years old. The boy grew up with his maternal grandparents, in a family constellation where everything revolves around his manipulative and intrusive grandmother. Worrisome symptoms had already made their appearance in childhood: he was closed off, presented speech regression, outbursts of anger, talking to himself out loud, and more. Adolescence, on the other hand, had represented a new traumatic impact that the patient had attempted to overcome with a reorganisation that initially seemed to announce a possible perverse outcome.

The mother had an intense but inconstant relationship with him and seemed to have fantasised about generating a child on her own. She gives the child her own surname and shortly afterwards sneaks away from her partner, taking the child from him and returning to her parents' home. According to the grandmother, Andrea's mother had a "morbid" relationship with the child, as if she used the child, as later substances, for her own narcissistic balance. Around the age of one, the mother is said to have suddenly detached from her son, who then presented an arrest in speech development and a regression to communication by gestures.

Throughout his primary school years, Andrea exhibits peculiar behaviours that often attract the teachers' attention, but the family does not agree to have him treated. He is described as a child who lives in a world of his own, speaks out loud to himself and has sudden outbursts of anger and aggression. When agitated, he fears physical contact and being poisoned. He has an imaginary companion who emits urine, faeces and spit, flooding everyone. At the end of fifth grade, Andrea, scolded for an act of aggression towards a classmate, threatens to throw himself out of the window.

I will now describe the beginning of therapy.

For a long time, Andrea fills the sessions with stories he has invented. Horror stories in which humans vainly attempt to oppose the invasion of prehistoric monsters and aliens who mercilessly lacerate and kill. At the same time, the theme of identity enters the scene, brought into session in a characteristic manner through the interest in women's and men's clothes, compared with each other in minute detail: collections of old jackets (from when he was a child to the present day) and embroidered fabrics, with the insistent request made to the therapist to personally contribute to the latter collection. From the start, all the elements that would develop in the following months are present in a nutshell: for him, being male or female is determined by the clothes one wears. Andrea then confesses that he is drawn to wearing female clothing. He does this secretly at home by looking at himself in the mirror. He asks the therapist to help him with his make-up, even though he publicly attempts to construct an acceptable image for himself made of a fragile and artificial male identity. An erotic transference emerges at some point, complicating the relationship, but the therapist's gentle but firm response appears ultimately effective, although Andrea certainly experiences burning frustration. He reacts to the frustration by threatening to interrupt treatment and by provoking through cross-dressing. As the sessions continue, the work carries on around identificatory themes and what comes to light seems to be the link between dressing up in women's clothes and the abandonment of the mother, "being the mother since one cannot have a mother." After a year of treatment, in a dream Andrea expresses the need to rob and then hide the male identity that is experienced as threatening: "*me and a friend were going to a concert. Suddenly I am in a place full of bicycles, I see an abandoned jacket and I take it. My friend gets scared because he's afraid the owner's reaction. I, on the other hand, reply that it has been there for more than a week and can be taken at this point. Then we are on a beach and he digs a hole to bury and hide what has meanwhile become a studded belt, so nothing will happen. My friend is afraid, instead I laugh.*" As Andrea does not associate, the psychotherapist asks who the friend is and which concert they are going to. The patient explains that it is his school friend and that he has had a great influence on his recent change because he introduced him to music. The band is the Sex Pistols and just a year earlier, when he heard one of their songs on TV, there was "the turning point," taking them as a model. The black jacket that then becomes a belt is something that is now very fashionable and that some girls wear, "even though it has nothing to do" with girls. The analyst interprets that the change and turning point Andrea speaks of seems to be in the sense of a somewhat transgressive male identity. The friend is his double, together they find a male thing (which females misappropriate) and hide it for fear of being found out.

With this dream, we might wonder whether Andrea is saying that, through the friend he relies on and the transgressive band (the Sex Pistols), he is robbing that male identity that no one has given him. The hole is in his mind, in his unconscious, where he buries the male identity so that no one will notice that he is a male. Being male is indeed dangerous and deadly, and the boy struggles with the impossibility of integrating his being male within his own body image because this would mean definitively recognising the difference of the sexes and separation from his mother.

The sessions then document the boy's constant search for a seemingly unsolvable dilemma, alternating moments in which he attempts to put together a male identity, reassuring himself and the therapist, with moments in which he directly acts out the symbolic equation and dresses as a woman.

This alternation is also documented in the sessions, where the patient's struggle to define his identity is occasionally evident, emphasising masculine aspects and reinforcing himself through idols that are typical of adolescence or through a friend.

In later stages, it will be observed that Andrea seeks a masculinity that is initially located in clothing, in appearance, in a kind of aesthetic identity that he experiences as a way of achieving it. Intense work on the mourning for his parents, both of whom died (his father committed suicide), reveals the extent to which the impulse to wear women's clothes is connected to the need to "put himself in a woman's shoes," to become a woman, perhaps so as not to lose the mother he lost so many times until she disappeared. The acknowledgement of mourning and of certain good qualities of the parents emerges after intense work.

In a dream at this stage of the work, Andrea recounts: "*I went to a monastery and asked a friar to visit a person's grave. It was a person from the Middle Ages and he was being slandered because, the friar explained, he was a saint but everyone presented him as a devil. Other dead people were also slandered. The ghost of the character in question arrives, and a "negro" shows him around. I wake up.*" The dream's connection is with his dead parents' grave, which he perhaps feels the need to rediscover, re-evaluating even good aspects of the self that were buried and can now return, albeit as ghosts.

He ends by talking about how the studded chain he wears on his trousers gives him an identity, just like the Sex Pistols band that built its success on transgressions. He insists to such an extent on this topic that the therapist asks him how he relates it to himself. Andrea answers that "with these things, even strange things like the chain, he can get noticed, appreciated, build himself."

In the later stages of therapy, the patient struggles between his masculine and feminine identities and his inability to creatively integrate them, while increasingly developing attraction for girls with an interest in them. He is also ashamed of his impulse to cross-dress, always less and less present, and eventually admits that in recent months the fantasy is to wear the analyst's clothes, dressing like the analyst when he is alone at home and feels a sense of emptiness. He speaks of the pleasure he derives from the fantasy of wearing the therapist's clothes, because he believes it reminds him of being in session with the therapist. Again, the therapist comments on the symbolic equation that leads Andrea to want to be his mother so as not to lose her, and to dress as the therapist in fantasy when he feels the absence of the sessions and the therapist is far away.

Gradually and despite his grandparents' fear of him entering the adolescent world that was so dangerous for his parents, Andrea enters peer groups, goes to discos, smokes his first cigarettes, and dates his first girlfriends. The male identity, which was previously avoided through inhibition and isolation, is now sought and flaunted as a transgression, as a distinctive sign of masculinity. This will characterise the final year of work.

Comment

Amidst the utter sadness of this unfortunate boy's story, one can clearly observe the vicissitudes of the identity processes surrounding gender identity and the possible risk of a perverse solution. For Andrea, the suicide death of his father confirms that male identity is dangerous and that being male leads to death; the loss and abandonment of his mother pushes him towards the symbolic equation of being the mother, in an attempt to take possession of something important that he had lost, and through this symbolic equation, Andrea actualises that fusion with his mother that he had occasionally experienced.

In session, he re-actualises the same need in transference, and this was very useful information.

We might also add that the fantasy of an erotic transference perhaps also represented the boy's attempt to re-present himself with a masculine identity, avoiding the need to elaborate mourning and make contact with the depressive void that he carried with him and that had led him to a suicidal fantasy at the age of ten.

From this perspective, the erotic transference might also bear the same meaning as transvestism, that is, a defence against an exceptionally primitive depression, but now experienced in a more mature relationship, such as the relationship with the other, with the therapist.

From yet another viewpoint, it could reveal its paradoxical usefulness if considered as a means of reopening the game of object investments, and therefore of working indirectly on identificatory vicissitudes, a project that might not be omnipotent if we consider the very young age of the boy.

Having established, as the psychoanalytic literature on adolescents teaches us, that at this age one cannot diagnose a perverse structure, it is important to question oneself on the significance of this choice in the boy's psychic economy, and to understand whether it represents a dam against psychotic breakdown. In the words of André Green (1990), the institution of a sectorial delusion can be a means of avoiding schizophrenic dissociation while preserving the relationship with reality.

Along these same lines, most authors agree on the need to integrate the Freudian conception of perversion as the negative of neurosis, given that in numerous clinical situations perverse solutions have turned out to be complex defences against possible psychotic outcomes. Thus for McDougall (1995), deviant erotic scenarios present themselves as techniques for psychic survival, the only ones able to save the feeling of subjective identity from psychotic anguishes of internal death.

The solutions implemented by Andrea represent desperate attempts at self-therapy to defend himself due to the inability to create an area of illusion in the experience of separation. Also, they are attempts to cope with the confused sexual identity, the terror of castration and the loss of ego boundaries, while protecting internal objects from his own hatred and destructiveness.

It almost seems to me that precisely that body, which has created problems with its new needs, precisely that adolescent body, is the foothold with which, however modified, negated, made partial, exploited or abused, one can construct a defensive reality that prevents a complete breakdown into far more severe pathologies, such as fragmentation and confusion. As Cahn (1991) argues, transitions from one organisation mode to another are frequently observed in adolescence. Sometimes, adolescents with rampant primitive anguishes who cannot cope with reality adopt the perverse solution. It is a less "costly" solution because it modifies reality yet maintains it by combining it with fantasy and allowing the body to remain in contact with the other while simultaneously experiencing itself. Eglé Laufer too believes the distortion of the sexed body image, in the subject's unconscious relationship with his or her own body, can therefore be the way out from adolescent psychotic decompensation, "a solution to anguish through splitting and rejecting those aspects of sexuality that they feel are a threat to their psychic equilibrium" [tr. by O.M.] (Laufer, 1989, p. 209). I will discuss this more extensively in Chapter 9.

Notes

1 This patient is described in more detail in Chapter 8. He was treated by Dr. Laura Ballaré as psychotherapist and by me in supervision. My thanks to Dr. Ballaré.
2 The patient was in treatment with Dr. Simona Olivieri, under my supervision. My thanks to Dr. Olivieri.

References

Aulagnier, P. (1975). *The violence of interpretation: From pictogram to statement.* London: Routledge, 2001.

Aulagnier, P. (1986). Les deux principes du fonctionnement identificatoire (permanence et changement). In J.J. Baranes, R. Cahn et al. (Eds.), *Psychanalyse, Adolescence et Psychose*: Colloque International mai 1984, Ministère de la Recherche. Paris: Payot.

Bollas, Ch. (2013). *Catch them before they fall: The psychoanalysis of breakdown.* London: Routledge.

Bronstein, C. (2019). *Adolescent breakdown: Rupture or fracture?* Personal communication – Committee Forum for the Psychoanalysis of Adolescents – EPF.

Cahn, R. (1986). L'inquiétant étranger. In J. J. Baranes, R. Cahn et al. (Eds.), *Psychanalyse, adolescence et psychose*: Colloque International mai 1984, Ministère de la Recherche. Paris: Payot.

Cahn, R. (1991). *Adolescence et Folie: Les Déliaisons Dangereuses*. Paris: P.U.F.

Cahn, R. (1998). *L'adolescent dans la Psychanalyse*. Paris: P.U.F.

De Masi, F. (2011). Alcune considerazioni su come impostare la terapia analitica con un paziente psicotico. In Carnaroli F. and Giustino G. (Eds.), *Psicoanalisi delle Psicosi: Un Tema da Sviluppare* Dibattito SpiWeb https://www.spiweb.it/wp-content/uploads/oldfiles/images/stories/dibattito_su_psicoanalisi_delle_psicosi.pdf.

De Mijolla-Mellor, S. (1998). *Penser la Psychose: Une Lecture de l'Oeuvre de Piera Aulagnier*. Paris: Dunod.

Freud, S. (1900). The interpretation of dreams [Note added in 1925], *S.E.* 4-5, London: Hogarth Press.

Freud, S. (1907). Delusions and dreams in Jensen's *Gradiva*. *S.E.* 9: 1–96, London: Hogarth Press

Freud, S. (1919). The uncanny. *S.E.* 17: 218–256, London: Hogarth Press.

Freud, S. (1938). An outline of psychoanalysis. *S.E.* 23: 139–208, London: Hogarth Press.

Gaddini, E. (1982). Early defensive fantasies and the psychoanalytical process. *International Journal of Psychoanalysis*, *63*, 379–388.

Garcia, Badaracco (1986). Identification and its vicissitudes in the psychoses. The importance of the concept of the "maddening object". In *International Journal of Psychoanalysis*, 67.

Green, A. (1990). *On private madness*. London: Routledge, 1996.

Ladame, F. (1991). L'adolescence: entre rêve et action. *Revue Française de Psychanalyse*, *55* (5), 1493–1544.

Ladame, F. and Perret-Catipovic, M. (1998). L'adolescence. In *Jeu, Fantasme et Réalités: Le Psychodrame Psychanalytique à l'Adolescence*. Paris: Elsevier Masson.

Laufer, E. (1989). La solution perverse, aménagement d'une décompensation psychotique de l'adolescence. In F. Ladame, P. Gutton, *et al.* (Eds.), *Psychose et Adolescence*. Paris: Masson.

Laufer, E. (2002). Le corps comme objet interne. Relazione presentata al Centro di Psicoanalisi Romano, novembre 2022. *Adolescence*, *23* (2): 363–379.

Laufer, M. and Laufer, M. E. (1984). *Adolescence and developmental breakdown: A psychoanalytic view*. London: Routledge, 2018.

McDougall, J. (1995). *The many faces of eros: A Psychoanalytic Exploration of Human Sexuality*. New York: Norton Press.

Nicolò, A.M. (2020). Notes on change of technique in psychoanalysis. *The Italian Psychoanalytic Annual, 14*: 81–97.

Nicolò, A.M. (2022). Unconscious/unconsciouses: A reflective note. *The Italian Psychoanalytic Annual, 16*: 43–54.

Segal, H. (1990). Phantasy. In *Dream, phantasy and art*. London: Routledge.

Winnicott, D.W. (1963a). Fear of breakdown. In *Psycho-analytic explorations*. London: Routledge, 1989.

4

THE NEGATED, REPUDIATED, PERSECUTORY BODY

Foreword

Most psychoanalysts agree with Freud's assertion that "the ego is first and foremost a bodily ego; it is not merely a surface entity, but is itself the projection of a surface [...] the ego is ultimately derived from bodily sensations, chiefly from those springing from the surface of the body" (Freud, 1923, p. 26).

These two statements, which have never been refuted by either psychoanalysis or neuroscientific studies, contain in a nutshell potential developments that are, however, only now – almost one hundred years later – finding an initial delineation. Still today, we are lacking a general theory in this regard that explains the functioning of this inseparable body-mind unit and illustrates its characteristics and clinical repercussions, increasingly common in psychologists', psychiatrists' and psychoanalysts' practices. This is also because to-day's society has made body-related issues almost epidemic. Even now we juggle within ourselves two visions: the body we are and the body we have, repeating the Cartesian dualism between *res extensa and res cogitans*, quite outdated by modern philosophy.

The psychoanalyst who most pioneered a unified conception of the mind-body pair was Winnicott, who spoke of "psychosomatic collusion." He asserted that personalisation is a process, the result of the settlement of the psyche in the soma (1949), sustained by the tendency to integration with its alternating phases of non-integration, and is the result of handling, namely, the manipulation that the mother makes in the holding period, that is, the containment of the child in the phase of absolute dependency.

DOI: 10.4324/9781032663371-6

Scholars in developmental psychology and Infant Research have confirmed Winnicott's observations, and there is currently a new neurocognitive approach based on a different perspective from that of the cognitive neurosciences of the past, which effortfully yet reductively attempted to localise brain areas in order to explain the workings of the mind. This new orientation acknowledges that bodily expression plays "a central role in constructing exchanges with others, with an implicit intentionality that gradually becomes more explicit in awareness of Self and Others" [tr. by O.M.] (Ammaniti & Ferrari, 2020, p. 75). Winnicott himself had paved the way for these discoveries, pointing out that the interaction with the environment was constituent of the infant's self, that there is no such thing as an infant, and that the core of the self, as it emerges from the infant's relationship with the mother, presupposes in a continuous process (going-on-being) the integration between the soma and the psyche.

The soma, the mind, and the environment are thus the fundamental actors in this scenario.

The environment will exert its own stimuli that will direct and shape the development of the psychosomatic unit; the soma will be the source of the stimuli that the mind will integrate and progressively symbolise. There are therefore a lived body, a symbolic body, and a body mirrored by the other, and these three dimensions are in continuous relation to each other.

The lived body is primarily the producing body of sensory and kinaesthetic stimuli, among which the tactile ones, as Freud then Winnicott had first told us with the reference to handling, are decisive in delimiting the body surface and therefore the skin. As Ammaniti recalls in this regard, Susan Isaacs, foreseeing current discoveries by decades, asserted that sensations related to bodily functions and rhythms generate unconscious fantasies. She also added that "the first bodily experiences begin to build up the first memories, and external realities are progressively woven into the texture of phantasy" (Isaacs, 1952, p. 93). Sensation, therefore, is the physical substrate of fantasies. But even before Isaacs (1943), it was Melanie Klein (1957) who had described how memories were contained in sensations, namely, "memories in feelings." I will not dwell further on this fascinating topic, which moreover is largely unknown, but I do wish to remind how crucial the articulation between these three dimensions, between the lived body, that is, the body of sensations, the symbolic body and body image, is in adolescence.

Body and adolescence

In adolescence more than in other ages of life, the body and its vicissitudes assume structuring importance. In Chapter 2, I have already discussed what the developmental tasks of this age are. I also added that adolescence is not just a phase of life; instead, it is akin to an enzyme that stimulates our minds towards new functioning. Monniello (2016) considers it a process of neuro-subjectivisation. Allowing adolescence to function in the mind is complex work that raises conflicts and fears, and much can be played out at this stage to allow, in some cases, the beginning of a new story. Thus, if at birth we can speak of the settlement of the psyche in the body, in adolescence it is the body that imposes itself to the attention of the mind (Ferrari, 1992).

Eglé Laufer (2002) formulates the notion of the body as internal object. It arises from the conjugation of the libidinal body, linked to memories of early mother-child interactions, and a body constructed from sensory experiences. In normal situations, these two aspects merge, while in problematic situations, following Eglé Laufer, there is a split in such integration, a source of perverse solutions or hatred for one's body or aspects of it. In adolescence, new sensations emerge that have never been experienced before; they are connected with the transformation of puberty: hormonal impregnation, new muscularity, new physical stature, sexual maturation and new experiences related to menarche, pubarche and sexual initiation, are some of the events that produce new sensations. Particularly, sexual initiation triggers novel sensations that may at times be explosive (Laufer, 2002; Nicolò, 2011).

In fact, this new sensoriality stimulates the sensory memories of childhood and infancy, allowing, if possible, the emergence of a new integration. With great precision, Gutton distinguishes puberty from pubertary. Puberty is a bodily event, and pubertary *is for the psyche the equivalent of what puberty is for the body* (Gutton, 1991; 2000; 2008). The pubertary originates from the archaic renewed by genitality. More specifically, Gutton speaks of the genital archaic in that the genital experience is found and not found again; that is, it is not the second half of childhood sexuality, but the intrusion of the neurohormonal biological event (Gutton, 2004, 2008). The new adolescent experiences in any case "revisit" the antecedent ones, particularly the more primal ones, and sometimes succeed in offering it a new course[1] by promoting better integration, for example.

New sensations are also offered at this age by masturbation. Masturbation and the central masturbatory fantasy[2] (Laufer & Laufer, 1984, p. 6) that accompanies it constitute a rehearsal act that allows one to experience "thoughts, feelings, or gratifications" by investigating which "are acceptable to the superego and which [...] must not be allowed to become part of the person's image of himself or herself as a sexually mature male or female" (*ibid.*, p. 38).

If the adolescent gradually comes to experience pleasurable and affective romantic and sexual experiences at this age, this contributes to his or her growth, given that it confirms the possibility for self-acceptance through experience with the other, and in the possession of a body that is differentiated from the parent's. These experiences will allow him or her a further step towards the integration of sexuality and identity.

Yet, the new sensations were preceded by the mother's sensual investment in the child. Sensorial experiences, through maternal care and autoerotic investment, favour the child's libidinal investment in his or her body and allow healthy sensuality to emerge.

Gutton (2003) posits that archaic experiences are the immediate effect of the "sensual sensory."

Elsa Schmid-Kitsikis stresses the importance of sensuality, affirming that through the relationship with the other, the care of the mother, "sensuality incorporates and binds sensoriality to desire" [tr. by O.M.] (2005, p. 395). This experience, generated by the relationship and pleasure with the other therefore lies, according to the Swiss psychoanalyst, at the crossroads between autoeroticism and object relations, and therein finds meaning and delimitation. The absence of this early experience "keeps the child in a state of arousal and the adolescent in a catastrophic experience in the face of any form of penetration, sexual, verbal or relational" [tr. by O.M.] (*ibid.*, p. 393). The experience of sensuality therefore features two sides, one towards the inner world and another towards the outer world and the non-self.

The body and the other

From the very beginning, sensory experiences related to hearing, sight, smell, touch, being touched and thus the definition of the skin and body temperature, require maternal care in order to be integrated. From here originates a process that will lead to personalisation, to the distinction between ego and non-ego, and to the demarcation of the boundary of the self (Bonaminio, 2009). A great many psychoanalysts and developmental psychologists emphasise the crucial presence of the other in this process, and of course the first other is the mother. Maurice Corcos firmly expresses this by stating that "every sensory interaction is an affective interaction, and the mother is the multimodal source, the first source (as echo and as reflection) of sensory and affective information. The mother is the mother-world that with her sensory–motor and affective interactions allows the *infans* to essay and then represent the beginning of the world" [tr. by O.M.] (Corcos, 2014, p. 859). However, if it is the mother who will enable this process for the child, in adolescence, when the parents are to be abandoned and are in any case burdened by the excitatory storm due to the renewed Oedipus, it is the other, the new object, the partner, the best friend, the teacher, the group, that will play a crucial role. On the one hand, this indeed supports us in the possibility of altering an adolescent's fate; yet on the other, it increases the weight of the psychotherapist's ethical responsibility in that person's future, given the enormous developmental potential of the moment.

The symbolic body

Adolescence is the time of drastic questioning of previous identifications and even previous representations (Cahn, 1998). The adolescent needs to create new representational systems that reflect the new objects of investment and the new storms. It is a complex, arduous, and sometimes even painful process, because the new can come with disturbing attributes: what is truly happening is the end of the world that has belonged to that adolescent up to that moment. To do this, the adolescent mind will use the new sensations that are implanted on the archaic ones, but it will need to symbolise them, to represent them, carrying out a process that is in some ways akin to that already experienced early in its life in relationship with its mother.

The slow transition from sensations to thoughts, to representations, is reported by many authors. For example, Piera Aulagnier points out that sight, hearing, and taste can be a source of pleasure or displeasure, in the latter case rejected, thereby also rejecting the representation of the organ that is a source of arousal (De Mijolla-Mellor, 1998, pp. 114–115).

She meaningfully describes the transition from hearing to understanding, that is, from a series of sound fragments that the infant hears, sounds that carry pleasure or suffering, "to its investment in and finally appropriation of the semantic field" [tr. by O.M.] (*ibid.*, p. 139). Yet hearing, which the child cannot prevent, is not separable from seeing or feeling caressed. If it is a pleasurable experience, it generates the desire to hear. She describes three ways in which the psyche elaborates the information it derives from its relationship with reality. Indeed, "every act, every experience, gives rise conjointly to a pictogram, to a *representation* and to *sense-making*" (Aulagnier, 1975; De Mijolla–Mellor, 1998, p. 147). Thus, there is a shift from the pictogram representing "the partial experience of an encounter between a sensory area and an object designed to complete it" [tr. by O.M.] (De Mijolla–Mellor, 1998, p. 117) to a figurative dimension, and then to a symbolic dimension. The pictogram connected to sensoriality is therefore at the roots of thought. Nonetheless, all this will be the result of a process in which two actors construct it: the other will always be necessary in its unfolding.

Because everything has been called into question, anguishes of annihilation and death may challenge the adolescent mind. Given that in this struggle to acquire a new system of representations the adolescent may fail, there may be momentary depersonalisations. In other cases, he or she may re-experience an absence originally ex-perienced, and the path will then open to a dangerous disinvestment of the object, a loss of its representation. This is what Winnicott said about the fact that what is dangerous and pathogenic is not so much the loss of the object, but the loss of its representation. Green links this aspect, which he calls the "fading of internal representations," to the negative, and goes on to say that it is "'a representation of the absence of representation', as I say, which expresses itself in terms of negative hallucination or in the field of affect of void, emptiness, or, to a lesser degree, futility, meaninglessness" (Green, 2000, p. 87).

These adolescents will then manifest suffering, a sense of futility and destructiveness. The natural traumatophilia of adolescence will thus be made more dangerous by these mechanisms.

In a healthy process, radical requalification (Levy, 2016, pp. 84–85) and symbolic reorganisation are set in motion (Ruggiero, 2016, p. 38). The body will need to be represented and the mind will need to contain these symbolic representations of the new body, the new emotional experiences, as well as non-symbolised emotions. What will prove pivotal is the balance between the ability to symbolise these new experiences, their violence, and the existence of a new object that is able to facilitate these processes.

Therefore, the symbolic reorganisation of the body represents the final stage of a complex work that is rooted in archaic sensations but eventually results, through sharing with the other and their mirroring, in the ability to think the body and symbolise it.

Every so often, this complex process comes to a halt; the adolescent then, in an attempt to cling to experiences that sustain the self and provide some identity, will turn towards the image in search of narcissistic stability and of the mirroring that was originally lacking. Again, Winnicott shows us the importance of the mother's gaze, the other's gaze, when he shows us that the child sees himself or herself when he or she sees the mother's eyes. Furthermore, he adds: "when I look, I am seen, so I exist" (Winnicott, 1967, p. 114).

In search of existence and mirroring, the adolescent today makes use of image much more than in the past. Ours is also a culture of image, where aesthetic identity is now certainly one aspect of how identity is declined.

The problem arises when underneath the aesthetic identity the adolescent does not find himself or herself. He or she will then react with a continuous spasmodic search that will not come to fruition.

The myth of Narcissus and Echo seems to be the representation of this process, where withdrawal from the relationship with the other and a sensory disorganisation that leads to the transformation of the body prevail. As we know, Narcissus, in love with his image and unable to love anyone other than himself, falls into the water killing himself, and is transformed into a plant, a flower, the narcissus. Similarly, Echo, in love but not reciprocated by him, turns into a rock and in another version of the myth into a sound, the echo. Both therefore operate a sort of sensory disintegration and bodily dismantling. Moreover, what is also striking in the myth is the absence of the other and his or her gaze.

When Narcissus looks at himself in the water, he sees himself for the first time and no one else. No one has ever mirrored him before. He will thus be unable to recognise himself in his identity and mistakes a mirror image for a real person. In another version of the myth, Narcissus longs to feel and see the nymph Echo, but not her body; therefore, when she longs to embrace him, Narcissus pulls back, frightened and horrified. Yet a terrible transgenerational secret weighs on him: he is in fact the child of abuse, of violence suffered by his mother, the nymph Liriope, by the river god Cephissus. Liriope is the nymph of the spring in whose water Narcissus looks at himself, and he thus grows up without a father. What is lacking for him is the possibility to access the Oedipal dimension with all that it means for mental life, that is, the ability to separate and individuate, to recognise the non-self, accessing reality and the possible elaboration of the depressive position. This is precisely what has prompted some authors, such as Racamier, to assert that certain narcissistic pacts, such as those observed in the relationships between severe patients and their parents, are anti-Oedipal and ante-Oedipal, therefore constructed prior to the Oedipus and anticipatorily against its constitution.

Acting on the body, acting with the body

The struggle to define identity, as occurs in our current society, increases the need to cling to the body to anchor oneself in reality, giving importance to acting and acting out as replacements of the symbolisation process. Bullying or new forms of youth sexuality are but some of the phenomena that our society and culture must grapple with. Acting out replaces reflecting, verbalising by putting feeling in the place of thinking, and operating an affective dissociation of the body. An experience that we might call borderline and that characterises our adolescents today is represented by acting fleeting and superficial, momentary and ephemeral sexual experiences. These forms that we might call "neo-sexuality" do not prelude romantic relationships; they are ends in themselves. They are often consumed in an evening and bear a strong connection with the group to which the adolescent belongs. They allow for sensations to be experienced and constitute a prologue to talking about them with others. The adolescent thus privileges sensations over experiencing a relationship with the other (Gutton, 2004, p. 218) with its richness and creativity, but also with the natural limitations that arise in the relationship with the other. In most cases, in benign evolution, these operations are *in fieri* experiments that can also allow the adolescent to cope with the anxiety over the loss of the infant body and the primitive relationship with the mother. A gradual transition to more adult sexuality is thus generated, allowing the construction of a more personal "sexual scenario [...] that also provides a sense of continuity with one's childhood story" [tr. by O.M.] (Marion, 2009). Nevertheless, sometimes there is instead a sort of affective dissociation from the body. The body divides an "object of speech," a "source of sensations," that is not integrated into the mind and therefore into the adolescent's developing subjectivity. The adolescent looks at himself or herself as if from outside, he or she is the spectator of himself or herself and exists in feeling, in the sensations felt, on the surface of the skin, seen from the outside or experienced on the sensory plane.

Maria, in the second year of high school, conceals her continuing search for sexuality from her parents. She makes no distinction between one or the other of her classmates, as if she were constantly playing a seduction game. The group in which she talks about it is extremely important. Yet ultimately, her sexual activity does not bring her pleasure; it is continuous acting out, a split feeling that upholds arousal but denies affect. She notices what is happening only indirectly, when people at school start talking badly about her. She wonders why this is happening, and is surprised to see the angry or jealous reactions of one of her boyfriends, the only one who had attempted to have a relationship of a different quality with her. She understands the meaning of her actions only when, after a year of psychotherapy, she falls in love with a boy.

In these activities, friends and the group are often of great importance, consequently leaving intimacy and secrecy with no place. Experiences are communicated to one friend or the other, or are the subject of approving or disapproving comments within the group. In this regard, the behaviour of girls is quite different from that of boys. In my opinion, sexuality today has become more precocious, with a disappearance[3] of latency or its premature eroticisation. In many cases, we observe the split between love bond and sexuality, with the appearance of a sort of hyper-investment of the sensory plane.

Massive sensation-seeking to feel they exist is common among some adolescents who use sexuality not to get know themselves and get to know the other, not to feel pleasure and give it, but rather to cling to the body they cannot integrate.

When sexuality, losing its affective connections, fails to organise the symbolic integration of the body and the maturation of the object choice, it then merely serves as a narcissistic confirmation where the other and their body can be used in a masturbatory way. This often results in acting out that rules out affection or thought, lying in an ambiguous area between normality and pathology. In this landscape, there seems to exist in some adolescents a hunger for sensation and sensory stimulation, so as to somehow construct some sort of body image providing the illusion of a stable identity.

I am clearly describing a picture that does not fit all adolescents and fortunately, in its most pronounced forms, only the most problematic ones.

The search for a perfect body, or one that appears so and is therefore acceptable, is one of the most topical problems of adolescence. This is also due to the fact that, as Alessandra Lemma (2015) has exhaustively discussed, the body today can be omnipotently manipulated, changed, negated, and reconstructed.

Society as we know it multiplies the excitatory stimuli that come from the outside, imposing the need for a surplus of integration and a greater number of elaborative tools.

If the adolescent cannot "bind" these sensations and excitations, or is unable to find an object that may organise and contain them, he or she will attempt to multiply acting out in order to be rid of them.

The repudiated and persecutory body

When it becomes impossible or arduous for the tasks I have described in the previous paragraph to occur, the possibility of breakdown becomes concrete. At this point, body and mind enter into opposition (Lombardi, 2011) and it is as if the reality of the body itself took on a persecutory meaning (Laufer, 2002, p. 369).[4] But so do the other and their gaze. The body turns foreign and extra-territorial, as Gutton (2003) puts it. The adolescent feels besieged by new and particularly sensual sensations that he or she feels as coming from the outside and especially from the inside. These sensations can be pleasant, intriguing, seductive but also massive, frightening, shameful, or intrusive if the ability to modulate them, integrate them and begin to process them is lacking. A possible defence will then be the denial of the "real" sensorial experience emerging from the body, which inevitably alters reality testing. Henceforth, it is reality itself that is negated. The struggle for the adolescent then takes place between two possible options: the active reappropriation of his or her body and desires, or the helpless and resigned blocking of growth in order to maintain the "omnipotent phantasm of the union or fusion with the pre-Oedipal, idealised body of the mother" (Laufer, 2002, p. 370).[5] The adolescent may then enter in standby, a stalemate, unable to choose between the fear of abandoning the prepubescent body and the integration of the new sexed body, because this also means the loss of a safe and protective object such as the parent, confronting incestuous and aggressive desires, accepting that he or she is not omnipotent and perfect, but real and active. Hence will arise the terror of losing control of the body and its equivalent, namely, the loss of control of his or her mind.

This is one of the reasons for the higher frequency of psychotic onset in late adolescence, although other challenges such as the renewal of growth-related mourning processes (developmental mourning), and the integration of aggression, may concur in bringing about these problems.

Yet this is also one of the advantages of studying adolescent processes, given that it allows us to better understand the psychotic problem and the reasons for its eruption.

We might hypothesise that the breakdown explodes when the adolescent is unable to integrate this storm of new sensations generated by the body, subject and object of new sexual and sensual urges. But not only! In fact, these new sensations threaten a personality that carries an integration that has never been fully experienced before,[6] but also a basic and latent identity problem that awakens precisely because of the inability to achieve the various and complex developmental tasks.

Yet, there may be situations where clinging to the body may be the last bastion in order to exist. Let us then see how the body might be used as a defence against a possible developmental breakdown or rupture. This can be seen in a brief clinical fragment.

Paolo is seventeen years old and travels around Italy because he believes he has droopy ears. He undergoes surgery in a city in central Italy. He will then have surgery on his nasal septum, but his anguish persists and is now located in his eyes. In his opinion, classmates and girls do not have a good relationship with him because of these physical defects. He believes his eyes are fixed, his gaze limited, but woe to whoever may suggest he might be talking about a different kind of gaze. An ophthalmologist in a small northern town sees him once a month, he who is from the South, and gives him "eye movement rehabilitation" exercises that seem to contain his anguish. In the meantime, his trips take him away from his distressed parents, who realise they must tolerate this oddity.

To what is this dysmorphic symptom due?

In this case, we might speak of the existence of "psychotic islands" (Rosenfeld, 1998) that concentrate in one organ, thereby protecting against the invasion of psychotic panic. Or, are we faced with:

1   A body experienced as filthy and imperfect, exposing to the world the ugliness of the self, its inability, its powerlessness? (Lemma, 2010)
2   Or is Paolo confronting himself with an idealised, unattainable body?
3   Or, in specifically investing that part of the body, is he attempting to operate a sort of reappropriation of it?

In any case, this sort of backward path by which the patient explores his sense organs, separating them from time to time in treatment, is striking. Indeed, it appears as the preview of a broader disintegration that he attempts to avoid and from which he attempts to protect himself by focusing, concretely, on one organ at a time.

In Fabio's case, the surgery to his finger tendon, which he had sought with all his might, had a profoundly destabilising effect. The remodelling or removal of a part of his body, of such importance to him, was an attack against a hated self, identified with a bad and persecutory object that he felt as capable of limiting and occupying his body.

Fabio, sixteen, a piano student who used to be brilliant, is the son of a tyrannical musician and an insignificant mother, an absent presence in her relationship with her son. His father devoted his life to him in the hope – compulsory for him – that he would become the new Glenn Gould, thus also preventing him from any smallest autonomous movement. Fabio presents a progressive withdrawal from previous, albeit modest, socialisation, alongside the appearance of pervasive anxiety. Inside him persists the distressing idea that his supposed failure in piano study depends on an abnormality in the tendon of his middle finger. All this leads him to laboriously attempt psychotherapy, but his parents, particularly his father, are paranoidly concerned about this psychotherapeutic experience of his and control him by attempting to invade even the analytic space. He is desperate. He continues to believe and say that his not being brilliant depends on this tendon. He eventually succeeds in getting surgery for his tendon, which will be performed in a private clinic.

However, the very operation, which he had sought with all his might, utterly destabilises him. The remodelling of such an important part of his body was a self-destructive attack on a hated self, identified with an evil, persecutory object that he felt as capable of limiting and occupying his body. It was also an attack on an intrusive father whom he was unable to stem.

His mother called me a week after surgery, reporting with anguish the deterioration of her son that was beginning to creep in. When we resume, after the interruption for the operation, Fabio comes to the session at the height of his decompensation. He asks me if I see his body splattered on the wall of the analysis room, blended with the white of the wall. I feel his and my dismay, which I attempt to modulate. That feeble defence that was represented by his clinging to a finger – his and mine – had completely collapsed. Splattered on the wall, though physically sitting in his chair, he feels himself getting lost and blended with the object, without boundaries or demarcations. After that session, I never saw him again.

Admitted to involuntary psychiatric treatment, he will no longer resume his three weekly sessions, which had begun three months earlier. His father will tell me that they have decided to move, with the whole family, to their small hometown.

Fabio's inability to cling to the last feeble defence that bound him to reality, brought about by the stupid and criminal surgery, had dispersed his body, fused and confused with his environment. The ego ideal had collapsed. The persecutory paternal superego, which had haunted him since childhood, had prevailed.

I will not insist on the obvious associations we might make. "The phantasy is that this persecutor is killed-off through the reshaping or removal of the reviled body part—this is the only way of separating from the other felt to now 'reside within the self'" (Lemma, 2010, p. 80). Fabio's self-mutilating act was aimed at ridding himself of his mediocrity and impotence, of his sexual fantasies and, finally, of the parent who expropriates his self.

But we can also witness other manifestations, such as the following case I personally supervised[7]:

Alberto has had a difficult life since his premature birth. His mother, who brings him into the world with a depressive illness and the emergence of an autoimmune disease, will die when Alberto is ten years old, but the funeral will be kept hidden from him. Apart from his stuttering as a child, Alberto shows a surprising sort of anaesthesia that characterises his body. At a very young age, he fractures his arm, but returns home almost without asking anyone for help. Yet his indifference to his body is also noticeable by his neglect of a serious infection that secretes pus that only others notice. After his wife's death, Alberto's father is very close to him until he decides to marry a woman who notices Alberto's difficulties, who is now seventeen years old. A few months after the marriage, a car accident, with the fear of the death of the whole family, precipitates the situation. Persecutory fantasies emerge around the father and his partner. Alberto begins treatment and pursues it with care. Despite successfully attending university, Alberto has no friends outside the extended family circle. A year after beginning therapeutic work, he falls into a new crisis triggered by another incident, this time psychological. His father's wife, Giovanna, accidentally sees a video on the internet where the ever-gentle and inhibited Alberto, for fun, mimes a rape scene on a colleague. Giovanna scolds him, but Alberto's attempts to defend himself are to no avail. Alberto thus begins to spiral: in a session after the weekend, he recounts that on Friday, after going to bed, he felt as if many thoughts had taken over. They are insistent and out of control until the moment he feels a force emanating from him, heat coming from the lower right part of his belly and then rising up towards his heart. Marked tachycardia then begins. He gets up, afraid he is about to die, and asks his father for help. Over the next few days, he does not leave the house, yet slowly a seemingly more confident attitude grows within him that leads him to undertake sports training with his cousin, and to change his Facebook page by introducing himself as a wrestling enthusiast.

This will be the onset of a decompensation that appears over the following weeks, when he verifies in the mirror a disharmony in his body related to the functioning of his right side. Objects fall out of his hand and he feels less strength in the right side of his body, which "almost goes by itself." He goes on to say that he feels male and female parts inside himself, but separate, and will be caught up in a fantasy of meeting a girl he knows, which will of course prove unfeasible. These themes will evolve into a franker psychotic episode that will later recede. Currently, Alberto continues his psychotherapy and is successfully attending university.

The discussion of this severe case allows me to illustrate the dynamics mentioned so far.

The weekend absence had awakened anguish over separation and loss, leaving him alone. Alberto was uncovered in his sexual fantasies and their aggressive nature (rape). He can neither split them nor negate them any longer. It is a second trauma: his father's wife, representative of all incestuous Oedipal fantasies, strictly reprimands him. Giovanna may therefore represent both the superego ban and the incestuous mother, the object of desire that terrifies him. Yet the relevant pressure is also unleashed, which we see placed around bodily sensations that seem alien to him. Hence, he seems to return to being a small child who turns to his mother to return to her bed.

The once erotic, or potentially erotic, body thus becomes a child's body again. To use Aulagnier's expression, we see the regression from a body of desire to a body of need.[8]

He therefore attempts numerous defences. The first is a defensive split that seems to run through not only his mind, but also his body starting from the right side as opposed to the left. Yet this mechanism cannot be withstood for long, precipitating his heterosexual and homosexual drives in a short time. Added to this is the never processed mourning for his mother, a mourning that was taken from him. Unable to have the woman, he becomes the woman; unable to accept the mourning for his mother, he becomes the woman his mother had been. Yet luckily (so to speak) there is a way to defend oneself from total decompensation.

His masculine and feminine aspects can be placed in the soma, where he feels them located in the lower abdomen. The sensations and arousals of his sexed body are re-read and re-signified within his somatic dysperception.

What happened?

The bodily changes experienced uncontrollably are soon transformed into a sort of "pseudo-hallucination," immediately accompanied by terrifying tachycardia, as anguish of imminent death, so much so that he is driven to wake his father.

Was it the perception of his aroused body that gave rise to a fantastic theory, out of touch with reality? Or was it the psychotic organisation that made him feel the heat pervading his body?

By being both male and female, he is the omnipotent bisexual, the prepubescent boy who does not define himself, but also the lost maternal object from which he cannot differentiate himself. Concurrently, he avoids being the latency child who has lost his mother, the adolescent who is overwhelmed by sexual arousal and developmental needs, as well as the infant who was unable to find in his ailing mother the containment and care necessary for the continuing process of integrating sensations and sensuality.

In Alberto, as in other similar patients, the body as internal object suffered a severe blow in its constitution due to early maternal deprivation, which also significantly influenced the later elaboration of the Oedipus complex. In such an intricate situation, failures abounded, among which that of body integration was but one. Nonetheless, it is precisely in adolescence that the possibility of a new re-founding of identity opens. In fact, unlike in other ages of life, adolescence allows for games to be reopened, whereby we might witness dramatic chronicization, but also spectacular changes, or restructurings of personality, or in other cases defensive re-organisations that are useful for survival.

The disavowed body

Finally, there is another use of the body that we see presenting itself almost epidemically due to the increased frequency of anorexic syndromes. On the use of the body in the case of anorexics, numerous interpretations chase one another, from the omnipotent fantasy of controlling and negating its arousal, to its emaciation as a gateway to differentiation and distance from a mother with whom one feels fused and confused. According to other authors (Gatti, 1976; 1977; Kestemberg et al., 1972), the disavowal of the body in anorexics has a perverse nature: the body becomes the equivalent of a fetishistic object, thus perpetuating a focal symbiosis with the mother.

In particular, the sexed body is disavowed and bodily mortifications, which at first are a means to emaciation, eventually become almost an end in themselves. This pursuit, when conducted to the point of spasm, leads to what Kestemberg calls the "fasting orgasm." She also points out to us that the phantasm of the idealised body, connected with the fantasy of an omnipotent mother ultimately expresses the need for fusion with this ideal mother whose loss is unbearable. In other types of anorexic functioning, there can exist more striking signs such as paranoid experiences around anything that might enter the body or mind, with fears of poisoning or contamination.

Finally, the last form of anorexia is related to a defence from breakdown. In this case, it is constituted by a set of symptoms that are used as a defence against decompensation because, thanks to the obsessive control of reality and of the body that they allow, omnipotently nullifying hormonal drives as well as conflict in the internal and external world, they offer a sort of protective shield against collapse (Nicolò & Russo, 2010).

Notes

1 Pellizzari (2010) spoke of "second birth."
2 The central masturbatory fantasy proves to be very useful, providing insight into the patient's current fixations and evolution. There are

situations in which the masturbatory fantasy contains regressive and shameful desires that the adolescent hates, and that will prevent him or her from experiencing himself or herself and his or her body and related sensations. In this regard, the Laufers stated that in assessing central masturbatory fantasy it is necessary to consider (1) the direction of libido (objectual or narcissistic); (2) the distortion in sexed body image; and (3) the place occupied by genital sexuality in adolescents' fantasies and object relations, and whether sexuality is sought or has been abandoned. It is also important to assess the fixity, repetitiveness, rigidity and non-transformability of such daydreams that usurp the elaborative space (Laufer & Laufer, 1984).

3 As a consequence, epistemophilic drives are not structured around the primal scene phantasm, which defines the recognition of sexes and generations (Guignard, 1997).

4 The page of the quote refers to the French edition of the text (see bibliography).

5 The page of the quote refers to the French edition of the text (see bibliography).

6 De Masi (2012) writes that one of the possible solutions is for these children to enter a state of withdrawal centered on sensory experience and in which awareness of psychic reality is abolished. This self-produced sensoriality is different from the search for bodily pleasure in the affective relationship, as is the case in the normal child.

7 I will not name the psychotherapist I supervised for reasons of confidentiality, but I thank her for allowing me to report the case.

8 Piera Aulagnier, quoted by De Mijolla-Mellor, argues that reality will be seen, tasted, and heard through the body, which represents "a relational mediator" between the psyche and the world, and between two psyches (De Mijolla-Mellor, 1998, p. 22) giving rise to both a body as bearer of needs and a body as bearer or receptor of desires.

References

Ammaniti, M. and Ferrari P. F. (2020). *Il Corpo non Dimentica: L'Io Motorio e lo Sviluppo della Relazionalità*. Milano: Raffaello Cortina.

Aulagnier, P. (1975). *The violence of interpretation: From pictogram to statement*. London: Routledge, 2001.

Bonaminio, V. (2009). *The psyche in-dwelling in the body: States of integration, unintegration and the primary identification*. Presented at the 13th Francis Tustin Memorial Lecture, Los Angeles, 6–7 November 2009.

Cahn, R. (1998). *L'Adolescent dans la Psychanalyse*. Paris: P.U.F.

Corcos, M. (2014). Sensorialité = fragments épars – morceaux vivants. *Adolescence, 34*, 4, 857–864.

De Masi, F. (2012). Alcune considerazioni su come impostare la terapia analitica con un paziente psicotico. In F. Carnaroli and G. Giustino (Eds.), *Psicoanalisi delle Psicosi: Un Tema da Sviluppare* - Dibattito SpiWeb, https://www.spiweb.it/wpcontent/uploads/oldfiles/images/stories/dibattito_su_psicoanalisi_delle_psicosi.pdf.

De Mijolla-Mellor, S. (1998). *Penser la Psychose. Une Lecture de l'Oeuvre de Piera Aulagnier.* Paris: Dunod.

Ferrari, A.B. (1992). *L'Eclissi del Corpo. Una Ipotesi Psicoanalitica.* Roma: Borla.

Freud, S. (1923). The ego and the Id. *S.E.* 19: 3–68. London: Hogarth Press.

Gatti, B. (1976). Il corpo come luogo di verifica del principio di realtà e dell'identità femminile in un caso di anoressia mentale. *Rivista di Psicoanalisi*, 22, 51–88.

Gatti, B. (1977). L'anoressia mentale. *Rivista di Psicoanalisi*, 23: 184–200.

Green, A. (2000). *André Green at the Squiggle Foundation.* London: Routledge.

Guignard, F. (1997). *The infantile in psychoanalytic practice today.* London: Routledge, 2002.

Gutton, Ph. (1991). *Le Pubertaire.* Paris: P.U.F.

Gutton, Ph. (2000). Il pubertario, tra l'infanzia e l'infantile. It. Tr. in *Psicoterapia e Adolescenza.* Roma: Borla, 2002.

Gutton, Ph. (2003). Esquisse d'une théorie de la génitalité. *Adolescence*, 21 (2): 217–248.

Gutton, Ph. (2008). Le pubertaire savant. *Adolescence*, 25 (2): 347–358.

Gutton, Ph. (2004). Souffrir pour se croire. *Adolescence*, 22 (2): 209–224.

Isaacs, S. (1952). The nature and function of phantasy. In J. Riviere (Ed.), *Developments in psychoanalysis.* London: Hogarth Press; 67–121.

Kestemberg, E., J. Kestemberg, and S. Decobert (1972). *La Faim et le Corps: Une étude Psychanalytique de l'Anorexie Mentale.* Paris: P.U.F.

Klein, M. (1957). *Envy and Gratitude and Other Works, 1946–1963.* London: Hogarth Press, 1975.

Laufer, E. M. (2002). Il corpo come oggetto interno. In A. M. Nicolò and I. Ruggiero (Eds.), *La Mente Adolescente e il Corpo Ripudiato.* Milano: Franco Angeli.

Laufer, M. and Laufer E. M. (1984). *Adolescence and developmental breakdown: A psychoanalytic view.* London: Routledge, 2018.

Lemma, A. (2010). *Under the skin: A psychoanalytic study of body modification.* London: Routledge.

Lemma, A. (2015). *Minding the body: The body in psychoanalysis and beyond.* London: Routledge.

Levy, R. (2016). Adolescenza: la riorganizzazione simbolica, lo sguardo e l'equilibrio narcisistico. In A.M. NicolòI. Ruggiero (Eds.), *La Mente Adolescente e il Corpo Ripudiato.* Milano: Franco Angeli.

Lombardi, R. (2011). "Chi ha paura del lupo cattivo? Una nota su psicoanalisi e psicosi". In F. Carnaroli and G. Giustino (Eds.), *Psicoanalisi delle psicosi: un tema da sviluppare*, www.spiweb.it.

Marion, P. (2009). Commento alla relazione: *Pelle per comunicare, pelle da danneggiare, pelle per esistere: Riflessioni su scarificazioni e self-cutting in adolescenza* presented by A.M. Nicolò at the *Centro di Psicoanalisi Romano*, March 2009.

Monniello, G. (2016). Psicoanalisi dell'adolescente e processo di neuro-soggettivazione. In A.M. Nicolò and I. Ruggiero (Eds.), *La Mente Adolescente e il Corpo Ripudiato*. Milano: Franco Angeli.

Nicolò, A. M. (2011). Sexual Initiation and Romantic Love During Adolescence. Talk presented at the panel: *Current Day Sexuality and Psychoanalysis. More than One Hundred Years form the 'Three Essays*, 47th IPA Congress.

Nicolò, A. M. and Russo, L. (Eds.) (2010). *Una o Più Anoressie*. Roma: Borla.

Pellizzari, G. (2010). *La Seconda Nascita: Fenomenologia dell'Adolescenza*. Milano: Franco Angeli.

Rosenfeld, H. (1998). *Herbert Rosenfeld at Work: The Italian Seminars* (F. De Masi, Ed.). London: Routledge, 2001.

Ruggiero, I. (2016). Il corpo ripudiato. In A.M. Nicolò and I. Ruggiero (Eds.), *La Mente Adolescente e il Corpo Ripudiato*. Milano: Franco Angeli.

Schmid-Kitsikis, E. (2005). Corps et psyché: théorisation. *Adolescence, 23*, 2, 381–401.

Winnicott, D. W. (1949). Mind and its relation to the psyche-soma. In (1958), *Through paediatrics to psycho-analysis*. New-York: Basic Books, 1975.

Winnicott, D. W. (1967). Mirror-role of mother and family in child development. In *Playing and reality*. London: Tavistock, 1971.

5

SENSORIALITY AND DEVELOPMENTAL RUPTURES

Treating young people and adolescents with developmental ruptures, I was quite struck by the frequency with which they reported disturbances pertaining to sensoriality, or dreams and fantasies involving this realm. As is now well known, these aspects are often experienced by the analyst in resonance with emotions and sensations, including somatic ones, thereby allowing the analyst to contact primitive levels of the patient's mind.

Many works highlight the fact that in psychosis sensory reality predominates over psychic reality. De Masi explicitly states that in psychotic patients, "the psychotic part uses the mind not as an instrument for relating to others (as an *organ of knowledge*), but to generate a sensory world in order to obtain a special, regressive type of pleasure. Hence the primitive infantile withdrawal into a world of sensory fantasies" (2015, p. 306). According to this author, this process is one of the most important in producing illness.

In a most interesting book, neuroscientist Northoff reports his studies on schizophrenia, which he refers to a breakdown of the world-brain relationship capable of producing a "social disconnection" of the patient from the reality around him or her. After reminding us that in adolescence the brain undergoes a transformation, particularly with regard to interneurons and a GABA neurotransmitter, he argues that this reduction is relevant precisely at the expense of the sensory system. Comparing the brain to a city that is flooded by water due to the collapse of its dams and bridges, Northoff suggests these patients can no longer

DOI: 10.4324/9781032663371-7

block and filter incoming input, being thus easily inundated with sensory information (Northoff, 2016, p. 155).

Of course, this is only one of the features illustrated by Northoff in schizophrenia, in which "symptoms such as delusions and identity change can be seen as the reaction to a break of the boundaries between world and brain" (*Ibid.*, p. 159).

Further, reviewing the psychoanalytic theories in this regard, we cannot forget Bion's monumental work with his emphasis on the fact that the unconscious we must deal with is not only the repressed unconscious but also the inaccessible mental states, which are neither part of the conscious nor the unconscious. At that level, there is no possibility of thought, and communication follows other pathways.

Riccardo Lombardi states that Bion highlights "the relationship between the *bodily sensory trace* and the *representational phenomena of a mental nature*" [tr. by O.M.] (2012, p. 99), observing the pathway from the sense organs, to the preverbal weave, and finally to verbal organisation. Among the sense organs, particularly sight[1] stands out as decisively important for mental functioning.

Also in this regard, in his work *Attacks on Linking* (1959), Bion shows how the child uses projective identification: "[it] makes it possible for him to investigate his own feelings in a personality powerful enough to contain them" (*Ibid.*, p. 298). The lack of the mother's containing function due to her deficiency, or to the child's hatred and envy, will result in an impaired tendency towards curiosity, and "the way is therefore prepared for a severe arrest of development".

Therefore, the altering of this process leaves the child in the grip of his or her own chaos of feelings, which he or she will attempt in various ways to cope with.

The failure of the relationship between the mother and the baby was also pointed out by Winnicott, for whom traumatic impingements by the environment, occurring at a period of life when "the ego is too immature to gather all the phenomena into the area of personal omnipotence" (Winnicott, 1963a, p. 91; 1963b), leave a trace that produces a distortion of the ego; traces that are not included within the dynamic unconscious, but that rather create modifications, alterations in the structuring of thought. To defend himself or herself from the disintegration caused by the mother's absence, the child then – according to Winnicott – will use the sophisticated defence of disintegration (1962, p. 60), produced by himself or herself. In this type of functioning, Winnicott refers to the period he called "personalisation". At this stage, "the ego is based on a body ego, but it is only when all goes well that the person of the baby starts to be linked with the body and the body-functions, with the skin as the limiting membrane" (*Ibid.*, p. 58): this process is fostered by the mother's holding and is care that is aimed at containing the child on the sensorial level and in fact "takes account of the infant's skin sensitivity – touch, temperature, auditory sensitivity, visual sensitivity, sensitivity to falling (action of gravity) and of the infant's lack of knowledge of the existence of anything other than the self" (1960, p. 48).

Unintegrated sensory stimuli due to environmental deficiency thus produce a deficiency in personalisation and body-mind integration, which, through various vicissitudes and in later stages of life, can remain "frozen", "catalogued", or generate personality disorders and thought defects.

An inability to manage and integrate this myriad of sensations, which moreover characterises our relationship with the self and the world, or an overload of them, will block that developmental path described by Bion that leads us to the development of thought. For some, such as Giustino (2019), when, in the relationship with the child there exists a relational context that provides holding and signification, then pleasure will emerge in emotional exchanges. Failing that, the child will "use his body for excitatory purposes. In this case, sensoriality is in the foreground but lacks the relational character" [tr. by O.M.].

Several vicissitudes may unfold and many authors have sought to clarify these aspects, however, this discussion would move us away from the goal of this chapter.

Clinical work with these patients allows us to come in contact with these modes of functioning and with the most primitive areas of the mind, still largely charged with sensations, with primitive emotional states, yet also very much invaded by different bodily sensations and perceptions, with unrepressed somatic memories, "a part of the body, a visceral emotional experience, a sensory-motor experience, an object without which and on this side of which it is impossible to feel oneself existing" [tr. by O.M.] (Racalbuto, 1997).

Sensoriality and adolescence

The situation becomes particularly complicated in adolescence when the young person is confronted with a quantity of sensations from the newly sexed body, with hormonal, environmental and phase-specific psychological changes. Inevitably therefore, a surplus of psychic work is required of the adolescent in order to integrate them. As I have pointed out in previous chapters, these new sensations are inserted within the previous ones, onto that world that Gutton (2003) calls the *genital archaic*. The adolescent will be able to use the capacity to integrate that as an infant and child he or she had developed thanks to the contribution of the mother, with her mirroring and signifying of his or her sensations. To complicate this process, in this period of life the para-excitatory screen function performed by the parents is lost, thus leaving the adolescent confronted with new arousals, without the function of modulating and signifying reality that the parents previously performed. Multiple authors emphasise this point. For example, Novelletto states that to avoid "the short circuit between stimulation and outlet, which adolescents attempt, often unsuccessfully [...] a filter capable of dividing drive energy into absorbable and processable quantities [is necessary], otherwise the exaggeration of the erogeneity of stimuli paradoxically leads to a decrease in narcissistic libido. It is only if one is able to secure this state of respite that one can create the personal space necessary for the unfolding of the various processes [...] required for the passage of the adolescent crisis" [tr. by O.M.] (Novelletto, 2009, p. 112). Therefore, if integration has not taken place, or has only partially taken place, the adolescent will find himself or herself at the mercy of a marasmus world that he or she will not know how to manage. This is why he or she will at best turn to new objects, asking that they perform that function that the original caretaker had not performed. Varied manifestations and symptoms may therefore arise, often bearing the traces of the lack of sensory integration or somatic trace that has become enclosed as the *locus minoris resistentiae* in their mental functioning. Often, disturbances in the falling asleep phase will occur. The appearance of images testifies the breaking of the dream boundary, being this the time of the greatest fragility of ego boundaries, of the lability of the psychic skin that creates a protective barrier between self and other, between reality and fantasy, between inner and outer worlds. Nightmares, body sensations to the point of somatisation or hallucinations should not be considered as they would in adult pathology, but are sometimes transient as the psyche/soma matures. A number of these manifestations will find their place in a hallucinatory area: there is a wide range "of intermediate experiences, placeable on the ordering axes of the attributes of *sensoriality* – degrees of sonority – and *spatiality*, and this in the twofold sense of *localisation* within or outside the bodily limits and of *provenance* from the ego or the other [...]. We might also observe, and not only in adult patients, the (predominantly auditory) 'pseudo-hallucinations' of obsessive patients – which take the shape of 'sonorized thoughts', localised in psychic space and by definition coming from the ego, although with egodystonic and disturbing content" [tr. by O.M.] (Ballerini and Stanghellini, 1992, p. 29).

In any case, in adolescents in particular, this world of images is remarkably alive and central: "the hallucinatory is at the origin of daydreaming, at the origin of thinking in images that feeds the world of conscious fantasies, the world of *rêverie*, which plays a fundamental role in the course of adolescence" [tr. by O.M.] (Ladame, 2006). Above all, it is propulsive towards an activity of thought, although it is of course important not to lose sight of reality testing.

Hence, this fluid area that we see in this age can take a number of different paths depending on different factors, one of which is the relationship with the new object, which might also be the psychotherapist, who in addition to an understanding of what is happening, allows for the creation of space, time, holding and the digestion of content. According to Gutton (2003, p. 33), "dreaming and hallucinating manage the genital quantitative and perceptual excess by preventing a delusional response and somatic disorganisation" [tr. by O.M.] (which is why adolescent insomnia must always be thought of as an important symptom). Particularly, in some adolescents, the new sensoriality coloured with strong sensuality invades the oneiric scene and, due to the massiveness of stimuli or to the insufficient ability to handle them, it fails to integrate or remain latent. However, the dreamwork in any case contributes to the adolescent's subjectivisation, and its absence prevents it. Even in the case of the operating dreams or action dreams mentioned by Freud, the somatically based infantile dreams that Freud had recalled from his observations of his children, always represent dreamwork because they constitute a trace that can later be developed.

The importance of sensoriality is clearly seen in the two clinical fragments of Alberto and Giovanni, which I discussed in Chapters 3 and 4.

I briefly summarise the two cases here for the reader's convenience.

Alberto is seventeen years old, motherless and presenting with a break-down following a traumatic environmental event that had involved him and his family. Subsequently, his father marries another woman, but a few months later a car accident, with the fear of death for the whole family, precipitates the situation. Persecutory fantasies appear around the father and his partner. Alberto begins treatment that he pursues with care. A year after beginning therapeutic work, a new crisis is triggered by another incident, this time psychological. His father's wife, Giovanna, accidentally sees a video on the internet where Alberto fakes a rape scene on a female companion for fun. Alberto begins to present more marked symptomatology of confusion. Over the weekend, disturbing and uncontrollable thoughts take over. He goes to bed at night, at some point however, he feels a force emanating from him, a warmth coming from the lower part of his abdomen, to the right, and then rising up towards his heart. Marked tachycardia ensues. He is afraid of dying and asks his father for help. Over the next few days, he locks himself in the house but slowly develops a seemingly more confident manner, decides to take up sports training with his cousin and change his Facebook page by intro-ducing himself as a wrestling enthusiast.

In the following weeks, looking in the mirror, he notices a certain dis-harmony in his body between his right and left sides. Objects fall out of his hand; he feels less strength in the right side of his body. He goes on to say that he feels male and female parts inside himself, but separate, and will be caught up in a fantasy of meeting a girl he knows, which of course cannot be actualised. These disturbances will recede. Subsequently, Alberto will con-tinue his psychotherapy. The follow-up of this patient is very positive, both in terms of his school record and romantic life.

Comment

Alberto, admonished by his father's wife, who may be reminiscent of a maternal parental figure yet not burdened by the taboo of incest except in fantasy, possibly in the falling asleep stage where ego boundaries blur, presents a sort of hallucination. This hallucination will later flow into a somatic sensation, connecting the lower part of the abdomen (genitals?) to the heart, a somatic expression of an affective involvement of which Alberto cannot be aware. The phenomenon also continues in the following days, when Alberto feels his omnipotent bisexual confusion materialised in his body.

The symptomatology erupts after an event that he experienced as traumatic, and that retrospectively repeats a childhood trauma of his own. It is represented by the emergence of a phenomenon that we might refer to a somatic hallucination, a body that speaks through its sensations, the erotic feature of which he is unaware as he repeats the death anguishes that had been his first trauma.

Bion reminds us that hallucination is far more common than one might think and this "depends upon the fact that, the senses being two-way, an object may be to the patient an excretion, or, as we should say, an hallucination, rather than something existing independently of himself" (Bion, 1958, p. 85). The sense organs are two-way because they can take in sensation but also excrete it, as Bion illustrates by interpreting to the patient: "taken in and transformed by his ears and ejected by his eyes" (*Ibid.*, p.70).

Giovanni's dream

Of interest is the case of Giovanni, who presents a dream somewhere between hallucinatory and dreamlike.

Giovanni is a highly intelligent sixteen-year-old boy.

The move with his family from his hometown was a true earthquake for him. Despite maintaining as best he can the relationship with his friends, whom he sometimes sees on weekends, he is in fact alone in his new environment. In the sessions, which initially struggle to take off, Giovanni claims that he and his two friends have code names taken from cartoon heroes. They are actually special beings with a mission to defend the planet from an alien attack. At the moment, the three of them must acquire special powers and learn to control the force. Giovanni is convinced that every night a long dream, which he is able to command, unites him with his friends. He recounts, in the second diagnostic session, one such dream: in a grey city of stones in the future, scenes of life take place. The master teaches him to concentrate so as to avoid fighting as he would like. He and one of his friends cook food because they do not like to eat raw. They have a point in the centre of their body that will gradually heat up, and that will be a dangerous moment given that they cannot distinguish right from wrong. Giovanni believes that he is able to control his dreams and get out of them whenever he wants. For example, if, while falling asleep, he dreams of falling, then he can wake up.

Thanks to psychotherapy, Giovanni's situation seems to improve and the boy gradually opens up to his new environment and new social relationships, while over time, the themes he used to report in dreams and daydreams fade.

Comment

With this dream, we are perhaps dealing with a very peculiar event: we might consider this a sensory dream, permeated by sensations.

As Gaddini (1982) points out, these dreams refer to the fear of the boundaries of the self being overstepped. They might also refer to a fantasy about the body that, in the young child, might constitute the visual fantasies that gradually develop and lead to the consolidation of the boundaries of the self and body image. In fact, we might ask whether such a fantasy is not instead an evolution of a fantasy *in* the body, namely, an early somatic sensation that fortunately found an outlet in Giovanni's visual fantasy. From the "centre of the body at a point that will warm up", which Giovanni dreams about (fantasy *in* the body), a fantasy *on* the body develops, which is represented by this special dream and hallucinatory-like phenomenon. Transformation is important, and moreover, in the same dream narrative, Giovanni indeed narrates a transformation: *he and one of his friends cook food because they do not like to eat raw. And, through concentration, the master will teach him to stop fighting.* The transformation from raw food to cooked food represents a first digestion of a material that would have been at the very least difficult to elaborate, a material that, like the fantasy *in* the body, is split and not integrated.

The fantasy on the body, this sensory dream (Giustino, 2019), is thus a developmental stage towards later integration and towards the development of unconscious fantasy, it is a response to the separation trauma that Giovanni had experienced several times, but also in the dream, as in real life, the boy sets out to actively fight with his friends, with methods that are certainly megalomaniac but are also very adolescent-like. He also sets out to be helped in the dream by his friends and master, and in reality by the psychotherapist, accepting the dependency that is so difficult at this age.

Although in the case of Alberto and Giovanni we are faced with a developmental breakdown, I agree with Giustino's (*Ibid.*) observation, according to which psychotic patients "tend to make a 'sensorial' use of the mind; the body, with its status as generator of sensations (and memories of sensations), seems sometimes capable of a 'lay over' in their 'dreams' by reproducing the delusion and, at times, feeding it with sensory hallucinatory productions" [tr. by O.M.].

An integrative possibility

In turning to another case, that of Paolo (reported in Chapter 4), who travelled around Italy having his ears operated on only to end up adding eye rehabilitation sessions in another region, it seems clear to us that his need to intervene, particularly on the sense organs, concretises in the soma what should rather have been a coordination of the various senses that he felt were dissociated from each other. We might sometimes observe in our patients, when they improve, a greater care for their bodies, in their way of dressing, in their image, but not only. A patient who had risked dying from severe anorexia, undertakes psychotherapy three times a week after hospitalisation. After three years, her improvement is marked: her weight improves, and she decides, urged by her mother, to see a gynaecologist to resolve the delay in the resumption of her menstruation, which in spite of everything had still not returned. While anxiously looking forward to her period, she becomes much more elegant and groomed as she resumes a normal life. She brings up a dream that in my opinion deals with these issues: *through a telescope, she was looking at the starry sky, and it seemed to her that she was seeing something yet she did not know how alien it was, but if she had listened carefully to the signal coming in she could have made better use of the two instruments (sight and hearing) by coordinating them, and achieved the goal.* She associates the telescope with the new glasses she must buy because she wants them prettier and needs new lenses to see better. She adds that the gynaecologist, who had the same tone of voice as the analyst, told her that she would soon get her period. Apart from the obvious transferential references, I believe the most significant element is this coordination between the eyes and ears, between seeing and hearing, that comes with the resumption of healthy body functioning. Even though the target is still alien and distant, it is possible to begin to see it. In all these cases, we must not forget the crucial element that is the presence of the analyst to whom, in various ways, all patients refer to, directly or indirectly.

All the experiences and dreams that I have narrated so far, apart from the case of Paolo who was travelling around Italy to integrate his sensory organs, relate to patients in treatment. This is of great importance and in my opinion these phenomena were triggered by the analytic process, by the analyst's holding and his or her ability to be a new object, allowing for the opening to areas of the mind that would have been completely split off and denegated. These areas are sometimes hidden within the very dreams or acting out that patients bring to us. They may be frozen traumatic areas or areas that were never formed. When a child learns to walk, he or she sometimes falls and has a wobbly gait; when these patients begin to make contact with memories or parts of themselves that they have never known, a number of borderline phenomena will inevitably emerge: illusions, imagination, hallucinosis, alterations in body image, derealisation and depersonalisation, sensory dreams, acted out dreams, and still many others that I believe unnecessary to mention here.

In session, all this is either part of a shared discourse with the analyst who signifies it, or from it the field of knowledge with the patient can be expanded. I realise that these phenomena are complex to assess, and that analysts who are not accustomed to dealing with adolescents or developmental breakdowns may stigmatise them. Instead, when present, one must consider the developmental perspectives they may represent in order to make full use of them and not dissipate that trace that the patient's unconscious has shown the analyst, in direct or indirect communication, through verbal, oneiric, somatic, or acted out paths.

Note

1 Bion writes: "My experiences have led me to suppose that some kind of thought, related to what we should call ideographs and sight rather than to words and hearing, exists at the outset." (1957, p. 268).

References

Ballerini, A. and G. Stanghellini (1992). *Ossessione e Rivelazione: Riflessione sui Rapporti tra Ossessività e Delirio*. Torino: Boringhieri.

Bion, W.R. (1957). Differentiation of the psychotic from the non-psychotic personalities. *International Journal of Psychoanalysis, 38*, 266–275.

Bion, W.R. (1958). On hallucination. In (1967) *Second Thoughts*. London: Karnac Books, 1984.

Bion, W.R. (1959). Attacks on linking. In (1967) *Second Thoughts*. London: Karnac Books, 1984.

De Masi, F., C. Davalli, G. Giustino, A. Pergami (2015). Hallucinations in the psychotic state: Psychoanalysis and the neurosciences compared. *International Journal of Psychoanalysis, 96*, 293–318.

Gaddini, E. (1982). Early defensive fantasies and the psychoanalytical process. *International Journal of Psychoanalysis, 63*, 379–388.

Giustino, G. (2019). Psicosi e Sensorialità. Relazione presentata al Convegno della Società Psicoanalitica Italiana: *Allucinatorio / Allucinazioni: Psicosi e Oltre*. Bologna, Italy.

Gutton, Ph. (2003). Esquisse d'une théorie de la génitalité. *Adolescence, 21*, 2, 217–248.

Ladame, F. (2006). Adolescenza e autodistruzione: Valutazione clinica e note teoriche. *Richard e Piggle, 14*, 2, 191–201.

Lombardi, R. (2012). Il corpo nella teoria della mente di Wilfred R. Bion. *Consecutio Temporum. Rivista critica della postmodernità, 2*, 96–111.

Northoff, G. (2016). *Neuro-philosophy and the healthy mind: Learning from the unwell brain*. New York: Norton Press.

Novelletto, A. (2009). *L'adolescente. Una Prospettiva Psicoanalitica*. Roma: Astrolabio.

Racalbuto, A. (1997). Pensare: L'originario della sensorialità e dell'affetto nella costruzione del pensiero. *Bion Conference*, Torino, Italy.

Winnicott, D.W. (1960). The theory of the parent-infant relationship. In (1965) *The Maturational processes and the facilitating environment: Studies in the theory of emotional development*. London: Routledge, 1990.

Winnicott, D.W. (1962). Ego integration in child development. In (1965) *The maturational processes and the facilitating environment: Studies in the theory of emotional development*. London: Routledge, 1990.

Winnicott, D.W. (1963a). Fear of breakdown. In *Psycho-analytic explorations*. London: Routledge, 1989.

Winnicott, D.W. (1963b). Dependence in infant-care, in child-care, and in the psycho-analytic setting. In (1965) *The maturational processes and the facilitating environment: Studies in the theory of emotional development*. London: Routledge, 1990.

6

FEAR OF BREAKDOWN AND BEYOND [1]

In 1963, Winnicott wrote one of his finest, partly incomplete works: *The Fear of Breakdown* (1963a). He resumed this topic later, notably in *Psychology of Madness: A Contribution from Psychoanalysis* (1965). In these works, which proved extraordinarily dense and rich with insights, Winnicott started from the hypothesis that certain patients' fear of breakdown is in truth the fear of a breakdown that has already occurred.

To illustrate my reflections on this work, I will report a clinical case that I deem particularly fitting.

I meet Pierugo, twenty-two, in a family session. He has locked himself at home for the past three years and refuses to go out for any reason. The failure of his first university exams caused him deep shame; no one must see him. His life revolves around lunch with his family and his room. The internet, the numerous novels he downloads from the internet for free, or sleep, are his daily companions. At first, the patient refuses any help, and therefore the parents turn to me. The family sessions he attends with the idea of helping his siblings, both of whom are in need, allow us to get to know each other and this will start our relationship. In time, the path is always similar: it will take a long time (even one or two years) to inaugurate each new activity, such as going to the tobacconist to buy cigarettes, but once started, it will persist. Thus, after a few months, Pierugo agrees to start treatment, and this will coincide with couples therapy for his parents.

The scenario that unfolds before me from the start is quite complex. Pierugo enters the office like an automaton, under a large mass of hair that he has not cut in a long time. Everything is mechanical: from his extreme punctuality at the beginning of the session to his way of speaking, filled with hard facts, without inflection of tone or apparent emotion. If emotions exist, they always refer to experiences of unworthiness for his failure. The world is dangerous and

   DOI: 10.4324/9781032663371-8

everything must be controlled. This is implemented by physically and psychologically building a refuge and withdrawing. I am quite amazed that Pierugo consistently attends the sessions and I feel the oppressive climate, as if a large black cloak covered the whole apartment. My various interventions appear to bring no result. However, Pierugo is a young man of extraordinary intelligence. He knows three foreign languages, two of which he speaks perfectly, and in his time spent exploring the internet, he has attained quite an extensive culture for a young man of his age. At home his assigned task is that of repairman, fixing electrical problems, the water heater, sinks, and cabinets. The house the family lives in (as I seem to gather) is damaged and poor, although the family is upper-middle class and the father a very well-positioned manager with an important salary. A year after this first period of treatment, Pierugo plummets into a worrisome state. He misses two sessions and I learn that he spends day and night crying in his room.

This coincides with a departure of the parents. I hypothesise that he might dangerously act out to free himself from this state of severe distress and, worried, I warn his parents. When he comes to the sessions, I can only watch helplessly as his desperate crying continues at home. Pierugo begins drug treatment, but he reassures me: he does not want to attempt suicide, although death might be an evacuation from this disorganised state. He will return to this episode several times in his analysis as a chilling experience that he must avoid at all costs, as he will tell me again and again. Gradually, flashes of his internal world dominated by intense persecution begin to appear. Continuous, incessant internal reproaches rule and annihilate him. We agree that we could call these internal voices (which do not sound like auditory hallucinations) the "tyrant" and somehow relate them to the difficult experience that lasted for years and culminated in his puberty. During this long period, his father had had a long crisis of a paranoid quality during which he had obsessive, controlling, and abusive behaviours towards all family members.

I will now report a session that took place three years after the beginning:

Pierugo walks in happy. This morning he suddenly went out to McDonald's and had a cheeseburger. It went well, successfully. He did not feel the tyrant. He explains to me, in a seemingly lucid way, that the tyrant wants to progressively create a void, and the solution is to reach nothingness, which, however, is unattainable. It is not death he wants, but the disappearance of sensations, emotions, pleasure and pain. Emotions scare him and he is ashamed of them. As long as you stay in bed you feel nothing. He wants to achieve nonexistence. Like when he was little and was afraid of the dark. One night he got up and closed the door from which some light came.

"Of course", I comment, "It reminds me of a very small child that no one hears and who then decides to do it himself, deny the fear. He gets up, goes to the door and closes it. He then becomes the one who leaves the world out; it is no longer the world that abandons him". I add, "But don't you like a little light?"

(I do not believe this episode has anything to do with the terrifying primal scene.) As I say this, my mind spins around the topic of nonexistence. Never have I had a patient with such lucidity talk to me about this. It is even difficult to understand what "nonexistence" means. My mind goes to existentialists and their description of forms of nonexistence, but in this case Pierugo is describing a state of the mind that does not seek death, as he confidently says. Death could be an active process that occurs after the experience of having lived and being born. Nonexistence is non-being, and it can only be described by another and not by the subject. If we exist, we run the risk of losing something or being responsible for what we do or lose. Nonexistence is the negation of this.

Comment

As is clearly observable, Pierugo is a difficult patient. We can speak of him in terms of a breakdown. This term is of great use to us, because – as Winnicott says – it is "rather vague and because it could mean various things".

From the perspective of an adolescent psychoanalyst, Pierugo had a developmental breakdown. To make this statement, I refer to the adolescent onset at such a crucial time as entering university, which marks the reorganisation of identity and separation from early parental objects. But all this was preceded by an attempt at rebellion, shortly after puberty, and serious difficulty in the early stages of life. This event is considered by Laufer (1984) to be a developmental stalemate. In fact, upon his entry into university, Pierugo stalled his growth and reversed his development. The failure of early relationships with his mother and the family environment, with highly traumatic and indeed psychotic and psychoticising patterns, generated in Pierugo a mode of survival to which he clings strenuously, made of withdrawal, refuge, and closure from the world around him. The world is dangerous, all interpersonal relationships are, but he himself carries an internal persecutor, a tyrant who gives no respite with his constant sadistic and cruel reproaches. Certainly, this echoes his identification with an aggressing father before whom he felt powerless, but also his sadistic omnipotence, with which he checkmates any other before him, as well as the sane parts of his personality.

Yet the real problem was or still is at the bottom of his personality, his defensive search for nonexistence and in the paradox of this search. In it, nonexistence is a defence against persecution, as well as against deep depression. Winnicott sheds light on this matter, stating that nonexistence is part of a sophisticated defence that helps the person avoid responsibility in the depressive position or persecution in the so-called "the stage of self-assertion": "the self-assertive state, that is, the 'I am' state with the inherent implication 'I repudiate everything that is not me'" (Winnicott, 1963a, p. 95).

I would like to further discuss the defence of nonexistence because Winnicott devotes a significant paragraph to it, and point out my use of Winnicott in Pierugo's case. In the presence of a depressed or absent mother, the child may become the mother's manic defence, as Winnicott (1935) told us in another work, or become a dead object, albeit continuing to live a futile life thanks to the false self or a semblance of life, as perhaps happened in Pierugo's case. As a commentary on Winnicott's work, Green defines "object nothingness" as "the feeling of nonexistence proper to the dissolution of being, which follows from destruction" and differentiates it from the "silence of disinvestment, a source of peace" [tr. by O.M.], a term by which I believe Green refers to the experience of non-integration (Green, 1977, p. 71). Certainly a paradox, such as those to which Winnicott has accustomed us.

In the presence of an absent mother, the child who has experienced a sufficient dose of illusion can become disillusioned, which allows him or her to cope with the onset of external reality and approach symbolism (Winnicott, 1945). An abrupt transition from the fusion state to reality without a sufficient dose of illusion allowing a gradual approach, as in the case of a depressed or dead mother, will instead generate pathology, emptiness, and a sense of nonexistence. The child will attempt to cope with these experiences with various defences, such as massive intellectual activity, *rêverie* to fill the void, or, as in Pierugo's case, withdrawal, isolation of the true, completely dissociated self.

In this case non-communication is an active and reactive phenomenon and it is a pathological defence. In these situations, withdrawal, a reactive noncommunication, helps the individual feel real because the communication arising from the false self is felt as false and unreal given that it is detached from the real self (Winnicott, 1963c).

Pierugo's withdrawal therefore paradoxically served as a solution to feel alive and real. Yet there is another particularly important aspect to the story of this treatment.

The days of long, continuous and exhausting weeping that Pierugo presented after the first year of his work had puzzled me: I did not quite know how to deal with them in the silent, almost wordless sessions with him, despite my trying to urge or even console him. In retrospect, I believe that Pierugo unconsciously wanted me to simply be there to watch him, to assist, and not to run away as had already happened with his mother, who was, immediately after Pierugo's birth, very busy because of the family's move abroad to follow her husband. At that time, her rejection of the child, which was exhausting for her, had led to a total and very early disappearance of breast milk, and Pierugo was starving.

I must confess that I was very impressed and still question the nature, the meaning, and the origin of his crying fit, which lasted for days. This had been a new event for him, who had locked himself in his room for years and was striving for nonexistence as the absence of emotions. The triggering event for the crisis may have been his parents' absence. That desperate crying had been crucial for me, making me feel anguished, desperate and helpless. In hindsight, I wonder whether it might have been the patient's way of allowing himself the regression he had always avoided and the attempt to repeat the primitive traumatic experience.

Did this episode have anything to do with the intense agony, the disorganisation of the infant, abandoned to itself and away from its mother's eyes, who can do nothing but scream and cry? I believe that two events had come into contact: the departure of the parents, of the mother in particular, and the presence of the analysis. The latter offered the opportunity to be welcomed, seen, and also – no less important – to arouse in the analyst an emotional experience of sharing. But while a patient with a relatively healthy ego, who has what Winnicott calls an "observing ego" (Winnicott, 1971), can enter into regression and subsequently exit it, patients like Pierugo are forced to act: this outward manifesting, or "enacting" (Abram, 1996, p. 291), is the only way they can experience something they carry but have not been able to experience, and it is also the only way the patient communicates to the analyst emotions and experiences that he or she has not been able to experience.

I will now continue with another brief excerpt from treatment with the same patient. After this episode, as the process progresses, I become aware from intangible clues that I have become an omnipotent and reassuring character for him and this, albeit laboriously, allows him to slowly undertake new experiences. Dreams begin to appear, often featuring experiences of getting lost or estranged without being able to receive answers from anyone, especially from his mother. The patient nevertheless takes steps forward: he rides his moped, goes to the supermarket, goes alone to the pharmacologist, begins attending socialisation groups within a community and finally, after four years of effort, accepts the dreaded responsibility of having a cat, which seems to bring him much joy.

This session, five years after the beginning, is an example of the persecution that lingers, yet the material also provides a glimpse of transformative possibility.

Pierugo begins by saying that he is feeling better. He has been assembling furniture from Ikea for the new house his parents bought, but he has not finished yet. He needs to go back to the pharmacologist. He feels guilty because he is exploiting his parents and perhaps that is why he should move out on his own.

I comment around possible fears and anxieties in going alone and separating from parents, and perhaps all of this is hidden beneath the guilt of still being at home.

He tells me about the dream he had the previous night: "someone discovered his different accounts, and this would allow him to be traced. The different accounts would lead back to him". He does not like this dream. His hiding place is discovered.

I reflect upon the evident transferential references, such as being discovered by the analyst in his anguishes or even his identity, but also upon the fact that the patient refers to an integration activity he is doing (assembling furniture) that may cause him distress. I decide to comment on his referring, in the dream, to the fact that he himself may know different aspects of himself, his different accounts, but perhaps this frightens him. Instead, he should be happy about it.

He answers by reminding me that in his house, as long as he can remember, talking about personal facts is not possible. None of the brothers do so, to avoid being vulnerable to their father's criticism. "Do you talk about trivial things then?", I ask him. "No" Pierugo tells me: "we talk about financial matters (the father is very anguished about whatever expenses can be made in the family), or political or social facts, or my father explains something". The feeling is that the patient is communicating the extent to which he must protect his unattainable self, his true self, and the extent to which even the other's intuition might be felt as a cannibalistic intrusion, as Winnicott tells us in the work Communicating and not Communicating *(1963c).*

What is breakdown

I pondered Pierugo's case at length, asking myself many questions and points for reflection, two of which I would like to recall here. The first concerns the definition of breakdown.

In a well-documented article, Ogden (2014) poses a question that in his view Winnicott had implicitly asked but not developed: "What is breakdown?"

a   The break of the mind in psychosis?
b   A defensive organisation against psychosis?
c   A defence against primitive agony?

Ogden concludes that, in his view: "the term 'breakdown' refers to the breakdown of the mother-infant tie, which leaves the infant alone and raw, and on the verge of not existing. The infant, in this state – disconnected from the mother – is thrust into what might become an experience of primitive agony". He then adds that "the psychosis lies in the defence against the experience of the break in the mother–infant tie" (*Ibid*, p. 213). Ogden hereby fully echoes Winnicott, who argued that psychosis is the defensive organisation against breakdown, against the collapse of the Ego because it is the organisation of the Ego that is threatened. Pierugo, having reached the threshold of adulthood, had experienced the inability to exist as an autonomous subject and define his own identity as a person, therefore developing a psychotic defence characterised by physical and psychic refuge and withdrawal. Very early on, he had organised himself as the non-existent knight that Calvino tells us about. His life and socialisation, which had accompanied him until late adolescence, was made of an empty armour. Pierugo was simply not there; he was stuck at the early breaking of the bond with his mother and his inconsolable crying that could nonetheless not be manifested. The creation of shelter and his emotional cut were organised to defend himself from a primitive agony he had experienced at the origin of his life. Pierugo constantly felt threatened by impending annihilation that led him, in Bionian terms, to hatred of his internal reality and hatred of awareness, as seen in the dream. The possible experiences of integration confronted him with additional anguish, not only because of the attack on awareness but also because of the destructive omnipotence that characterises these patients. However, in the course of the analysis, the possibility of reliving them in a containing situation that differed from that of the past had perhaps arisen in time. Indeed, in order to continue his development and subjectivise himself, he was to face the primitive agony of his early separation from his mother.

The extraordinary intuition

"The patient needs to 'remember' this but it is not possible to remember something that has not yet happened, and this thing of the past has not happened yet because the patient was not there for it to happen to. The only way to 'remember' in this case is for the patient to experience this past thing for the first time in the present, that is to say, in the transference. This past and future thing then becomes a matter of the here and now, and becomes experienced by the patient for the first time" (Winnicott, 1963a, p. 92).

In this statement, Winnicott implicitly broadens the concept of the unconscious, which is no longer the repressed unconscious, but rather refers to a traumatic memory that was stored, but never recorded, a memory that occurred when "ego integration [was] not able to encompass something" (Winnicott in Ogden, 2014, p. 212). Winnicott, in his work *Mind and its Relation to the Psyche-Soma* (1949), distinguishes between two types of memories: memories that are thinkable because the child has not experienced excessive interference from the environment, and another type of memories, the unthinkable ones. The latter due to traumatic impingements by the environment when the child is unable or not yet ready to deal with them. These constitute an interference for the continuity of being and are "catalogued", frozen, waiting for the hope of trans-formation to open. Winnicott believes that everything that happens to us, from the trauma of birth, is remembered on both the emo-tional and bodily levels. Other contemporaries of his also posited the same insights. Klein (1957) spoke of "memories in feelings". Freud (1914, 1915) in one of his extraordinary insights, but especially Bion,

109

also referred to this same problem. In fact, Bion asserted the existence of "ideas which cannot be more powerfully expressed because they are buried in the future which has not happened, or buried in the past which is forgotten, and which can hardly be said to belong to what we call 'thought'" (1974, p. 43). This is the field that Bion calls inaccessible mental states, which are neither part of the conscious nor of the unconscious.

Thus, it is not just a matter of remembering what was frozen in the soma, but what was never really constituted. It is a memory that was never formed, but that leaves a negative trace in the ego, the trace of an experience with the object in which the most important thing is not what happened but what was not, what never happened. The subject is thus stripped of a potential capacity for signification, a capacity for symbolisation. We are therefore not in the realm of splitting, even less so of repression; rather, we are talking about an experience in the Ego that is in the order of the un-constituted. It is the very capacity to think that is called into question – Levine tells us – hence we cannot rely on the search for what has been "hidden". We may be faced with the formless, something that may not yet have reached a specific form such that it comes to "exist" and is consequently concealed. "There exists a paradox whereby this formless part might constitute a foundational 'unlived experience', in which experiences that could never be thought are condensed, albeit potentially active" [tr. by O.M.] (Nicolò and Accetti, 2015, p. 15). With these patients, the repetition of trauma is not a punctual event. In truth, we are facing an ongoing process that lasts a lifetime, precisely because it is inscribed in the global functioning of the personality. A process of continuous remodelling based on primitive impingement, in a continuous interaction with the environment, an interaction that can repeat or transform the traumatic mode of functioning. In certain cases then, as Winnicott tells us at several points in his work, "the unthinkable anxiety that some people have to carry round with them all their lives [...] contains – at root – the deepest source of your own psychic energy, so that when you have to blot it out (or it happens to you that it gets blotted out) you lose the taproot, so to speak" (Winnicott, 1969, p. 119). This may partly coincide with the clinical observation that certain trauma patients organise their self around trauma. Finally, we must consider that each of us carries different levels of representability (Aulagnier, 1975, p. 75), which I believe allows us to live a life that is in some ways acceptable despite the deep traumas that might accompany us. A number of these traumas will remain pre-symbolic throughout life or find symbolisation outside representability, as some research in developmental psychology states (Beebe *et al.*, 1997), even though the psychotic functioning with which we are in constant balance does not always predominate in our lives.

Yet, there is another aspect to be taken into consideration in this work and it concerns the introduction of temporal meaning into the subject's mind.

In a work on the autobiography of the psychotic (Nicolò and Accetti, 2015, p. 15) we observed that "the psychotic or the borderline do not have access to what concerns the origin of their life and the meaning of their experiences. These patients have constituted secret areas of the mind that cannot be accessed by thought or memory. Secreted areas in which secrets concerning origins or evoking themes concerning doubts about existence can be contained. The isolation of these parts brought about by the lack of a self that is able to contain thoughts about one's existence will generate the continuous search for answers, precisely with the function of compensating for this lack. This operation confirms the timeless repetition that is typical of psychotic functioning. The perception of time allows one to take a historical perspective of one's life and to feel the existing self. In the psychotic, on the other hand, thinking is a closed and circular phenomenon, time remains concrete, the narrative factual, lacking a chronological axis that ties the various episodes of existence together" [tr. by O.M.].

As Winnicott (1963a) teaches us, the event of repeating breakdown in transference (which the holding of the analytic environment and regression allow) inserts this event into the patient's history, providing temporality in both the present and the past. In the present, because it is occurring in the here and now, but also in the past, because of the analyst's imaginative activity and his or her interpretive hypothesis. Indeed, the latter gives meaning to the breakdown as he or she observes its connection between the present agony and the primitive agony that was lived, but not experienced.

In *Fear of Breakdown* (*Ibid.*), where Winnicott's full clinical maturity shines through, we find the coagulation of many of his findings, beginning with his work on early stages and emotional growth, on primitive agonies, on the importance of regression in the analytic process, on psychosis as a defence against a deficient environment, as well as on the fear of death, emptiness and nonexistence.

The future of our patients

When analysis is able to represent the hope that these patients have not had up to that point, different outlooks for their lives can open, although development for them is never easy nor definitively taken for granted. It cannot be taken for granted because a young adult, especially, must recover developmental experiences, such as adolescent developmental milestones that he or she did not have in the past. Another crucial point, which psychoanalysts very frequently forget, is that the traumatic functioning of the family ties in which they are immersed may continue almost unchanged unless something has been done to change it. Bion speaks in this regard of how, in the interaction between the child and a rejecting mother, an obstructive object is generated, and I believe that these patterns persist in the families of these patients. Winnicott by his own account was very precise in this regard: psychosis is an illness of environmental deficiencies, and these deficiencies are unpredictable failures of what was provided as a basis, and "they result in the annihilation of the individual whose going-on-being is interrupted" (Winnicott, 1963b, p. 256). He also adds that in these patients "the ego cannot organise itself against environmental failure insofar as dependence is a living fact" (Winnicott, 1963a, p. 88). In Pierugo too, the primitive dependence on the environment and the need to relive or experience what he had failed to remember but had re-experienced in disorganisation and paralysing crying remained alive within him.

Yet, the crucial problem for us concerns the tools we have to help them, because attention to these levels, which are not subject to the functioning characterised by repression, imposes new methodological approaches on psychoanalysis. I believe that an important transformative moment, which I did not realise at the time, was the long crying crisis that lasted for days, which Pierugo allowed himself by seizing an occasional traumatic stimulus, but also finally having present in him an element of trust, born thanks to the continuity of my presence in the setting. That occasion allowed us to share a meaningful experience, for him with despair, endless falling and anguish of annihilation, and for me with confusion, not knowing what was happening before me, but containing my anguish and being alive and affectively present. The person of the analyst and his or her position in the setting are crucial to restore hope. I will not dwell here on issues that presently seem to be the current trend in psychoanalysis. In my experience with these patients, what is of great importance is the analyst's emotional participation, his or her sharing of the patient's distressing experiences, modulated by the analyst's holding capacity, sometimes supported by his or her thinking capacity and sometimes instead characterised by his or her ability to wait and question. In the most fortunate situations, the analyst associates for both, dreams for both, symbolises for himself or herself and for the other, and also arranges his or her mind towards the emergence of unconscious and unpredictable aspects. From this viewpoint, the analyst's psychic functioning is an integral part of both process and material.

Note

1 This work was published in the book edited by Busato Barbaglio, C., Macchia, A., Nicolò, A.M., *Winnicott e la Psicoanalisi del Futuro* [Winnicott and the Psychoanalysis of the Future], Rome, Alpes, 2017 (revised here).

References

Abram, J. (1996). *The language of Winnicott: A dictionary of Winnicott's use of words*. London: Routledge, 2007.

Aulagnier, P. (1975). *The violence of interpretation: From pictogram to statement*. London: Routledge, 2001.

Beebe, B., Lachmann F.M., Jaffe J. (1997). Mother-infant interaction structures and presymbolic self- and object representations. *Psychoanalytic Dialogues*, 7, 133–182.

Bion, W.R. (1974). *Two papers: 'The Grid' and 'Caesura'*. London: Routledge, 1989.

Freud, S. (1914). Remembering, repeating and working-through (further recommendations on the technique of psycho-analysis II). *S.E.* 12: 154–156, London: Hogarth Press.

Freud, S. (1915). The unconscious. *S.E.* 14: 159–215, London: Hogarth Press.

Green, A. (1977). Il regno appartiene al bambino. In V. Bonaminio and A. Giannakoulas (Eds.), *Il Pensiero di Winnicott*. Roma: Armando, 1982.

Klein, M. (1957). *Envy and gratitude: A study of unconscious sources*. London: Routledge, Classic from the Tavistock Press, 2002.

Laufer, M. and M.E. Laufer (1984). *Adolescence and developmental breakdown: A psychoanalytic view*. London: Routledge, 1995.

Nicolò, A.M., Accetti L. (2015). Introduzione all'edizione italiana. In H.B. Levine, G.S. Reed and D. Scarfone (Eds.), 2013, *Stati no n Rappresentati e Costruzione del Significato*. Milano: Franco Angeli, 2015.

Ogden, T.H. (2014). Fear of breakdown and the unlived life. *International Journal of Psychoanalysis, 95*, 205–223.

Winnicott, D.W. (1935). The manic defence. In (1958), *Through paediatrics to psycho-analysis*. New-York: Basic Books, 1975.

Winnicott, D.W. (1945). Primitive emotional development. In (1958), *Through paediatrics to psycho-analysis*. New-York: Basic Books, 1975.

Winnicott, D.W. (1949). Mind and its relation to the psyche-soma. In (1958), *Through paediatrics to psycho-analysis*. New-York: Basic Books, 1975.

Winnicott, D.W. (1963a). Fear of breakdown. In *Psycho-analytic explorations*. London: Routledge, 1989; (1974) *International Review of Psycho-Analysis*, l, pp. 103-107.

Winnicott, D.W. (1963b). Dependence in infant-care, in child-care, and in the psycho-analytic setting. In (1965), *The maturational processes and the facilitating environment: studies in the theory of emotional development*. London: Routledge, 1990.

Winnicott, D.W. (1963c). Communicating and not communicating leading to a study of certain opposites. In (1965) *The maturational processes and the facilitating environment: studies in the theory of emotional development*. London: Routledge, 1990.

Winnicott, D.W. (1965). The psychology of madness: a contribution from psycho-analysis. In *Psycho-analytic explorations*. London: Routledge, 1989.

Winnicott, D.W. (1969). To an American correspondent. In *The spontaneous gesture: Selected letters of D.W. Winnicott*. London: Routledge, 1987.

Winnicott, D.W. (1971). Playing: A theoretical statement. In *Playing and reality*. London: Tavistock.

7

DEVELOPMENTAL RUPTURES[*]

A transformative pathway

In this chapter, we recount the analysis of an adolescent girl who presented, at age fourteen, a severe breakdown. The case was treated with three weekly sessions by Lara Bancheri with the supervision of Anna Maria Nicolò. Support was also provided to the parent couple, one of whom was undergoing analysis.

We felt it was important to report the salient stages of this process, highlighting how difficult it can be and the extent to which these patients test the analyst, his or her emotional experiences, as well as the setting. Maintaining a strict working model, as if we were dealing with a neurotic patient or a candidate in training, is a dangerous illusion that often results in the interruption of psychotherapy. With such patients, the setting is always a complex and bumpy process of construction, and when one finally reaches an orderly setting, this means that a great deal of work has been done and that the patient has finally internalised the distinction between reality and fantasy, between the inner and outer worlds, and that a container and a space where to begin to think has finally been constituted within him or her. In these situations, the analyst is forced to resort to his or her emotional presence, to his or her fantasy, to his or her receptive unconscious, given that many times communications flow from unconscious to unconscious and sidestepping the conscious, as Freud had pointed out (1911).

[*] *Psychiatrist, associate member of the* Società Psicoanalitica Italiana [Italian Psychoanalytic Society, translator's note].

DOI: 10.4324/9781032663371-9   115

Generally, the technique with adolescents is, by international convention, different from that with the neurotic adult. Classic interpretation must often be replaced or channelled within the dialogue (Nicolò, 2013), often also allowing for a mirroring of the patient, without ever passivising him or her.

All this may even shock the analyst who needs to anchor himself or herself in rigid rules. In fact, given the great difficulty for an analyst to have verification of his or her work, he or she often sticks to the rules as if they were an unbreakable taboo. We personally believe that the best verification is effectiveness, improvement and healing, whenever possible, of the patient.

We recount the different stages of this process, interpolating comments where necessary to facilitate the reader. Throughout the chapter, we delve into the characteristics with which breakdown presents itself in Gaia and its evolution. Gaia breaks with herself by depersonalising herself, also breaking words, keeping her mind busy by dividing words into groups of three. She thus blocks the possibility of turning the many dreams she recounts into constructive thoughts and actions, confining herself to a place where she can neither turn back nor proceed with her growth. We will describe the way in which meeting the real parents allowed the analyst to experience first-hand the existence of alienating identifications that had passivised the patient, enabling a better understanding of the extent of anti-developmental pressure from the environment.

Gaia

Gaia is fourteen years old. The description given by the referring doctor portrays her as a provocatively dressed girl with a coarse dialect vocabulary. Gaia uses her body as a foothold to construct an omnipotent and triumphant defensive neo-reality full of excitation: as early as seventh grade she dresses hypersexually and impacts against parental prohibitions. The father comes across as weak and confused, while the mother is impermeable to the girl's developmental needs. The parents are separated and in perpetual quarrel. Two events stand out as significant in her childhood: the birth of her brother, which occurs when Gaia is fifteen months old, and the move to another city that causes Gaia, at eight years old, to lose all her references by triggering conflict with her mother because of her protests. Coinciding with this opposition are night terrors and episodes of sleepwalking in Gaia.

The pain of growing up

Upon arriving at the consultation, Gaia is overwhelmed by an anguished feeling. The preliminary phone call preceding the first meeting is long: the father initially speaks, alarmed, reporting that his daughter has been feeling bad for the past week and that just then she is asking him to help her die; Gaia threatens to kill herself, he then hands her the phone. On the phone, the father shows live his difficulty in containing the anguish of the girl who, left in terror, cannot speak. The analyst attempts to calm her down as Gaia cries. She then begins to say that she is very sick and starts to talk about what is happening: she wants to understand right away why *that thing* happened because now everything seems different and strange and she no longer remembers what it was like before.

The analyst seeks to grasp, in the midst of that crying, the slightest information that might help encourage her to come for an initial meeting. Gaia listens to her and stops crying, which reassures the analyst in the time leading up to the meeting, given the counter-transferential fear that the girl might be on the verge of a breakdown.

Gaia arrives at the first meeting with a tracksuit and a sad expression, although her eyes seem able to open into a smile when the analyst approaches her emotionally. She recounts that it all started a week ago: she was sitting on the couch at home with her boyfriend Simone and her mother. She says that just as she stood up she was seized by this bad feeling that never left her: "I had the feeling that I saw him in another way, it was as if I weren't able to be with him anymore. I didn't want to see him anymore but at the same time I wanted to talk to him". She describes an experience of estrangement, something made Gaia no longer recognise reality.

In the two consultation sessions that follow, it emerges that Gaia's experience of feeling estranged from herself may be connected to an early sexual initiation that was traumatic for her mind.

She says she is agitated about Simone, because he has reconnected with certain friends who deal drugs and distribute fake money, and that in order to be well, she feels she must help him. Gaia presents Simone as her "double", onto whom she projects parts of herself to distance them. She explains that she cares so much for Simone but that now, unlike before, agitation comes to her even when she is with him, "I don't know if it is for other reasons that I unloaded on him". The analyst asks her to explain what she is referring to: she

117

recounts that she melted a large necklace of her mother's that her father had given her, and a small necklace of her own, because she was angry with her. She is now very afraid to do it again. She says that her mother, after finding out, started crying saying that she did not expect this from her, and this disappointment never went away. About this, Gaia, dark and dull, remains silent.

The analyst comments that in talking about the two necklaces, the small one and the big one, she seems to be talking about the two dimensions of existence, being small and being big, both lost "because of her". Gaia answers that when she argues with her mother, her father first listens to her and agrees with her, only to then tell everyone what she said and agree with her mother. Gaia feels her father is childish and unreliable.

In later consultation sessions, Gaia talks about her mother: "she talks too much, she says a million things at once, she yells because I am messy and she is repetitive. We started fighting when I was in seventh grade because she didn't want me to go out, she says I always go out. In seventh grade, I woke up. Several times I stole money from my mother's wallet." (The analyst imagines her waking up in seventh grade with that vulgarised adultomorphic body of which there is no trace now, on the one hand to explore aspects of the self by acting them out, and on the other hand to triumph over her mother.)

Gaia accuses her mother of not allowing her any space-time to go out and experience herself in her no longer childlike being. Until a week ago she was "awake", now she spends her days sleeping while her nights are sleepless. "I never want to fall asleep and when I sleep, I never want to wake up". She therefore stopped going to school and locked herself in the house.

Comment

It was perhaps intense anger that drove the girl to melt the link/ necklace between her mother and father, and between her and her mother, as if she had made a "phantasmal robbery" of her mother's sexuality. Perhaps she acted out an aggressive fantasy directed against the link, which the conjugal separation made disappointing to her. The fusion of the two necklaces seems to represent a drive towards undifferentiation with the object, but also, in an ambivalent way, hatred towards the mother by whom she feels abandoned. Certainly though, it is the sexual initiation that she reports as the triggering cause. Rather than having developed pleasure in sexuality and love sharing with Simone, Gaia precociously acted out. With early sexual intercourse she could thus have felt like an adult, a woman like the mother she was trying to rob of that mysterious area of sexuality of which she was previously the sole possessor. The response, however, is tragic. Gaia senses her mother's violent retaliation, a mother who is no longer the same with her and rejects her. The situation becomes worrisome. Gaia is locked at home, withdrawn, depressed, and has reversed her sleep/wake rhythm.

Trying not to think

Gaia begins analysis with three weekly sessions, without drug treatment. She arrives at the session accompanied by her mother, who waits in the car. She tells a secret she has never told anyone about: "It's a kind of prayer, if I do it things go well. I divide the words I hear into groups of three letters. If a word is odd I repeat it until I form all groups of three". After a few months, she announces that maybe next week she would like to start going to school again to "try not to think", to see how it goes if she resumes school. Yet Gaia spends her days on the couch, alternating between sleeping and watching TV, and so the announced intent to go back to school turns out to be false. She has stopped going out and does not know whether to see her boyfriend again.

In the first session of the second week of analysis, after a month from the start of treatment, she recounts two dreams she had the night before. She says she had them while she was not really sleeping.

> *I dreamed about a yellow thing, not sticky but it was like an eraser trying to take shape. The ones that if you pull them form all those threads. Then there were yellow shoes that had a face, eyes, mouth and nose like monster faces.*

At this point, she says she gets up and goes to sleep in her mother's bed. There she has this other dream:

> *There was me and a brownish cloth with holes in it. The cloth was like a reality that continued when I got up.*

Although prompted, Gaia does not make any association.

In many moments of the session the locus of exchange is the body rather than the word: Gaia looks at the analyst making her feel that

119

she is making contact with her, she smiles at her. In the intensity of that smile, the analyst feels an authentic closeness that remains in her as a vital element of affective certainty in the relationship, making Gaia's attacks on linking – the constant resetting of everything that has been conquered in the session – more bearable to the analyst.

Comment

Her wanting to "try not to think" connects to her need to regain control, to the words divided by three. The analyst wonders to what extent she has divided by three the things said to one another. The meaning is lost and the attempt to keep everything under control appears to want to take over. The three suggests the need to control the entry of the third. Perhaps, Gaia also feels the thought as an unbearable third element, pulling her away from the need to remain fused with the object. Gaia describes a terrible condition: the impossibility of moving forward as Simone's girlfriend, and simultaneously, the impossibility of going back as a daughter, to her disappointing family. The request seems to be for an immediate magical solution that will free her from this utterly tormenting confusion.

Gaia still manages to dream, although much could be discussed around the nature of these dreams. There seems to be an element of confusion between sleep and wakefulness, between reality and fantasy, with the risk of a rupture of the contact barrier to watch out for. They have the characteristic of sensory dreams (Giustino, 2019) that at times seem to enter the realm of the hallucinatory, blending in with reality and crossing its boundary. Yet, the yellow thing seems to represent her self as it attempts to take shape. As in reality, after trying on the guise of the vulgar woman, she has transformed into the sad girl. Both the yellow thing and the blanket with holes have a strong sensory character. In particular, the latter recalls a container with holes in it, a pierced maternal container, as the setting becomes pierced because of her constant skipping sessions, attacking the therapeutic link and reducing it to a cloth with holes in it. Even the relationship with Simone, which represented containment for her, shows its holes, like her pierced self and body.

Sexual initiation

In the course of the analysis, Gaia fails to recount anything about her first sexual experience; she says that even recently she accepted

120

Simone's attempts and dismisses the sexual relationship as "don't know ... normal". She had attempted to omnipotently and hypersexually forge ahead, which did not hold up and fell apart.

In the first session of the week, at the end of the second month of analysis, after talking at length about her boyfriend, whom she sees as happy as if nothing had happened, she recounts a dream.

"Simone's sister wanted to give me her cell phone, but from the pictures on it, it was as if that was Simone's cell phone. I thought Simone got it for me to check up on me, to see if I was texting anyone. Then there was a room with a ladder, he was under the ladder, laughing and trying not to be seen, and then he leaned out. Then I went into a room, I was wearing a black dress and black heels. He said, 'You're wearing heels'. But they were all broken. I changed and put my zebra-print Converse shoes back on. He had dressed up, black T-shirt, black suit and ugly brown shoes. I was hiding because I didn't want him to see my shoes. I laughed, it was the entrance to my grandmother's house, there was an ice-skating rink and all the male skaters had wooden skating clogs, the kind you use in the mountains". End of dream.

As always, she makes no associations, but the persecutory fear of being controlled emerges, and the analyst notes that Gaia watches her furtively.

The analyst tells Gaia that the ladder and the heels, make her think of a part of her that wishes she were older, that she seems to be torn between doing something that pleases Simone and being more comfortable in her Converse shoes. Gaia tells her that when she was with Simone, she avoided doing things that might bother him, and she begins to wonder if she really was as comfortable with him as she thought she was, begins to realise how she lost sight of other things she liked to do in order to please him. Gaia does not know whether to continue the relationship with him, who now says hurtful things to her, and she does not know what to do.

Comment

There is a spying couple in the dream: Simone and her sister. Simone's sister's eye may be the incestual eye, her parents' eye, her father's eye that always phones both her analyst and Simone. The analyst's eye looking in on her may repeat a traumatic intrusion of her mind, invading a secret space of intimacy. Gaia's heels have broken, her broken omnipotent phallic part, triumphant over a powerful mother, who instead of talking to her, controls her. The breakdown has broken her self. Gaia puts her zebra-print Converse shoes back on, more appropriate for little girls. The spying from under the ladder, as Simone does in the dream, as she does in the session when she scrutinises the analyst without being seen, also hints at Gaia's need to be able to find a space under the ladder where she cannot be seen, a secret space where she can feel protected, where she can decide when to show herself and when to hide in the relationship with the analyst. Simone's shoes are ugly, Gaia did not like what she discovered under an attractive appearance. Everything turned to ice because of this experience, and she was unable to build a bridge between emotional experiences and bodily experience, she split off and her sexed body became frozen. Freezing is both a symptom and a defence against dangerous arousal, uncontrollable anger, and persecution. For now, Gaia's solution is withdrawal into the house and freezing. The dream also seems to describe her experience with Simone as a traumatic submission to the male hard hooves passing over her.

The freezing continues.

After several months, another dream addresses this experience of freezing: "Gaia finds a frozen moth on the bed and it disgusts her. Gaia had to do something with it and touches it".

Comment

The moth, a nocturnal butterfly, seems to represent a fragile self, a still immature and frozen female sexuality. Gaia tries to touch it, finally approaches it, but does not know what to do with it.

In "normal" experiences, the love illusion is felt as a protected passage because it promotes the integration of sexuality and allows the developmental mourning of the first parental objects by offering itself as a metaphorical bridge between bodily experience and mentalisation (Nicolò, 2012). This is not the case for Gaia who cannot even talk about this experience. The moment she got up from the couch, both Simone and her mother were next to her, perhaps Gaia may have felt a violation of the boundaries of the self on both sides. A traumatic intrusion seems to have been repeated with Simone, with the violation of the body from the inside and outside. Similarly, Gaia also considers what she feels to be foreign, clandestine, and has frozen it just as she has now frozen her autonomous initiatives. The shape of this unbearable third element begins to take shape.

The first summer break

On the eve of the first summer break, Gaia says her head aches and spins and her heart beats faster, that she would like to take Simone with her on vacation because she does not know if she can make it away from him. The analyst points out that she seems very worried about being alone facing her difficulties without the analysis. Gaia says this is also the case because she is constantly fighting with her parents and cannot make a vacation plan: "I feel like everything is going back to the way it was before, like this period was all pretend and that it will always be like this. There are too many incomprehensible things, I think I'm crazy".

The real parents and their attacks

Gaia's parents ask to speak with the analyst; at the end of the first meeting they are brought in with Gaia. They are very alarmed, immediately pointing out that they have been separated for three years. The mother says that according to her, Gaia is in the throes of panic attacks because of her fear of being abandoned. She says that she is now refusing food and wants to sleep in bed with her. She compares her daughter to a volcano that has erupted. Recently, they have come to blows because Gaia is rebellious and never obeys, she still feels that in her relationship with her there is a wall. In fact, contact between Gaia and her mother occurs in an exasperated manner, both in regressive attempts at closeness and in angry and unsuccessful attempts at distancing.

The father talks at length about Gaia's abrupt change in seventh grade, recounting that they were taken aback by the "arrogance and irreverence" with which their daughter began to address them: "All of a sudden, she no longer recognised our authority and challenged us". Several times, the father hints that Gaia's problems stem from her relationship with her mother. With bitterness he concludes, "Too bad, because Gaia was an intelligent and sensitive person". This last sentence comes with the violence of condemnation.

During the session, the atmosphere is very tense. There is a strong conflict between the parents; they take turns talking, and while one is talking, the other becomes estranged. Gaia remains closed, almost impassive throughout the meeting. Intolerance and irritation circulate, the girl's parents seem unable to integrate themselves into the narrative, although they seem very much in agreement in describing Gaia as a daughter that is no longer recognisable: disappointing and incomprehensible, a small delinquent.

Comment

The "ban on thinking", just as Piera Aulagnier (1986) understands it, is palpable within the family system. Parental fantasies violently intrude into Gaia's mind, hindering differentiation. From this relational perspective, Gaia's attempts to not think seem to be the only possibility that guarantees her survival within her family.

The story continues

The parents begin couples therapy, only to discontinue shortly after the summer break, asking for a reduction in Gaia's sessions, and pointing out that they want to be constantly informed about Gaia's therapy developments, as they see no improvement since *their daughter does not respect them and listens exclusively to her analyst*. The father's often expressed feeling of gratitude for his daughter's improvement has vanished since the summer break, addressing the analyst with hostility and suspicion, with his wife's complete agreement. The analyst experiences the relational difficulties described by Gaia.

After the summer, the parents ask to be received alone and not in the presence of their daughter. Several telephone calls will be needed to contain their anguishes. During the session that Gaia will also attend, however, the parents openly show themselves allied against Gaia. Her experiences of distress are not believed and are judged false. The father complains that Gaia behaves badly with them. The mother, to underline the extent to which therapy has been a failure, makes a list of disrespectful actions committed by Gaia. The impact of the disconfirming violence of the parents on the analyst causes an experience of helplessness and dejection to prevail in Gaia; in the session, she initially defends herself but then falls silent: the analyst feels the veil falling on this silence of hers of a "defining hypothesis" from which neither she nor the analyst seem to have any escape. The analyst verbalises the elements that the parents feel as threatening: she reassures them about their fear of being dispossessed of their parental role, brings them to reflect on their experience of not feeling acknowledged and respected by Gaia for what they do for her, and explains to them that Gaia does not feel seen by them in what she does, showing evidence of improvement: Gaia feels better and has returned to school.

The alliance with Gaia and the alliance with the parents at this point come across as communicating vessels that cannot be separated; the parents do not want to go to another therapist: Gaia is the site of projections of the parents' unwanted parts that they do not want to face, but that they want to continue to keep under control by placing them inside their daughter.

Throughout the months, the anti-developmental acting out against Gaia's individuation is manifested violently by both parents: the mother disowns any of her daughter's differentiating characteristics, zeroing in on the existence of resources and capacities in Gaia; the father insistently telephones the analyst and puts himself in his daughter's place to be nurtured himself, showing his childish and deprived side that always seems to want to collect a debt. Eventually, the parents demand a reduction of sessions and create problems in payment. The analyst must therefore impose herself by threatening to interrupt therapy, a firm position that produces an internal shift in the father who seems to begin to conceive of a boundary beyond which it is possible not to be invaded. During the monthly parent sessions, he begins to talk about difficulties with his family of origin and, accompanied by the analyst, begins individual therapy with another therapist.

From then on, the climate in the relationship between the father and the analyst will be in favour of an alliance for the well-being of the daughter. The mother instead, throughout the course of the analysis, will not change her devaluing position towards her daughter, and will fail to accept and process the numerous therapeutic interventions made both in the presence of her daughter and in the sessions in which Gaia decides not to participate.

Comment

Hence, the theme of the exclusion of the third appears again; the family has a tyrannical organisation of control with relational patterns along the lines of "controller-controlled" and "persecutor-victim". Yet, control is not exercised over behaviour, but instead over each person's emotions and thoughts. Gaia cannot be recognised as non-self, but must be owned and colonised: the parents demand an alliance-agreement with the analyst that excludes the girl and takes away any element of individuation that the analysis is fostering in her. They want to exclude Gaia as they have felt excluded themselves from her space, which for this reason has become threatening.

It was very important for the analyst to experience the way in which the real parents were connecting with Gaia and the emotional climate they were creating around her in order to bring relational meaning to the symptoms. The analyst could also bring to light, through temporary identification with the patient in the family session, both the parental projections that colonised her and the existence in Gaia of vital resources that could temporarily be freed of the parental relational barrage, precisely because they were being directed by the parents onto the analyst.

The internal parents

In January, after the first year of analysis in the first session after the Christmas vacations, Gaia will tell a dream that will show the shape of her internal parents.

> *I was riding my bike by the sea and saw a huge snake. I looked at him and hoped he would not see me. There were other children and the snake was chasing us. There were two leopards in the village eating people. A friend of mine was forcing me to stand in a dead end, and the leopard had surprised me by telling me that if I stayed there, he would spare me. I did not trust him, I only trusted myself and ran away. I see the two leopards, my friend following me while I jump over the garden wall and tell her to hurry. The leopards catch her, maul her, then load her into the car and drive off taking her away. I saved myself.*

Gaia associates the dream with her mother's comment when she told her about it, "the snake represents sin". She explains that there was an ambush in the alley and that she pleaded with the leopard to leave her alone, and that he replied that he would spare her only if she let herself be found in the same spot when she returned. She remembers with pain that her parents, a few months before analysis began, had locked her in her room and both beaten her, terrorising her.

The analyst comments on how the *snake*, "the sin", seems to represent her encounter with the sexuality that chases her, the *leopards* seem to show how she experiences the two parental figures, as two leopards who ask her to stay put in the dead end of a growth that Gaia cannot make. Otherwise, she will be mauled.

Comment

The dream seems to point to the partial overcoming of the breakdown situation, yet now Gaia seems to find herself between the hammer and the anvil, between the snake that can poison her and chases her as time passes, making her increasingly adult, and the two aggressive leopards, the internal parents that imprison her. Sexuality and the body have taken on persecutory significance. We might also hypothesise that the violence with which she perhaps experienced the arousal felt in the sexual relationship prevented the possibility of thinking about the experience. Also, the transference shows Gaia's difficulty in letting go and relying on the relationship with the analyst.

The Truman Show: Not living in reality

In the second year of analysis, Gaia begins to talk about her parents spying on her through cameras. She recounts that they themselves confessed to her that they had learned about the melted gold by spying on her social media profiles and monitoring her computer. At the same time, she begins to skip sessions and explains the reason, saying: "There are times I don't feel like coming and other times I think one thing and then I say to myself 'what if it's not true instead?', I come to a conclusion and then I think, 'but what if it's not true?' You're not feeling well and you're sick ... I get it in my head that I'm sick and I'm bound to be sick forever". One session shows that even the benevolent reception of the analyst is falsified in Gaia's mind: she talks about the movie *The Truman Show*. She fears that the analyst is like the director of the movie and is actually allied with her parents against her. The analyst thinks that on the contrary, the filmmaker Gaia never spontaneously starts talking or associating with her false ideal self full of unrealistic grandiose expectations, secretly watching and examining her analyst making her often feel disoriented, or in an ever repeating script.

Gaia asks the analyst to tell her the plot of the film, and manages to make the analyst feel her fear of not living in reality, of being confined to a suspended place that needs to be described with her.

The analyst decides not to interpret Gaia's request but begins to tell her about the film, responding to Gaia's need to lean on the narrative as a container that will bring order and give her thoughts orientation. A temporary interlude to the persecution is finally generated. Like a child listening to the fairy tale her mother tells, Gaia relaxes in the chair and listens.

In the following sessions, she will confess that she cannot remember what she was like before she was ill. Gaia cannot distinguish whether her thoughts are true or false; she observes herself from the outside and feels that a part of herself is inhabited by something unexplainable and foreign that constantly threatens her from the inside. She calls it "that feeling". At times, she seems to begin to express the need to reconstruct her story. Gaia and the analyst discover how difficult it is for the patient to contact her past given the gap there seems to be, a void on which the experience of the sexed body could not rest.

In one session she says: "For too long I have been confused, the fear of not knowing how I have been, how I was, this fear is due to the fact that for so many years I have been sick … if I have been sick like this all these years, it is scary". Gaia thus begins to recover the historical sequence of her feelings.

Comment

Gaia expresses the fear that in analysis the unknown part of herself, destined to be controlled and delegitimised, an alien part within her familiar world, so unacceptable in its diversity, will be highlighted. False thoughts and true thoughts blur, fearing at times that her real life does not exist, but is a kind of life in the *Truman Show* run by her parents, or a false part of her. The film's narrative seems to have served a profoundly transformative function, allowing that experience of contact, of true reciprocity that the girl needed. Gaia eventually allowed herself a regression that the analyst contained and transformed. As a mother tells a fairy tale to her daughter, so Gaia and the analyst found themselves sharing together in attunement ("at one moment") (Stern, 1985) an emotional experience of reciprocity. From that moment, it is possible to come out of the suspended dimension of breakdown, and Gaia, who has perceived the emptiness and rupture of the self, makes a request to recover a story (Nicolò and Accetti, 2015).

After the second year

Gaia returns from vacation in September and starts having frequent headaches. She cannot tell what her emotions are. It seems that Gaia is clinging to the body, to the headache as an anchor in the passage towards change. The months of analysis proceed, alternating periods in which Gaia manages to be constantly present in session with periods in which she skips them. She has resumed with the same alternation going to school. She recounts of increasing quarrels with her mother, one in particular fittingly describes the atmosphere in which she is immersed: after asking her mother to teach her how to wash and iron so that she could take care of her clothes herself, to keep them tidy, her mother refused and told her that she would not be able to do it anyway, teasing her. The analyst comments on how aggrieved Gaia must have felt at her mother's response, and comments on how in the past a part of her, like her mother, did not take seriously how important it was to keep things tidy, to give them a place, to define things outside and things inside, to define who she is. It would be important to do this in the sessions as well. She points out to Gaia that in this way, the inertia that removes importance from everything takes over. Gaia responds that she has a closet at home that looks like it is full of rubble, as if they were buried at home, that it is indecent, and that this clutter makes her feel very bad, as when something is missing.

In May, during the second session of the week, Gaia explains to her analyst that when she wants to do something that pleases her, that ban within her that requires her to split words is triggered. The analyst points out to her that these magical beliefs get in the way of her life and sessions. The girl replies that it is very tiring, and essentially helps her not to think. The analyst tells her that maybe she is afraid to think along with her. Gaia replies that she does not believe that analysis can help her and that there is no solution. The analyst then offers that perhaps she is afraid that she will not be able to produce thoughts independently. Gaia replies dryly, "Yes", and tells a dream.

I was asking for a ride and got into a yellow four-seater electric car, inside were two boys and a girl. As we were walking, a truck went by and managed to avoid us, another one went by and crushed us but everything was happening in slow motion. I was talking to the other girl, we couldn't move. When they came to help us they checked our ears to see if we were okay. The two boys in the dream looked dead.

After a few sessions she says she finally left her boyfriend and started going to the "Gay Village" with her friends. At the end of the third year, for three consecutive months, Gaia will not show up for sessions but will ask not to interrupt. She would like her father to continue to pay for the sessions in which she does not show up. Therefore, the analyst writes Gaia a letter in which she explains to her that it is not possible to do the analysis without her presence, pointing out that she would rather not interrupt because she feels that there are many resources within her: "Being on hold, stalled, in fear is not good for you or for me. I suggest you muster the courage to counter fear, to fight to defend who you are. I will keep waiting for you, and hope you will answer me". Gaia will not respond to the letter, and because of her repeated absence, interruption will become the only viable solution. This interruption will last for one year.

Comment

The analyst believes that the car may now represent her mechanical proceeding, the form now taken by the "yellow mushy thing" of the first dream. Gaia is defending herself with a mechanical proceeding in which feeling is unable to direct thoughts. The truck that crushes her seems to replay the experience of the breakdown by which she felt crushed. Her healthy part is related to being able to hear the words spoken in analysis. If her ears are free, she can listen and save herself. In the dream, males are being taken out by the part in Gaia that wants to get rid of the trauma of sexual initiation and control everything. The primary homosexual fantasy seems to offer her a way to recompose her self, through a homoerotic dimension: self-love projected onto the other of the same sex. The third is once again annulled, but Gaia needs mirroring. Once again, her mother seems to debase her by devaluing her intention to approach her as a woman and learn an activity that could be considered feminine.

Third year

After a one-year break, Gaia, who is now about eighteen years old, contacts the analyst asking to resume sessions: the contract calls for a single weekly session, with plans over time to increase the number of sessions, because now that she has graduated from high school, her father has found her a small job and wants his daughter to pay for the sessions herself. It becomes possible to meet Gaia without the parents. Work schedules allow Gaia to make sense of her days; she no longer has had boyfriends and does not go out. She spends her free time at her mother's house sleeping. She also complains of feeling passive and helpless, as she continues to distrust her thoughts, annulling the moments of understanding experienced in session. Doubt prevails and continues to make everything false. The analyst's words seem to be felt as a traumatic penetrating element, making her mind feel no longer hers, just as it did with her body after sexual initiation. The analyst tells Gaia that she seems to feel intruded by the analyst's words and that perhaps she is afraid of remaining passive. Gaia responds that this is the case, and it makes her feel that her progress is not her own accomplishment; she points out that before she did not understand what it meant to be passive, but now she feels she understands it well. After six months, again after the summer separation, Gaia will begin skipping sessions again, keeping the analyst sequestered in endless waiting. A year later comes yet another interruption, this time unspoken. On the phone, Gaia says that she will come to session but then does not show up.

Accepting to be treated

Following a year and a half of discontinuation, Gaia, who has turned twenty, calls again saying she no longer wants to run away. She thus resumes analysis once a week, paid for by her father, with the possibility of increasing the number of sessions as soon as she can find a job. Gaia has just returned to her mother's house after spending a long time at her new boyfriend's house. She wants to be helped because she is afraid of being ill again. On her way back, she brought two cats with her: a large severely injured one and a very lively kitten, imposing them on her mother, who became very angry. Through Skype, she shows her cats, her room and the drawings she

131

made as a child. She tells the analyst that her new boyfriend is very affectionate and that, like her, he is unemployed.

In a February session, after expressing a strong desire to see her boyfriend again soon, and concern about her difficulty in starting the search for an educational course that would qualify her for work, she tells a dream:

> *I dreamed that I was at home with my boyfriend, we were guests at his parents' house, his mother suddenly came in and was angry because everything was in a mess and she was cursing at me. I was in the bathroom; I was very anxious because there were so many things to clean. On the bathtub there were the cat's footprints, I was trying to remove them with the shower, they were melting but instead of going away they became more obvious. His mother comes into the bathroom and starts insulting me. She gets a text message from my mother wanting to say hello and she says: "What a nuisance this one, what does she want!" Then I get angry and take a photograph in which there was a portrait of some people and smash it in her face. Then my boyfriend didn't want me anymore, I try to apologise but he avoids me, but in the end, he is on my side. We come out of a supermarket and his father and brother were waiting for him outside, sorry that he had left.*

Gaia comments that her boyfriend's mother is actually not unpleasant. She expresses her concern that by getting a job and leaving home, she may lose her place in her mother's house forever, who would turn her room into a closet and instead have her boyfriend come home.

Comment

The regressive and fusive dynamics that still harness Gaia in her relationship with her mother become visible. The two faces of this internal mother are presented in the dream: the affectionate mother unjustly debased from whom she would never want to be separated, and the mother who reserves nasty surprises that mortify her by screaming against the prints her sexed body leaves and against the mess it has caused. The mother also screams against the other mother, the tender one, against the affectionate bond of childhood, and this evokes a violent reaction in the dream; Gaia breaks a photograph in her face, thus breaking with the memory that portrayed them together. She herself in the dream would like to clean up, to make the cat's footprints disappear; her sensual and sexual parts are considered dirty even by the superegoic part of herself that does not yet accept them.

Slowly, however, Gaia has reconciled herself with the figure of both the real father who is now more present and solicitous and the father who is waiting for her in the dream, and with an affectionate and tolerant male also represented by her new boyfriend. She can now dream of the continuation of an involvement that still does not tolerate shifting to other objects. The footprints recall her two cats, her small and lively body part and her large body part with a severe wound that is slowly healing; she takes them with her from her boyfriend's house to her mother's house, and finally into session, not giving up the struggle to build an autonomous space in which they might find their rightful place.

Gaia no longer questions what she thinks. She no longer breaks words and is able to retain in her mind what was said in session by remembering them later. The analyst can now be felt as a real person and the words she says as true. Gaia has stopped questioning her thinking perhaps because she has stopped questioning the existence of the container. The analysis may now be considered a place of constant reception, in which the analyst survived the endless interruptions and attacks on the setting that were also agitated expressions of the attacks Gaia had made and suffered from her mother. The analyst never ceased to preserve a place for her in the mind, the place that Gaia had perhaps never had in her mother's mind, and that in any case she feared she had lost when she woke up and used her body in an acted out and adultomorphic way in opposition to the prohibition to leave and separate.

Perhaps at this point analysis could begin.

References

Aulagnier, P. (1986). Les deux principes du fonctionnement identificatoire (permanence et changement). In J.J. Baranes, R. Cahn *et al.*, (Eds.), 1986. *Psychanalyse, adolescence et psychose*: Colloque international, mai 1984, Ministère de la Recherche. Paris: Payot.

Freud, S. (1911). Formulations on the two principles of mental functioning. *S.E.* 12: 213–226, London: Hogarth Press.

Giustino, G. (2019). Psicosi e Sensorialità. Relazione presentata al Convegno della Società Psicoanalitica Italiana: *Allucinatorio/Allucinazioni: Psicosi e Oltre*. Bologna, Italy.

Nicolò, A.M. (2012). Iniziazione sessuale e illusione amorosa. *Richard e Piggle*, *20*, 4, 354–366.

Nicolò, A.M. (2013). Pensando al futuro: In cosa (e se) si differenziano le interpretazioni nella psicoanalisi dell'adolescente? *Rivista di Psicoanalisi*, *59*, 3, 665–684.

Nicolò, A.M. and L. Accetti (2015). La narrazione autobiografica negli adolescenti con breakdown evolutivo. In M. Balsamo (Ed.), *L'Autobiografia Psicotica*. Milano: Franco Angeli.

Stern, D.N. (1985). *The interpersonal world of the infant: A view from psychoanalysis and developmental psychology*. New York: Basic Books.

8

PATHOLOGICAL TRANSPERSONAL LINKS AND ADOLESCENT BREAKDOWN

The perspective from which to look at the family

As far as my work is concerned, the focus I use is the study of the relationship between the intrapsychic, the interpersonal, the analysis of convergences, divergences and the intertwining between these two levels (Nicolò, 1992; 2002). This is the specificity on which I seek to intervene. Therefore, in my view, this presupposes that those who work with families or couples must also know how to work with the individual, and indeed, this is the first basis of their training. However, this also imposes a much more complex view in observation.

Many psychoanalysts around the world today are putting forward a change of perspective from the more classical psychoanalysis. They have understood that in order to read the inner world of the subject they can no longer be solely interested in the projections of the individual, but must also look at the response of the other to whom the projection is directed, as well as the modifications induced by these responses. Even in the dual setting, we can observe phenomena relating to the analytic pair, and, having banished the myth of neutrality, study our own and the patient's experiences as co-created within the relationship. However, we must not forget that the history of psychoanalysis is replete with references or insights on this point.[1]

Both Bion and Winnicott studied the relationship between the subject's internal reality and its incidence in the external reality of the other. Projection and its effect on the other, the use of the object, the way in which the other is parasitised, exploited, colonised or on the contrary used within oneself or in the relationship, in the economy of the individual or in the collective economy: these are the perspectives that these authors propose.

And yet, even though these studies have enabled enormous advances in clinical practice and research, they fail to fully explain what happens in complex phantasmatic organisations such as the couple or the family. This has given rise to a focus on what Kaës calls the third topography, namely, a psychic space that is characterised by a "psychic reality, common and shared, which includes the inter-subjective space between subjects [...] and is organized on an articulation between the psychic reality of the link and that of the individual subject" [tr. by O.M.] (Kaës, 2009, p. 120). The author goes on to state that "the task of a third 'topography' is to describe and make intelligible the complex relations that articulate, distinguish and in some ways contrast the intrapsychic space, of the individual subject, and that of these plural spaces, organised by specific psychic processes and formations. This is the epistemological stake" (*Ibid.*).

The adolescent and the family in co-evolution

In all developmental situations, in all crisis situations, the functioning of the individual and of the family are challenged. Nowadays, numerous authors point to the importance of considering adolescence not so much as a state but rather as "a decisive latent or manifest organizing agent, yet always operating the elaboration of the depressive position and castration anxiety" [tr. by O.M.] (Cahn, 1998). These organising processes, which then pertain to identity reshaping and separation-individuation, function within the family as a sort of catalyst, activating and triggering a similar reshaping process of the parental couple and of the family as a whole.

We might say that during this period family members, including the adolescent, must renegotiate a new way of "being with" the other and "with" the family, consequently also renegotiating the recognition of a new image of self and of the other. However, while new relationships and new patterns of interactions must be experienced and stabilised, continuity in the self must be maintained and found anew in the family.

Following the idea of a developmental parallelism between the adolescent's growth and that of the family, the continuous and unceasing circularity and complementarity between these is therefore observable: the adolescent's crisis of the body parallels the midlife crisis of the parents with the loss of biological creativity and the possible mourning of the grandparents. The loss of omnipotence will occur in parallel in the adolescent's and parent's minds. It is the child himself or herself who, presenting himself or herself as autonomous and individuated, functions as a reality test in the face of the parents' idealising projections and expectations.

All this leads to an identity crisis of each of the partners and of the couple itself, calling into question the models of solution to the Oedipal conflict, which both parents brought with them from their past.

Another comparison imposes itself, in this time, on the parent couple: that with the models of solution that their own parents had put in place with respect to the same problems. The issue of identification with the grandparent couple and their internalised relationship thus resurfaces again.

Among the many parental functions that characterise the family as a whole and the parental couple specifically, three functions are particularly tested in this work of identity renegotiation and redefinition in adolescence: *the parents' ability to change*; *the ability to mourn and repair*; and finally, *the ability to reflect on their own and their child's functioning, and on each other's changes, by restoring and sustaining the new changed image*. This restoring operation, which parents can provide, has a powerful recognition effect that the adolescent needs.

These functions belong not only to the parents, but to the family *as a whole*. For example, one member might be the bearer more than another, or the grandparents might be more explicit bearers than the parents. This is particularly important given the vicarious function grandparents or older siblings may sometimes exercise in this regard. Or, we may find that a capable or well supported child can help a parent in his or her own change.

In adolescence, perhaps far more than at other times of life, the developmental crisis generated by the need for separation thus becomes a crisis of identity and a crisis that re-founds identity. The work that is carried out pertains to a complex process concerning not only the adolescent, but each member of his or her family and the family as system.

For these reasons, far more than in other periods of life, at this stage, the boundaries of the normal family may blur and appear ambivalent and ambiguous in relationships, both external and internalised, in a state of constant flux. Nonetheless, it is also a powerful melting pot of change that allows for the resolution, even final, not only in adolescents but also in parents, of conflicts inherited from childhood or passed down through multiple generations.

In observing family links, we might find that they are co-constructed among members and at times inherited from generation to generation. Some of these are intergenerational, thus potentially passed on from one person to another, and are often conscious or preconscious. Others, however, are transgenerational and generally trans-subjective, and are therefore passed on between people, often stored in the interactive procedures that depict the concrete life of the family. They perhaps represent a part of those unrepressed memories that recent neuroscience tells us about, and are always unconscious. Transgenerational mandates belong to this category. In them lurk the brute or concrete, rejected or negated elements of unelaborated trauma. Such mandates are sometimes enshrined in family myths or secrets (Nicolò, 1993; 1996; 2014), unspoken, albeit often known by all to some degree. It is of utmost importance, moreover, to consider the world around the patient. Indeed, one should not overlook the family's resources, from its phantasmatic functioning to the possibilities of mobilising its energies, and the presence of a member with bargaining power, preferably a parent, who might offer therapeutic alliance and/or develop elaborative capacity.

The psychotic functioning family: some history

In the case of psychotic situations, the family becomes crucial both in assessment and treatment, given that the ties around which it is organised contribute to the genesis and maintenance of pathology.

From the very first signs of distress in the young person who consults us, an accurate diagnosis of the relational world around him or her is needed. Indeed, we must, if possible, highlight not only his or her mental functioning but also that of the family. In early emergencies, the patient in a crisis who will later show a psychotic onset carries with him or her that psychotic potentiality of which Aulagnier (1986, p. 419) has told us, as an inheritance in relation to the history and prehistory of that subject and as the existence of a psychotic core that is susceptible to actualisation into psychosis. If we neglect these aspects, the persistence of traumatic links in the family will continue to function as an attack on the patient's fragile self, often jeopardising the new experiences that reality offers. We might thus hypothesise a *family psychotic potentiality* that we must also diagnose in order to prevent decompensation as far as possible.

I believe modern research confirms the coexistence of an environmental psychotic potentiality that is grafted onto a vulnerability of biological origin, which has never, in fact, been clearly demonstrated. A most interesting study conducted in Finland by Tienari and colleagues (1983), on children of schizophrenic mothers given up for adoption, statistically significantly showed that in healthy environments, the children had similar functioning to other children. In contrast, in dysfunctional families, the children of schizophrenic mothers could develop far more problematic personalities than others. This research points to the interaction between the biological factor and the family pathological potentiality. Sound relational functioning is certainly helpful in protecting the development of a disorder in the psychotic realm. However, there are no definite statistical studies showing family patterns capable of generating psychosis or more specifically schizophrenia.

Nevertheless, over the years, countless clinicians have engaged in the study of these pathologies at the family level.

Since the 1950s, the study of psychotic families, particularly with regard to schizophrenia, has been divided into two major strands of thought. The first, psychoanalytically oriented, relates the phantasmatic and affective functioning of parents to the personality organisation of their children. Of interest here are the works of Bowen (1960; 1975), who described the family of the schizophrenic as an "undifferentiated mass of the family ego", finding the root of this sort of disorder in symbiotic or fusional-type processes that may involve multiple generations. Problems related to unlinking were also reported by Boszormenyi-Nagy (Boszormenyi-Nagy & Spark, 1962), who spoke of the invisible loyalties that bind members of these families. The systems studies that arose as an alternative to the psychoanalysis of the time, which was objectifying towards the patient and carried forward a view of linear causality, looked at the family as a single system, thereby underlining its overall relational functioning. Famous for describing these families is Sluzki's concept of double bind (Sluzki & Ransom, 1976) and the concept of mystification that Ronald Laing (1965) put forth. Furthermore, Haley (1967) also highlighted the perverse triangulation, which consisted of an alliance both acted out and at the same time negated at another level, between one parent and the child against the other parent.

In my view, all these studies document the existence of an apparent mutuality, absence of conflict in these families, constantly contradicted by a deep "schism" that characterises them.

The contradictory and conflictual double level that immobilises them, making differentiation and separation impossible and preventing a relationship of growth and mutual exchange among the members, is perhaps the richest contribution that systems studies on psychotic families have brought us. Finally, we must not forget the observations on the immobilisation of the time of growth and the rigidity of transactions that some systems scholars have highlighted (Andolfi et al., 1983).

Transpersonal pathological links

When we think of psychosis, rather than a pathology of the individual we must think of a true relational organisation that finds its spokesperson, or symptom-bearer, in the patient.

The massive use of projections and projective identifications, the fragility of the boundaries of the self, the acting instead of thinking and communicating, as well as the difficulty in symbolising that we observe in these situations, determine the specific concrete nature of these subjects' functioning and involve the entire relational world. We are thus faced with real transpersonal pathologies.

This term is useful to define those pathologies which, from their origin and in their perpetuation, reveal that the genesis is to be found in the encounter between the patient and the world outside the self, between the ego and the "psychotic potentiality", in Aulagnier's words (1975, p. 163–168).

There is a common and shared peculiar functioning among members, with respect to which each member of the family will react differently according to experience and ability. Certainly, the patient will become the spokesperson of this psychoticising and psychotic potentiality, but each will have their part in the puzzle, either in its origin or perpetuation, or in suffering or defending oneself from it. Along these lines, paraphrasing Meltzer and Harris (1983), we might ask ourselves some useful questions: who is the bearer of the group's suffering? To whom does it belong? By what mechanisms is it avoided, evacuated, or modified? To the detriment or benefit of which aspects of the family or which members, are these strategies organised? And so forth.

140

I believe we would be making a big mistake if we simply focused on the relationship between the patient and the parent, given that these processes involve all members of the family to some extent, each of whom performs an unconscious task in the group and is therein partly designated. Therefore, in working with these pathologies, we must think in terms of links and must distinguish between each person's intrapsychic defences and interpersonal defences. Transpersonal defences are a collective product that is quite stable over time, of which we might identify several types. The use of anything concrete, of acting, or of somatisation are an example of one type of transpersonal defences in the family. For example, in certain families somatisation may become privileged, trans-generationally passed on by multiple family members, together or alternately (Nicolò, 2014).

This defence can be observed in the interacting other or in the group as a whole. Indeed, there are countless ways of ridding oneself of mental pain, not only through normal intrapsychic defence mechanisms. Using the other in the relationship, healing through the other (Nicolò, 1990), through the relationship with them, inducing suffering or disturbance in the other, for example by putting them in the condition in which he or she expresses discomfort or suffering in our place, are some of the most common though largely unrecognised ways. The links thus constructed will be pathological, and in turn become pathogenic, and for this reason we must bear in mind that the permanence of such functioning increases pathogenicity over time.

The study and modification of such linkages is the first condition without which no individual treatment will bear results or can indeed be undertaken.

Every so often, the clinician might be confused, given that, particularly in the beginning, such situations are marked by severe tension and the parents generally and even understandably manifest great distress. We ourselves will also struggle to understand that they are not at fault. Unfortunately, we carry with us the legacy of the past where the concept of a schizophrenogenic mother was in common use. The parents themselves have been victims of an entrapment upon which an existential blackmail weighs heavily. They themselves may have been victims of mandates that belonged to other generations. Indeed, Murray Bowen (1960) argued that it takes at least three generations to make a psychotic patient.

Accurate recounting of the history of both the father's and mother's families of origin may be very helpful, though the most important element is to reconstruct the repetition of interpersonal links that may recur over several generations, and the trail of this is sometimes inapparent.

If a late adolescent tells us that in his or her head he or she hears a woman's voice insulting and commanding him or her, not only will this communication provide information about a difficulty or confusion in his or her personal and gender identity, but it will also speak of the kind of links he or she may have suffered over time with significant figures in his or her life. Perhaps it will speak of injunctions or disqualifications from a mother, a grandmother, or the female part of his or her father. If an adolescent informs us, as in the case of one of my patients, that she had a nightmare that woke her at night in which her father had an incestuous relationship with her, causing her to get up to lock the door to her room, we certainly will not believe *tout court* that her nightmare is real. We will, however, investigate the boundaries of the patient's self, her respect for her sense of secrecy and private space, we will delve into the seductive dimensions, that incestual air that, without being incestuous, she may have shared in the family. This will allow us to shed light on the quality of other pathological transpersonal links of a seductive and intrusive nature that may have led her to experience a breaking of the boundaries of the self, a confusion of tongues – as Ferenczi (1933) calls it – which, although never resulting in actual abuse in the subject's history, has nevertheless generated specific anguishes.

A classic psychoanalyst would call this position naive. On the contrary, I strongly believe Freud's (1907) assertion according to which there is an element of historical truth in any delusion, and this element is to be found in the traumatic links.

The psychotic patient's family

In an attempt to make an enormously complex discussion more vivid and simpler, I will begin by reporting a clinical case.

The case of Regina

I will now report a brief clinical excerpt of treatment with a family that was seen by two colleagues within a public institution.[2] We discussed the case in supervision as part of research on adolescent breakdown.

Regina is about eighteen years old, the youngest of four children. The eldest is Giacomo, whose role is that of the caregiver. At the start of the work and for a year, nothing is known of the second child, Carla. She has left the family, as if she had disappeared, for reasons unbeknownst to the family. At any rate, she seems to have suffered unspecified mental disorders. Elena, approximately twenty-six years old, had contracted Hodgkin's disease five years earlier.

Regina's first disorders arose with the onset of menarche at age thirteen, experienced with sadness and depression.

Anorexia ensues between the first and second menstrual cycles. At this time, Elena presents a metrorrhagia crisis following which she is diagnosed with lymphogranuloma.

At the onset of the second period, Regina manifests a state of delirious excitement, feeling possessed by the devil. She is therefore hospitalised for the first time.

After the failure of a psychotherapeutic relationship, Regina establishes a very close bond with her sister Carla. Regina's management is entrusted to Carla, who abandons her personal interests to follow her until she herself collapses.

Regarding her parents' history, her mother recounts her difficult function in her current family and in her family of origin. At the age of seven, she was providing care for her asthmatic and depressed mother, as well as for her younger sister. The father was described as a brutal and distant man. In the present family, she had her own craftsmanship work in addition to caring for the children. Elena says that their mother was very nervous with them, often beating them and feeding them by lining them up one after the other.

The father was always away, either for work or among his books, and for a long time even in session, he complained of hearing problems and spoke in a low voice. He was often dreaming about returning to his home country. Even their marriage had come about by calculation rather than by mutual feeling.

I will now report a fragment of a session in the eighth month of the weekly family psychotherapy.

Regina yawns and her mother complains that she always goes to bed at midnight. Elena had a restless night because of a movie she saw on television, *Alive*, and recounts some of its scenes of cannibalism that impressed her. She then recalls how in the film there was an air of danger among the characters, a hidden danger, of someone who could kill others in order to feed on them. (She describes the dream of the night: *she had both legs wrapped and immobilised by a belt. She was in the company of a green-eyed doctor who cared for children with eye problems*).

The mother reminds Elena that she herself suffers from conjunctivitis and goes on to report that she too has anguished nights. She wakes up and rearranges the kitchen and tells of her fantasy of leaving alone, with her suitcase, while everyone else is happy.

The family talks about the future prospect of vacations, and upon Giacomo's invitation, Regina says it is difficult to leave and tells a dream she had: *she was with her parents in the country house. Imprisoned on the upper floor was a stranger, perhaps a* mafioso, *and she was the jailer. Suddenly, she realises that he had managed to escape, leaving the door of the cell open.* Regina associates the *mafioso* with a recently captured *mafioso* seen on television.

The family resumes talking about travel and camping.

The father also went camping as a young man and recounts a dream he too had in which he was being *chased by the townspeople, took refuge in a shed in the country just when they were about to catch up with him, managed to pull himself to safety by going out a back door through the keyhole.*

The family goes on to talk about travel, and the father recalls the pleasure of being in familiar places and with familiar people.

Giacomo mentions when they were little and their happiness in being together on Sundays.

(End of session.)

There are many possible interpretations to this session. Among these, also for reasons of time, I will focus on one. Beginning with Elena's association on *Alive*, a covert persecutory dimension comes to light, characterised by the need to cannibalistically kill a part of oneself or family members to enable the survival of others.

Perhaps one might glimpse the reference to a primal cannibalistic and monstrous scene.

The persecutory climate is also apparent in Regina's dream and in her father's dream. There is an unknown, sequestered, captive character upstairs who manages to escape, as the father manages to escape through the keyhole.

Beyond possible transferential references, to how hunted the family feels by the therapy, we might think of a perverted and mafia-like part of the self that escapes control, but also of the existence of a sequestered and imprisoned dimension that in attempting to escape

144

(as for the family in its frequent associations to vacations and travel), nevertheless shows itself and becomes apparent.

A few months later, the family brings the news that Carla has turned up again. An apartment is arranged for her, and a cooperative atmosphere is created in the family among the siblings. Months later still, in a moment of confidentiality between the mother and Carla, about how the daughters reproach their mother for keeping the family away from the maternal grandmother, the mother confesses the long years of rape by her own father.

Hence, the story seems to find a conclusion that is frequently described in the literature in situations of psychotic adolescents, about the existence of these kinds of secrets.

The secret of rape retrospectively elucidates the attack on the body that all the women in the family suffered, the active seizure of femininity that was manifested early on with Elena's problem revealing Hodgkin's through a metrorrhagia, and with Regina's breakdown at menarche. Becoming an adult woman was experienced in a secretly dangerous way, and Elena's cancerous intrusion or Regina's demonic possession portray two variants of the same problem.

How can such links be described?

In Regina's case, we have seen these particular types of functioning in action, which we could summarise as the ban on thinking that group members manifest (Aulagnier, 1986). A ban that is perpetuated and aggravated over time, alongside a sort of robotisation. Family functioning is concrete and acted out. The boundaries of each member's self are fragile. These atmospheres are mostly characterised by what Racamier called an incestual atmosphere, "in which the wind of incest blows without there being incest" [tr. by O.M.] (Racamier, 1995, p. 21; Monari & Calaon, 2003, p. 145). According to Racamier (1995, pp. 132–135; Monari & Taccani, 2004, p. 117), the traits common to pathological incestuality are: deconstruction of origins, in the sense of generational confusion; loss of meaning of parental figures; disqualifications of the ego; uncertainties and distortions of judgment; paradoxicality, and I would also add a kind of perversion of links that are distorted and attacked.

Secrets that are never officially made explicit result in paradoxical functioning, characterised by the contradiction between official and hidden truth, unthinkable voids and brute elements in communication. Rigid family myths expropriate members' Selves and impose pathological as well as pathogenic objects of identification (Nicolò, 1996; 2014). Searles (1959) describes the relational ways in which the child becomes the bearer of parental alienating fantasies, showing the effect of those alienating identifications discussed by many French analysts, including Raymond Cahn (1991). In these situations, the external object weighs on the child's subjectivisation processes first and on the adolescent later, thanks to processes of intromission and submission in his or her mind of the parent's objects, conflicts and fantasies or even transgenerational ones, subjecting the child to the pathological links in turn suffered by the parent. Garcia Badaracco (1986) had spoken of maddening objects to explain the intrusion within the subject of parental phantasms that subjugated the subject's psyche, perpetuating a condition that thus becomes not only pathological, but also continuously pathogenic. This might explain why some psychiatrists now recommend the patient's removal from home as a means to avoid the risk of decompensation. Meltzer (1979) had also observed the existence of colonisation processes in the mind, which is thus parasitised from within.

In the communications between members, it is also possible to observe specific modalities that I previously described (Nicolò, 2005), namely, the fact that any link between two members is felt as persecutory, the tyrannical control organisation of communication, accompanied by the attempt to seize the other's thoughts even when he or she does not communicate them, as well as the reversal of parental roles and functions.

In such cases, the family system presents not only a difficulty in differentiation, as pointed out by many authors (including Searles), but also a difficulty in each member's subjectivation, given that "the interactive register prevails to the detriment of the intrapsychic one" [tr. by O.M.] (Racamier, 1986).

Racamier (1992) particularly illustrates the nature of the link between the psychotic child and the parent. He speaks of the narcissistic seduction that, in a perverse triangle, unites the patient, whom he refers to as the "predestined extra", and his or her parent, whom he refers to as "the perverse narcissist". This illustrates a psychotic relationship that does not bear the characteristics of sexual perversion, but instead those of a relationship whose stake is the subject's ego, subjectivity, real or psychic death. From this type of link, Racamier then derives the functioning of these families, which he describes as anti-Oedipal and anti-depressive. Anti-Oedipal because this functioning hinders the development of a healthy Oedipus complex, and is constituted before it. They are therefore ante-Oedipal types of functioning, prior to the Oedipus. Yet, these are also anti-depressive types of functioning, in the sense that they prevent separation-differentiation and therefore oppose the development of that Kleinian depressive position that is characteristic of healthier functioning.

To better explain these concepts, I will quote Racamier's words: "The Antoedipus [...] in one word, it is a transgression: an Oedipus subverted by narcissistic seduction [...] an Oedipus that endeavours to neutralise the Oedipus; [...] an anti-phantasm phantasm [...]. The Antoedipus brings into being a subverted triangle, in which the subject, in an incestuously narcissistic seductive relationship with his mother, occupies his own and his parent's place, while the father, excluded, appears only as pure and simple persecutor. Father of the son that he is, creator and creature, Antoedipus is self-generated [...]. The price of this subversion of Oedipus is high: one is no longer autonomous by the fact of being self-generated [...]. No Genesis, no thought is any longer possible in the psyche of one who accepts neither that he had no part in his own conception, nor the difference of sexes, generations and beings" [tr. by O.M.] (Racamier, 1980, pp. 94–95).

To exemplify such a link of narcissistic seduction, the story from a movie might be useful. In this story, we can observe the gradual creation of a core of confusion between the victim and his perse-cutor, to such an extent that at times one turns into the other. This might also remind us of those characteristics that Bleger (1966) had described as a confused agglutinated core.

An example from a film

I will begin by the plot of a very significant film, *Apt Pupil*, by Bryan Singer, based on a short story by Stephen King.

The story begins in an almost banal way. In a small American town in 1984, a professor finishes explaining the themes of the Holocaust to his high school students. Echoing in the background are questions asked by the professor about what motivated the Nazis' behaviour: economic, social, personal. Todd is particularly inter-ested; he has done special research. Soon he is seen behind the door of the house of an old gentleman, Mr. Denver. On the surface he just wants to talk to him. He is curious and knows something about him, about his past history. He even secretly took his fingerprints. The old man is very frightened even though the boy seems harmless at first, has an angelic face and asks for some milk. Slowly, however, the spider web closes. "I just want to hear about it" Todd tells the increasingly frightened Mr. Denver, and the latter is forced to submit to blackmail. Denver is in fact a fugitive Nazi criminal hiding in Todd's country.

Blackmailed by Todd, Denver thus begins to narrate the deaths of Jews in the camps by the different gases. Slowly and inadvertently, the atmosphere changes and in his daydreaming and nightmares, Todd sees the faces of the dying Jews.

A sort of complicity, of fascination, arises between the two. "A door had opened and could not be closed again", is said with respect to the Nazis' adventure. Thus, this open door between the Nazi criminal and the young adolescent begins to change them both.

In fact, while showering at the gym, Todd sees the emaciated faces of Jews again, isolates himself from the group and from his best friend, maintaining secrecy around his encounters with Mr. Denver.

It all culminates one evening when Todd shows up with a Nazi uniform and forces Mr. Denver to wear it.

The sadomasochistic relationship that has been in the working therefore becomes evident. This same relationship seems to extract an identity never seen in the two partners up to that point. "Be careful, boy, you're playing with fire", the old Nazi tells him. From that moment until the end of the film, violence grows.

The sadistic and insane Nazi is reactivated in the old man through the relationship with the boy. The co-constructed transpersonal link between the two complementarily activates sadomasochistic and insane aspects in both, ultimately leading to homicidal acts. Initially, the Nazi begins by taking pleasure in burning his cat alive in the oven, and then Todd, who has now lost most contact with his comrades, with the girls, and whose parents have received a summons from school for his poor performance, kills a wounded bird.

The unsuspecting school psychologist is oblivious to the conspiracy between the two and is manipulated, albeit for the good purpose of getting Todd back on track with his studies. Yet by now, any subsequent act with constructive or destructive purposes only serves to consolidate the shared madness.

"Do you really think I would let you drag me to jail without dragging you with me?" Denver asks Todd, who threatens him. At this point, too much time has passed and too many events have occurred. The situation is reversed. It is now the old man, previously blackmailed, who is in control; hence, it is the latter who, though he never wanted to tell, says to Todd, "Would you like one of my stories?" The boy replies "I don't care", but by then it is too late. In this situation, in which both are hiding something, the old man also arranges for evidence to protect him from the boy. He writes a memoir in which he tells about how Todd had forced his way into his house and blackmailed him, then informs Todd that he has rented a safe where he has deposited his story. In the event of his death, the manuscript would be turned over to public authority. This seems for a moment to finally create distance between the two, who both resume their normal lives.

But by now the demon has awakened. Denver, flooded with paranoid anguish, feels threatened by a homeless man who eventually tries to kill him, involves Todd in the murder, and Todd ends up killing the homeless man. Hospitalised due to a sudden heart attack, Denver, saved by Todd, asks him: "What sensations did you feel?" but the boy does not answer.

The film ends with the accidental discovery of the Nazi by the police. Denver commits suicide and Todd resumes his now perverted and criminal life, threatening the psychologist who would have wanted to communicate the truth to his parents.

What clearly stands out in the film are the shared constructions that I have called 'transpersonal pathological links'. Such links characterise the most severe pathologies and are re-actualised in the analysis rooms. Failure to decode these leads to the frequent drop outs of such patients or sometimes induces us into acting.

Therefore, it is useful to identify these transpersonal pathological links as they can be a key to understanding the severe pathologies we encounter in our clinical practice. It is essential to work with the family of the borderline or psychotic patient in order to hope for change. "We are sometimes surprised to find that even a single encounter with the family, the patient and the treatment team eventually triggers important and lasting modifications that have allowed a possibility of change for the patient" [tr. by O.M.] (Racamier, 1994, p. 109).

Notes

1 For example, Bion stated that we must address not only projective identification, but also what such projective identification *does* to the other. We must therefore observe the effect of such a defense mechanism on the other's reality, namely: the extent to which the fantasy expressed through projective identification can substantiate itself in the other's reality and modify it (Bion, 1962).

2 The material reported refers to a supervision I carried out on the case followed by Dr. Anna Bincoletto and Dr. Fernando Landolfo, whom I thank, and was published in the article *The transgenerational, between myth and secret* (1993, in *Interazioni*, 7, 1, 1996, pp. 138–151).

References

Andolfi, M., C. Angelo, P. Menghi, A.M. Nicolò (1983). *Behind the family mask: Therapeutic change in rigid family systems*. New York: Brunner/Mazel.

Aulagnier, P. (1975). *The violence of interpretation: from pictogram to statement*. London: Routledge, 2001.

Aulagnier, P. (1986). *Un Interprète en Quête de Sens*. Paris: Ramsay.

Bion, W.R. (1962). *Learning from experience*. London: Karnac Books, 1984.

Bleger, J. (1966). *Symbiosis and ambiguity: A psychoanalytic study*. London: Routledge, 2013.

Boszormenyi-Nagy, I. and G.M. Spark (1962). *Invisible loyalties: Reciprocity in intergenerational family therapy*. New York: Harper & Row, 1973.

Bowen, M. (1960). A family concept of schizophrenia. In D.D. Jackson (Ed.), *The Etiology of Schizophrenia*. New York: Basic Books.

Bowen, M. (1975). Relazione presentata al Convegno *La Terapia Familiare nella Comunità*. Firenze, 1975.

Cahn, R. (1991). *Adolescence et Folie: Les Déliaisons Dangereuses*, Paris: P.U.F.

Cahn, R. (1998). *L'Adolescent dans la Psychanalyse*. Paris: P.U.F.

Ferenczi, S. (1933). Confusion of tongues between adults and the child. In *Final contributions to the problems and methods of psycho-analysis*. London: Routledge, 1955.

Freud, S. (1907). Delusions and dreams in Jensen's *Gradiva*. S.E. 9: 1–96, London: Hogarth Press.

García, J.E. (1986). Identification and its vicissitudes in the psychoses: The importance of the concept of the 'Maddening Object'. *International Journal of Psychoanalysis*, 67, 133–146.

Haley, J. (1967). Toward a theory of pathological systems. In I. Boszomenyi-Nagy and G.H. Zuk (Eds.), *Family therapy and disturbed families*. Palo Alto: Science and Behavior Books.

Kaës, R. (2009). La réalité psychique du lien. *Le Divan Familial, 22,* 107–125.

Laing, R.D. (1965). Mystification confusion and conflict. In: I. Boszormenyi-Nagi and J.L. Framo (Eds.), *Intensive family therapy: Theoretical and practical aspects.* New York: Harper & Row, pp. 343–363.

Meltzer, D. (1979). Un approccio psicoanalitico alle psicosi. *Quaderni di Psicoterapia Infantile, 2,* 31–49.

Meltzer, D. and H. Harris (1983). *Child, family and community.* Paris: Organisation for Economic Co-operation and Development.

Monari, C. and S. Calaon (2003). Incestuale (Parte prima). *Interazioni, 2003,* 2.

Monari, C. and S. Taccani (2004). Incestuale (Parte seconda). *Interazioni, 2004,* 1.

Nicolò, A.M. (1990). Soigner à l'intérieur de l'autre: Notes sur la dynamique entre l'individu et la famille. *Cahiers Critiques de Thérapie Familiale et de Pratique de Réseaux, 12,* 29–51.

Nicolò, A.M. (1992). Verso una psicoterapia integrata. In A.M. Nicolò and C.G. Zavattini (Eds.), *L'adolescente e il suo Mondo Relazionale.* Roma: La Nuova Italia Scientifica.

Nicolò, A.M. (1993). Il transgenerazionale tra mito e segreto. *Interazioni, 1996,* 1.

Nicolò, A.M. (1996). Travail du rêve et secrets de famille. *Groupal, 2,* 123–134.

Nicolò, A.M. (2002). Die psychotische Erkrakung in der Adoleszenz. *Kinderanalise, 11,* 4, 395–415.

Nicolò, A.M. (2005). La famiglia e la psicosi: Un punto di vista psicoanalitico sulle patologie transpersonali. In A.M. Nicolò and G. Trapanese (Eds.), *Quale Psicoanalisi per la Famiglia?* Milano: Franco Angeli.

Nicolò, A.M. (2014). Family myths and pathological links. In P. Benghozi, D. Lucangeli, A.M. Nicolò (Eds.), *Families in transformation: A psychoanalytic approach.* London: Karnac Books.

Racamier, P.-C. (1980). *Les Schizofrènes.* Paris: Payot.

Racamier, P.-C. (1986). L'intrapsychique, l'interactif et le changement à l'adolescence et dans la psychose. In J.J. Baranes *et al.* (Eds.), *Psychanalyse, Adolescence et Psychose.* Paris: Payot.

Racamier, P.-C. (1992). *Le Génie des Origines: Psychanalyse et Psychose.* Paris: Payot.

Racamier, P.-C. (1994). Lo psicoanalista davanti alle psicosi e alla famiglia. *Interazioni, 1994,* 1, 103–110.

Racamier, P.-C. (1995). *L'Inceste et l'Incestuel.* Paris: Les Editions du Collège.

Searles, H.F. (1959). The effort to drive the other person crazy. An element in the aetiology and psychotherapy of schizophrenia. In *Collected papers on schizophrenia and related subjects.* New York: International University Press, 1965.

Sluzki, C.E. and D.C. Ransom (Eds.) (1976). *Double bind: The foundation of the communicational approach to the family.* New York: Grune & Stratton.

Tienari, P., A. Sorri *et al.* (1983). The Finnish adoptive family study: Adopted-away offspring of schizophrenic mothers. In H. Stierlin, L.C. Wynne, and M. Wirsching (Eds.), *Psychosocial intervention in schizophrenia: An international view.* Berlin, Heidelberg: Springer.

PART 2

THE DEFENCE AGAINST DEVELOPMENTAL BREAKDOWN

9

PERVERSE SOLUTIONS AND PERVERSION

Adolescent pathology is rather different from adult pathology, to the extent that major psychotic symptoms, such as paranoid delusions or hallucinations, may be a transient phenomenon related to the defence put in place against developmental conflicts. And yet, this very mobility of pathology rightly alarms and motivates us to remain alert, because the clinician must monitor the evolution of developmental ruptures or breakdowns whose outcomes may vary depending on the organisation of personality, on the subject's abilities, on the evolution of treatment, and intercurrent experiences. Partial healing often characterises the outcomes of such treatments. Furthermore, we must not forget, as already mentioned, that many types of typical adolescent functioning remind us of what occurs in psychotic functioning. Indeed, the chaotic internal world as well as the body that has grown foreign after puberty demand the necessary symbolic reorganisation, and along this perilous journey we might observe different gradations of these processes. From the outside, for example, the dysmorphic manifestations, which some adolescents present more frequently than in adulthood, may be an indication of impending decompensation, although in most cases, they are gradually overcome. Raymond Cahn is perhaps the author who to date has best described these issues by showing that a typical characteristic of the adolescent lies "in the contradiction between the initial taking shape of the main psycho-pathological organisations of adulthood and the often still labile and fluid character of mental functioning" [tr. by O.M.] (Cahn, 1991, p. 157). Inviting us then to a non-preconceived or predetermined view of the factors at play, he suggests we observe the lines of force

DOI: 10.4324/9781032663371-12

capable of acting on the "qualitative or quantitative variations in the responses available to the subject" when he or she must define his or her identity and object choices.

Some defensive or regressive modes may be used on this journey, for example, modes of relating to partial objects, which may represent steps towards a developmental path or instead, depending on the case, evolve towards a frankly pathological organisation.

A number of adolescents with breakdown come to us in urgent situations. We are sometimes forced to resort to hospitalisation, or instead might favour pharmacological treatment and initiate him or her to the difficult task of psychotherapy. However, the latter may not always begin immediately and certainly also benefits from integrated work with the parents, or if necessary with the family as a whole.

We may be faced with a suicide attempt, depressive symptomatology, dangerous acting out, or in the most severe cases, severe decompensation with possible hallucinations or delusional onset.[1] Of course, many breakdowns will not come to our observation at all, and not because they turn to another psychiatrist. Various reasons (the enormous prejudice that still invests this kind of disorder and the distrust that these young people have towards experiences of dependency, as well as the unbearable shame and humiliation that prevent them from seeking help) rather favour resorting to other solutions. At times, we may encounter these same solutions as an outcome of our therapies, and the analyst is forced to accept them knowing that, with certain patients, it is necessary to accommodate what the patient can do, therefore, avoiding the idealisation of analysis and its ideal termination.

Defensive solutions

In many cases, to avoid decompensation, patients put in place symptomatic personal solutions in late adolescence that nevertheless allow for survival.

In this chapter, I wish to reflect on some possible outcomes of such developmental pathologies.

Some of these were discussed in Chapter 4.

One in particular, the momentary use of polymorphic-perverse modalities in the relationship with one's own body or with the other, is far more frequent than clearly appears, and proves to be a sort of life preserver to navigate perilous waters. The development of temporary perverse modalities in the use of the body in severe adolescents is observed in clinical practice (Aa.Vv., 2006; Novelletto, 1989; 2009). As early as 1932, in studying the intermediate stages between neurosis and psychosis, Glover observed that such modalities "help to patch over flaws in the development of reality-sense" (Glover, 1933, p. 499). The centrality of the dynamics inherent in the new sexed body and the natural processes underlying its integration make these solutions more feasible.

In particular, the use of polymorphic-perverse behaviours, owing to their specific characteristics, can be useful in offering a powerful defence that is capable of stemming a more severe regression while providing time to ferry through a difficult and dangerous phase of development. Questioning some of these solutions, if not done with caution, care and within a therapeutic process that ensures the stability of the link and support to the self, can be extremely dangerous. Before delving into this discussion, I wish to mention that clinical observation has often highlighted several defences for surviving and coping with decompensation.

Winnicott, for example, shows that "freezing of the failure situation" allows the individual to defend himself or herself and therefore wait for another opportunity for a new experience when the environment offers an "adequate adaptation" (Winnicott, 1954, p. 281).

The condition of withdrawal, namely, "a condition in which the person concerned (child or adult) holds a regressed part of the self and nurses it, at the expense of external relationships" (Winnicott, 1988, p. 141), could also be considered one of the defences activated by these organisations to guard against decompensation. Still another is the kind of false self that Winnicott calls "split-off intellect" where thinking – understanding too much – becomes the substitute for maternal care (Winnicott, 1949; 1965; 1988, p. 177). Some of these solutions are widely discussed by analysts who deal with these states of mind, such as for example encapsulation, or encystment, used as a defence against the anguish of annihilation, as for that matter suggested by Tustin or Bion, who in 1957 observed that psychotic anguishes may be encapsulated within body parts.

A further possible solution is, in my opinion, the creation of a secret identity. This is one of the best solutions that not all of these patients are able to adopt because it presupposes a functioning ego within certain limits, and some ability to set the boundaries of the self and thus, a secret space in reality or in the mind.

Currently, all the role-playing games that adolescents engage in in chat rooms or on the internet lend themselves to effective use of this kind.

I believe these to be incredibly interesting dimensions that require careful evaluation. Adolescents can construct their own secret, or alternative identity from everyday life. Sometimes, these occasions prove useful given that, hidden behind another identity, they can experiment and experience the reality of relationships with others, including the opposite sex. They may attempt to be what they would have liked to be, but have failed to develop. They may also fantasise around negative or perverted identities that, as split elements of the personality, they struggle to integrate and instead explore, avoiding the danger of enactment. At times, however, the limitless use of such possibilities defies scrutiny and reality testing, and the adolescent who used the web to contain and experiment with his or her delusional content and enact a megalomaniac identity finds himself or herself instead reinforced in overstepping delusion into reality. In studying patients with an internet addiction, Gibbs observes that it constitutes a withdrawal into "the safety of an internal world" (2007, p. 11) and considers it in terms of what he calls "ordinary everyday psychosis" (*Ibid.*, p. 13) that might also come across as minor, not being accompanied by certain cognitive transformations.

Another of the defences that can be used is linking with the other through multiple mechanisms, perhaps the most important of which is externalisation. The most successful solution in this regard is love bonding. In this type of relationship, which is generally passionate, a conflict–free state is generated both between the ego and the other, internally within the subject, between the ego and the ideal, and between the ego and its unconscious parts. The invested object becomes the idealised substitute for all kinds of relationships and enables the resolution of all conflict.

I discuss this in Chapter 10.

We might find such a solution in young people who compensate by adhering to sects, fanatical groups or religious organisations, that is, groups that display rigid and primitive functioning, commanded by a leader or guru. Leaving these tyrannical and plagiarising organisations is sometimes difficult because of the submission they impose on the subject, who is forced to deny the truth and reality that the healthy part of his or her personality suggests to him or her, and replace it with the mad messages that dominate within the group.

There are then highly complex and articulated defensive modes that may crystallise with time, such as the use of perverted defences as a defence against breakdown or as a defensive evolution of it.

We might also observe the establishment of transient perversions that may persist, stiffen or continue to develop. In these situations, the analyst has difficulty diagnosing whether this symptomatology is due to perverse functioning used as a defence against decompensation, or instead represents the emergence of a truly perverse organisation that will begin to manifest itself after puberty. In the case of transitional forms, "the perverse experiences of these patients [...] are not organised in fixed and constant modes of instinctual outlet and are not ego-syntonic like true perverse practices. Instead, they are characterised by the subjective experience of regression and loss of one's body image, whereby intimacy fades into a feeling of fusion and identification with the opposite-sex partner" [tr. by O.M.] (Novelletto, 1989, p. 24).

If the patient is able to maintain a certain mobility in relations, without excluding an even small investment in a nonpartial object relation, that is, if polymorphous-perverse modalities are not the only vehicle for sexual gratification, if he or she is able to experience such functioning as egodystonic, if he or she is able to keep the link with the analyst or with another significant object alive, this defensive solution may recede. This can allow the personality undergoing analytic treatment, in time, to reintegrate oneself and reintegrate a genital sexed body, although we cannot exclude that the residues of such functioning will remain, influencing partner choices or the subsequent functioning of the personality, as in the case of the patient I will now describe.

Perverse modalities to exist

Polymorphous-perverse fantasies or acting out are almost always observable in the conflict elaboration of a large number of adolescent breakdowns. Yet, such behaviours may characterise the normal development and evolution towards genitality of certain adolescents who, though problematic, nevertheless do not present a psychotic or perverse organisation of personality.

The fact is that in adolescence, as Florence Guignard tells us in her book *The Infantile in Psychoanalytic Practice Today*, the preconscious, "a psychic skin whose osmotic function regulates the exchanges between psychic life and external reality, will normally become, for a while, more 'transparent' and more fragile" (1997, p. 125) until the adolescent has grown up, and it is precisely this transparency that allows us to see, without hypocrisy, what is happening in the adolescent's inner world.

Cahn (1991) points out that in breakdowns that make use of perverse defensive solutions the psychotic problem remains unchanged, even though the use of projection or delusion is no longer necessary. Only the defences have turned perverse. Freud himself in his description of Hanold's juvenile decompensation, in *Delusion and Dreams in Jensen's "Gradiva"* (1907), points out the protagonist's attention to the female foot, and indeed the very name Gradiva, "the one who advances" hints at it.

At this point, however, a distinction must certainly be made between perverse acts and daydreams with perverse content that often haunt these adolescents, filling their mental space. I believe that the use of acting out shows the failure of struggle in fantasy and constitutes a further step towards perverse immobilisation, although acting also offers the small advantage of reality testing.

In the adolescent patients with breakdown that I have seen personally or in supervision, such daydreams are often oppressive and imperative in their presence. The adolescent cannot get rid of them, so much so that he or she feels haunted by them. They become opportunities to manifest the degradation of Self and body, which they feel prey to unacceptable drives. Such fantasies are an expression of the difficulty in separating from the passivity that characterises and troubles them, yet they are also a manifestation of a broader regression that is also expressed in the sexualisation of family relationships, where the incestual dimension was present from the beginning. When they are, on the contrary, the debut of a perverse organisation, they remind us of what Greenacre pointed out: "[...] both separation from mother and castration being defended by the fetish" (1953, p. 85). To these patients, homosexual anguish is unacceptable, which is not itself a content with the character of perversion, and rather than expressing uncertainty about the choice of a partner more frequently refers back to childhood homoeroticism characterised by primary homosexuality. Such a position facilitates the "fundamental dynamic in the constitution of the ego and object" [tr. by O.M.], thus reinforcing identity construction (Gutton, 2001, p. 113).

A clinical case

Aldo is nineteen years old when he comes to me in an urgent situation because of the serious suicide attempt (he slit his wrists) he survived. I am struck by his extraordinary intelligence and sensitivity as well as his elegant, lean, slender body. Aldo describes his family's difficult situation: his depressed mother, on medication, is the only person on whose affection and support he can count. The father, unsuccessful in his work, separated at home from his mother, sleeps in the living room and is a man who humiliates his two children and is violent with the whole family. The family atmosphere is riddled with continuous conflict, mainly over financial reasons. The house is very small and Aldo gives me a claustrophobic description of it where the narrowness of the physical spaces mirrors the narrowness of the mental ones. The episodes that Aldo tells me about his relationship with his father arouse in me an experience of mortification for him, even for events of little importance: for example, his father's demand to win at all costs when playing cards and not to be found out if he cheats, but above all, the violence of his response and the risk of the scuffles, threats or insults if the son even jokingly notices his cheating.

The first few years of work, after nearly a year of antidepressant drug treatment, saw intense efforts to preserve the link and secure the setting. Aldo presents as motionless and blocked, with intensely self-destructive aspects. A sense of helplessness dominates the situation, and rare dreams refer to collapses and falls into precipices. Periods of paralysis and closure in his room, except for the time when he had to come to session, are pervasive. And in session he brings the sense of nothingness, of poverty of himself, the meaninglessness of life naturally contrasted with the high and unattainable ideals that characterise him. I feel worthless and frightened by the enormity of his expectations when Aldo tells me: "*My life is heading for destruction. The only thing against the current is therapy*".

Against this backdrop, the patient's intense struggle to resist is staged. Enrolled in university, he does not attend or give exams although when he does try, he gets very excited in the challenge and

161

hidden project of humiliating his examiner by showing his competence (which he does not find too difficult given his intelligence and culture, especially with the young assistants who are sometimes full of prosopopoeia). With difficulty, he eventually talks about his masturbatory rituals, which even go so far as choking to achieve orgasm, but of course, all this makes him feel lowly and miserable. Obviously, Aldo also has a kind of idealisation of the destruction he can enact, and apart from cautious interpretations, I am careful not to challenge him on this point, but neither can I collude with his destructive tendency towards analysis when I seem to have become the tender and seductive mother he had, yet powerless against the gratuitous destructiveness of the father by whom she was being abused. However, Aldo is very capable and sharp in his insights, he well understands the destructive eroticisation of humiliation that he carries and therefore begins to go out and look at the world outside of him. The anguish of being flawed, of carrying shameful experiences, but also the omnipotent and megalomaniac fantasies, lead him into an ambivalent position towards any relationship with peers, whether male or female.

Once his need to open to new spaces and relationships is defined, he reacts with fear. He has always felt discarded by successful peers. The best time was of course in elementary school, between the ages of five and eight, where he was admired for his delicate features and blond hair. Others, however, secretly prepared for life and managed aggression towards the world while he seemed helpless, slowly directing it against himself.

While in the first months of analysis I was faced with a patient who was motionless and open to the abyss as his very few dreams showed, the atmosphere changed greatly with the increase of his perverted fantasies that nevertheless haunted and alarmed him. I cannot, of course, rule out the possibility that they were not present from the beginning, but certainly Aldo began to hint at them or sometimes communicate them to me mainly to attempt to alleviate the persecution they caused him. Along with the fantasies, masturbation with strangulation and self-induced wounds for arousal increased. These behaviours were in Aldo's opinion not dangerous, in fact "*it is worse to ride a moped as he does, because when he drives he thinks of something else*".

These fantasies mostly took their cue from facts of reality, but generally involved situations in which Aldo was usually humiliated or mistreated, or in the most extreme situations hurt with contempt by men whom he sometimes met in his building and with whom he sometimes fell in love in a very fantastic way. We work on his falling in love with his neighbour, whom he does not know but about whom he very much fantasises. He spies on him, observes his motorcycle, and believes he ends up discovering that he is gay.

We work on his forays into the world of the internet, the homosexual and sadomasochistic sites he mentions that he frequents. His need for action is pressing. He goes so far as to make a date through the internet with a boy but, when he meets him, he desists after the first time. He does not like him and he seems insignificant to him. He has only one childhood friend, very much in love with him, whom Aldo instead endures and despises.

In this atmosphere he fortunately meets Olga, a young musician. This girl has a traumatic history that is very similar to his own, perhaps even more difficult, but she is very beautiful and there is a glimpse that she will prove to be exceptionally talented. Like Hanold who believed he had met the Gradiva, this idealisation helps him and facilitates the first approach.

During this period, we work intensely on the issues of his identity, on the eroticisation of the humiliation that his father inflicted on him, and also on the seduction of his mother who, with her protection and her fusional proposition, had in fact killed the very man inside him, as moreover recited by numerous dreams[2] that he brought to me.

In the session in which he tells me about his first date with Olga, I sense a different atmosphere. He begins with a dream: *he is in a car. Giovanna, an old friend of his, asks him to be accompanied. He says no because he has a date. He doesn't say he has an appointment with Olga. As he phones Olga, he notices that Giovanna is holding her first communion dress; it is a green dress* (he associates this dress with a short velvet dress that Giovanna used for a party). He criticises Giovanna's shyness, her sadness and inability apart from studying.

Olga has written him a letter in which she almost makes a declaration of love, and he is happy about the dinner they will have tomorrow. Neither he nor Olga has ever had anything like this happen to them. He quite agrees with my interpretation according to which Giovanna represents a feminine, confused homosexual (first communion) aspect of him that he wishes to abandon.

The relationship with Olga gets off to a happy start. Aldo tells me that since he has been making love to Olga, he no longer practices masturbation with masochistic aspects as was the case in the past. He feels a strong hatred for homosexuals, yet when I suggest that it is a projection of his hatred for his body, his homosexual aspects, and his permanent fear of becoming one, he informs me that in his opinion the reason lies elsewhere: *as a boy, he was convinced that gay men would adore him should he turn to them. He has discovered that this is not the case, that he is neither wanted nor loved by gay men, hence he despises them.* He thus shows the strongly narcissistic and regressive structure that characterises him, his majesty the overbearing child unable to come to terms with the existence of the other, due to being dropped early on by a depressed mother, towards whom he feels a destructive rage of which he is unaware.

Aldo's mother, stricken with a sudden illness, will die a year later. In this situation, Aldo manages to go live in a small one-room apartment that he inherits from her. However, he has run out of money to continue the treatment because his father does not give it to him. In truth, he wants to discontinue. The Giovanna he wants to abandon is also the analyst, and her mother's death weighs in this decision.

Three years later I receive a phone call. Aldo is expecting a child and has been living with Olga for a few years. He is working, albeit with a small income, and wants to resume treatment. In this new tranche he presents with a mildly depressive appearance and an inhibition of sexual desire, which, however, recede quite easily. We realise that homosexual fantasies recur when he feels distant or rejected by his partner. He has no longer reported sadomasochistic fantasies, nor has he ever again presented sadomasochistic masturbatory rituals. His approach to his young daughter is very maternal–protective and sometimes excludes his wife. On the other hand, Olga has difficulty with her mothering skills and has developed an intensely homosexual interest in her employer. Olga's rejection seems to have subtly re-activated his old issues, as we see in this session.

(In previous sessions, after recounting how Olga threatens to separate, he had talked about his interest in a gay friend, the son of an important man.)

In this session, the first of the week, Aldo reports feeling stuck and sad, and that a symptom from the past has recurred: once again he cannot tolerate seeing people eat or being seen eating by others; the smell of dirty socks always comes to mind. I connect his feeling of a dirty body to feeling rejected.

He reminds me that with Olga he had overcome this problem. Ironically, he mentions his job in which he must examine the bodies of other colleagues before choosing whom to work with. He also recalls that when he was very young, and particularly between the ages of fifteen and twenty-three, he only bathed at night. Olga spent years convincing him to undress and be seen naked. He always thought he had a different body from others. The parents of his schoolmates always complimented him on his table manners. I jokingly observe: "Do you mean you ate by following etiquette like a gentleman?" He replies: "They used to call me milord". His mother was insane before she was medicated, and she often humiliated him. For example, when he was very small, she would show everyone his dirty underwear, shouting: "See what I have to do? Clean the underwear!". Aldo is very distressed. I decide to make a joking intervention that also shows how he changed over time and say, "I wonder how many panties and underwear you cleaned with your daughter, and it wasn't that bad", I observe jokingly. Aldo relaxes a little.

(I feel very distressed by what Aldo says about his mother's reproaches, but I am greatly relieved by the memory of the patient's little daughter, whom he took such care of. Indeed, this leads me to believe that Aldo is now able to overcome his difficulties, regarding both the use of his body and his debasement and self-denigration. Moreover, the analyst as well symbolically cleans and repairs the most intimate and secret aspects of the patient. In contrast to a demeaning mother, the patient needs to experience acceptance and recognition of his abilities).

"You're right, doctor" he replies. "I've cleaned up my daughter's poop so much, but it doesn't upset me at all. A lot of water has passed under the bridge since then", I reply: "so you're saying we used this water to clean everything up?".

"Yes, we cleaned up, but do you know?" he continues, "even today sometimes I don't want to touch Olga or for her to touch me, I just can't".

"I think I have to tell you again that you want to be very clean, just like you did to please your mother when you were little. However, now your mother is dead! But your fixation on cleanliness keeps her alive! Only a machine without smell, taste or heat can be truly clean!".

The session continues, but it will become clear in later sessions that the relationship with Olga and his daughter (and in the past with the analyst) worked well because it allowed him to live through a primitive bond he had never before experienced with his mother. The current difficulties with Olga reactivated, to some extent, his anxiety about being abandoned, rejected, and mocked. Because of these feelings, the difficulty of integrating the body re-emerged. The marital crisis brings back to the surface, even if only in part, the difficulty in using the body, and the difficulty in touching and being touched.

Some of the patient's problems were overcome, such as the sadomasochistic fantasies and acting out. Subsequent work will highlight the patient's homosexual choice, which will be tackled later in a second analysis.

Comment

Aldo's case poses numerous problems: from assessing the kind of change the patient has achieved in the course of the work, to the more pertinent questions today around the fate of the patient's daydreams, the perverse nature of these fantasies, and their relationship to acting out and to the young man's mental functioning.

It was clear that the fantasies became massive and pervasive simultaneously with the disappearance of the feelings of emptiness, inanity, and annihilation that characterised the first year of work and had led him to the serious suicide attempt. Subsequently, the masturbatory fantasies disappeared with the appearance of Olga. We are all familiar with the intense and interesting debates around the topic of fantasy and daydreaming.

I will point out only a few elements pertinent to Aldo's case.

While on one hand the adolescent raises the question of which of his fantasies or regressive urges are acceptable, on the other we may wonder whether it is not helpful for him to allow himself access to these regressive fantasies and bear their impact. I believe that, in severe situations, there is an inhibition to daydreaming and not just thinking or imagining. Everything is concrete and acted out in a direct short-circuit.

The activity of fantasising, "fantasying" as Winnicott called it, which distinguishes it from imagining, "usurps life" by creating a sort of defensive retreat, a parallel and dissociated life, constituting itself as "omnipotent manipulations of external reality. Omnipotent control of reality implies fantasy about reality. The individual gets to external reality through the omnipotent fantasies elaborated in the effort to get away from inner reality" (Winnicott, 1935, p. 130), yet manages to delineate regressive drives and channel them into a limited space, a sort of refuge. It is necessary to observe the vicissitudes of this refuge and study it in order to understand whether it will constitute the ultimate prison in the patient's life, or instead promote the integration of regressive drives, or the composition in adult sexuality of the perverse components.

A number of authors, including Britton, rightly argue that autoerotic fantasy serves to fill the psychic space "to eradicate any gaps in the psychic space" (1995, p. 91). This is why, when Aldo produced fantasies, I witnessed a change in the atmosphere in the sessions and the sense of emptiness and annihilation disappeared.

Also, on the perverse nature of the fantasies present in many patients with breakdown and psychotic onset, we should note that this defence recedes (somewhat) when the breakdown is partly overcome, and serves multiple functions:

1 The sexualisation that characterises perversion allows for a defence that is useful for the adolescent's survival, namely, the transformation of the anguish of fragmentation and loss of identity into castration anxiety, as I believe happened in Aldo's case.

2 The perverse solution, although negating some of its aspects and modifying it, maintains a certain relationship with reality, which is not the case in psychosis.

3 This defence is useful because it expresses the attack on the sexual relationship between the parents, while allowing the adolescent to experience himself or herself in the relationship with the other, as well as to live through experiences and sensations related to the body and sexuality. In this case, the body exists and sends sensations that, where they do not exceed the subject's capacity for containment, are a testimony to its existence.

4 With this defence, such adolescents keep alive and locked in their confusive ambivalence between preserving a certain relationship with reality, by modifying their sexual body image, or destroying the Oedipal and incestual parent, simultaneously attacking themselves.

5 These defences allow for some separation from parents by enabling an investment in a different object and constituting a secret or clandestine area partly unknown to them.

6   In positively evolving cases, the homosexual investments of
    these adolescents are useful in strengthening identity, self-
    knowledge, representing a sort of "identificatory love" (Benjamin,
    1995, p. 134).

In other words, we could say that the patient is attempting integration, the split with reality has decreased, although he is not yet
able to tolerate it completely. According to Steiner, this mechanism
allows disparate versions of reality to coexist (Steiner, 1993, p. 121).
These adolescents also keep their confused ambivalence alive and
locked in because such a situation provides time to process the
conflicting issue, which would have been impossible had there been
an ongoing psychotic catastrophe.

Boredom as avoidance of perversion

In certain problematic cases, boredom is the active emptying of content,
conflicts, and fantasies that the patient operates to defend himself or
herself against their emergence and the anguish that might result (Nicolò
and Accetti, 2017). At times, we might glimpse the annihilation and
emptiness from which he or she defends himself or herself through this
evanescent emotion that is boredom. Yet, in boredom, the emptiness is
not only a defensive barrier but it can also be a content. In certain severe
psychotic onsets in young adults, the world can be experienced as empty,
having been deprived of all value and attractiveness. Then, the possibility
of understanding that boredom is within oneself, that it is one's own
content, constitutes a step forward for possible transformation, although
this step must be approached with extreme caution.

In *Nothing at the Centre,* Winnicott (1959) describes the case of a
thirty-year-old actress who, as a response to interpretation, reacted by
falling asleep in session. Winnicott told her that the emptiness she felt,
the hole in the centre, was herself, was actually her terrible hunger for
everything and belonged to her whole life. Falling asleep had been her
escape from anguishing awareness. Other patients do not fall asleep but
have difficulty associating. Some adolescents in particular present as
bored, lazy or indolent, sometimes shying away from the danger of
intense sexual fantasies because of the unconscious fear that they might
enact them.

In the phase of transition from narcissistic towards object functioning, a typical challenge of the mind's development at this age,

the adolescent might experience a state of stable "suspension" when, despite the drive towards the object, he or she senses that he or she is not yet ready. The adolescent might feel unable to replace autoerotic libidinal investments with object investments due to intense conflict or fragility of the self. This failure to invest may leave the adolescent alone and in touch with sensations from the body, which, in the absence of the object, may reverse their direction and goal by returning to the search for regressive satisfaction (Laufer and Laufer, 1984).

The state of boredom is an indication of a withdrawal of object investment on narcissistic libido, although it may be useful for the adolescent, as it could serve a para-excitatory function towards regressive pregenital desires and aggressive drives that might target the body from which the desire originates.

Boredom may function as avoidance, silencing the desire-related drive charge through the collapse of interest and the disinvestment of the relationship between the subject and internal and external objects. This form of boredom is what Fenichel (1934) and Greenacre (1953) called a restless form, expressed by that perpetual being in search of something. In this case, it is not the desire that disappears, but rather the *object and goal of the desire.*

If the patient claims there is nothing in his or her mind, we find that he or she has had a thought or feeling, or a fantasy of one kind or another that was quickly repudiated. According to Fenichel, it is related to a psychosexual conflict, usually of a sadistic-anal nature, and is the result of repression of unacceptable impulses by the superego, leaving the subject in a state of tension. This safety measure is burdened by an additional restrictive manoeuvre: together with the unacceptable contents, in fact, everything that accompanies them and that is associated with them, is also removed and segregated: thoughts, fantasies, memories and derivatives that bring affect back to memory. A connected portion of the psychic world is removed from consciousness and excluded by repression, splitting or dissociation, leaving only one phenomenon visible to oneself and to others: boredom.

Luigi: what was underneath that boredom?

Luigi,[3] aged fourteen, is the second and last child of a fairly troubled couple. The father, an executive, does not appear to be a significant figure. It is his doctor mother, unaffectionate and distancing, who dominates the atmosphere.

A hereditary disease has afflicted family life, and the parents became aware of it late in life when a congenital megacolon was discovered for their first daughter, Giovanna. Due to this disease, the mother spent a great deal of time inspecting and evacuating in various ways the intestines of this child, and later also Luigi's, who suffered from the same disease albeit less severely. Giovanna, having reached late adolescence, also developed a cyclothymic disorder, also present in the mother's family of origin. In this environment, there was clearly little concern for Luigi, except for his bowel functions, which his mother controlled. Escape into the intellectual dimension was then the only option that could be undertaken, and in fact Luigi is a brilliant student. Fearful that the mental disorder that had affected their daughter might also present itself for him, at the first signs of withdrawal, apathy, and difficulty socialising, the parents decided to send Luigi for treatment. In the first few months, the atmosphere proves heavy. Luigi arrives early to the sessions and waits as long as fifteen minutes in the waiting room. When the session begins, the boy remains silent and then comments on his fatigue, because of the little rest he has been able to get. He then updates the analyst on school and school progress. Everything is very matter-of-fact and interspersed with pauses for reflection. However, Luigi is a boy of great intelligence and is aware of his problems. He attends a scout group for which he is responsible, but the competitions end badly for him and his team. He does not know how to cook and criticises himself for doing the shopping wrong and breaking things. He wishes he could talk to others, find a girl who really interests him, but he just can't seem to find someone. They are all boring or interesting in only a few ways. He can't find someone he likes. Hence, he does not believe "the dating area" is possible. In short, he is not particularly fond of anyone he knows. When the analyst proposes some optimism by saying that the problem is not only to know but also to be known, he jokingly replies that he hopes it is possible for him, otherwise he will become a priest.

This adultomorphic and apathetic attitude worries the analyst greatly. Everything remains still until Luigi arrives at the session in a state of agitation, because he was faced with bullies at school and was forced to defend himself. He did so even effectively for that matter, yet inside him a storm suddenly broke out. The bullies called him "faggot", and he knows that according to scout regulations you cannot become a leader if you are gay. This troubles him deeply, although he does not know whether he is gay or not. He has decided to get to know a girl that a friend introduced him to; he wants to date her, a reasoned and studied decision. The analyst points out to him that it seems like a planned decision, with no momentum on his part but only logic. Luigi agrees and admits that this is the case.

170

A few months later a serious event complicates the situation. At the parish Luigi is accused of pulling down the trousers and underwear of a younger child and undressing himself as well. Luigi talks about his mother's reaction to this event. He was hurt because she did not help or comfort him, but instead burdened him with the burden she herself felt. The mother thought of the event as a further complication for the family. His father was understanding, and Luigi was grateful, happy and even somewhat surprised, while his mother made him feel guilty.

In later sessions, Luigi talks about his attempts to control his impulse to pull down smaller boys' trousers, which causes him constant checking and a great deal of mental fatigue. He is not serene; he knows that these impulses of his are impulses that need to be blocked because they are wrong. Luigi also talks about his attraction towards some of his classmates that he wishes he did not have. These attractions are powerful and unwanted. He feels this tendency is dangerous and specifies that he has two forms of attention, which are part of the same thing but differ: "A protective one he has towards younger children he knows, and another more manipulative, controlling and colder one", he says, "like the one for the boy at the parish".

The climate has now profoundly changed. The analyst is extremely concerned and sorry for Luigi. It seems to her that he is putting up a terrible fight. The boy agrees with her and adds that this second form of attention is dangerous because it gives him no way of knowing when to stop, and is also worried about his future at the idea of what he might become.

Comment

The connection between the problem presented by Luigi and the family dynamics appears clearly in all its tragic dimension: his sister's childhood hereditary disease, the mother's traumatising behaviour around anal emptying achieved in various ways, among which intrusive manoeuvres on the body with inspections of the anal cavity, enemas, etc. In addition, there is the absence of a father who could have played a third protective function. The tragic dimension is thus palpable, where each of these actors seems to be a designated victim of a story that exceeds and transcends them.

For the sake of clarity, I will therefore recall the obvious dynamics of this case. The trauma of bodily inspections passively endured by Luigi may have translated into paedophile fantasies and identification with the aggressor, a mechanism he enacts towards the younger child whom Luigi undresses while undressing himself. Castration anxiety is another of the elements that produce confusion in him regarding his sexual orientation. Yet the most relevant element is the sensory experience of a body that was precociously violated and intruded upon, both through gaze and through bodily inspection, by a defensively cold mother. It is a body that, in encountering the new bodily sensations produced by adolescence, falters. The emergence of perverse fantasies and acting out maintains it in an area that is not yet fully crystallised, which some might consider "transient perversion", a type of functioning that we sometimes observe in adolescence and that in some cases surprises us by its possibility of transformation. However, we might have to admit that we are facing the first signs of true perverse functioning.

Luigi's confession to the analyst seems to shed light on the whole clinical situation, beginning with the boredom that the boy felt and elicited in the analyst. It seems to respond to the desperate unconscious need to block any evolution towards the development of the perverse fantasy and to remain anchored in factual, concrete, operational thought. In this way, Luigi also kept at bay the deep depression that any perversion conceals.

In a historical article of great interest on boredom, Greenacre (1953) cites the case of an adult, an alcoholic and depressed patient who suffered from apathy and a sense of emptiness. The accurate description of the patient's behaviours allows us to see the promiscuous and perverse behaviours she had with numerous lovers, as well as with her husband, with whom she had intercourse only with the use of pornographic material.

As in Luigi's case, Greenson states that for this patient "the emptiness in boredom is in the first place due to the repression of the forbidden instinctual aims and objects along with the inhibition in imagination" (*Ibid.*, p. 16). All this was quite clear with Luigi: the boy was terrified by what was happening inside him, and at times the only solution seemed to be to escape from himself and his mind.

In encountering this kind of boredom, it seems we are dealing with a barricade against desire, desire that is removed from the psychic scene when the self needs to be protected. The gap between imagination and reality, between the ego's ideal expectations and the ego's actual ability to fulfil them, could be a threat.

Being emptied, the actively produced emptiness, shows itself to the outside world through boredom. A boredom sometimes experienced first-hand, but more easily with the more severe patients;

experienced on the analyst's skin in his or her experiences especially when in contact with those primitive states of the mind involving two-dimensional areas, or segregated and encapsulated parts.

Conclusions

The two clinical cases above highlight the extent to which behind the screen of perverse behaviours or fantasies we can find very different mental types of functioning. Diverse outcomes can open through treatment and through fortunate encounters in reality. The solutions the adolescent organises might be transient or turn into long-lasting defensive adaptations, such as withdrawal from social relations, transient perversions, a state of alienation in the other, or withdrawal into a fantasy world.

In this chapter, I have addressed the perverse solution as a compensation for breakdown, as I have observed in some of my patients. I have also illustrated the possible beginning of perverse functioning, still very fluid and unstable, in a borderline patient with perverse fantasies and occasional sporadic paedophilic acting out, which clearly created much anguish in the patient.

In conclusion, I wish to make a clarification: the term "perversion" was luckily replaced by the DSM-IV with the term "paraphilia", which defines them as "recurrent, intense sexually arousing fantasies, sexual urges, or behaviours generally involving i) non-human objects, ii) the suffering or humiliation of oneself or one's partner, or iii) children or other non-consenting persons" (APA, 2000, p. 566).

The term perversion is, on a cultural level, linked to a very discriminatory moral judgment that the clinician should also avoid in view of the enormous distress that characterises the mental functioning of these patients.

We must also consider that our culture currently abounds with behaviours, acts, and expressions that would have once been called perverse.

It is as if everything that the once respectable and religious society had banned with horror suddenly found a pervasive flourish today. The fact that a young person multiplies partners, alternates between homosexual and heterosexual behaviours, promiscuously acts out, or displays voyeuristic and exhibitionist behaviours on the internet, for example, amazes us much less than it used to, and we are more willing to consider these as tests and trials. I believe we need to delve far more thoroughly into what is meant by "perversion". In fact, as analysts, we are well aware that drive theory alone does not suffice to explain many of the perverse fantasies and behaviours, and that a read of the relational aspects of perversions is one of the inescapable parameters of understanding (Gabbard, 2014, p. 313).

Notes

1 I will not outline here a nosographic diagnostic distinction, which is certainly useful and which inevitably guides us in subsequent treatment, because I am convinced of the specificity of adolescent mental functioning. Hence, its specificity also colors pathology and its evolution in a decisive way. I therefore wish to emphasise the notion of a developmental checkmate, a stalemate in growth that can come in different hues depending on the underlying mental functioning.

2 In many of the dreams of this period, the mother unexpectedly killed a man, or a woman of similar age to the mother, forcing the children to conceal the murder she perpetrated. Of course, these dreams were also interpreted through his associations as the mother's (or a part of him identified with the mother) attack on the father or himself. They were also interpreted in a transferential sense.

3 Case treated in supervision.

References

Aa.Vv. (2006). Perversions? *Adolescence, 24*, 3.

American Psychiatric Association (APA). (2000). *Diagnostic and statistical manual of mental disorders DSM-IV-TR®*. Washington DC: APA.

Benjamin, J. (1995). *Sameness and difference: Toward an "Overinclusive" model of gender development*. Psychoanalytic Inquiry, *15*, 125–142.

Britton, R. (1995). Reality and unreality in phantasy and fiction. In E.S. Spector Person, P. Fonagy, and S.A. Figueira (Eds.), *On Freud's creative writers and day-dreaming*. London: Routledge.

Cahn, R. (1991). *Adolescence et Folie: Les Déliaisons Dangereuses*. Paris: P.U.F.

Fenichel, O. (1934). On the psychology of boredom. In D. Rapaport (Ed.), *Organization and pathology of thought: selected sources*. Columbia University Press, 1951.

Freud, S. (1907). Delusions and dreams in Jensen's *Gradiva*. S.E. 9: 1–96, London: Hogarth Press.

Gabbard, G.O. (2014). Paraphilias and sexual dysfunctions. In *Psychodynamic psychiatry in clinical practice*. Washington: American Psychiatric Publishing.

Gibbs, P.L. (2007). Reality in cyberspace: analysands' use of the Internet and ordinary everyday psychosis. *Psychoanalytic Review*, *94*, 1: 11–38.

Glover, E. (1933). The relation of perversion-formation to the development of reality-sense. *International Journal of Psychoanalysis*, *14*, 486–504.

Greenacre, P. (1953). Certain relationships between fetishism and faulty development of the body image. *Psychoanalytic Study of the Child*, *8*, 79–98.

Guignard, F. (1997). *The infantile in psychoanalytic practice today*. London: Routledge, 2002.

Gutton, Ph. (2001). Processus homosexuels de puberté. *Adolescence*, *19*, 1.

Laufer, M. and M.E. Laufer (1984). *Adolescence and developmental breakdown: A psychoanalytic view*. London: Routledge, 2018.

Nicolò, A.M. and L. Accetti (2017). Ennui et adolescence: entre défense et attente. *Revue Française de Psychanalyse*, *81*, 4, 973–983.

Novelletto, A. (1989). *Adolescenza e Perversione*. Roma: Borla.

Novelletto, A. (2009). *L'Adolescente: Una Prospettiva Psicoanalitica*. Roma: Astrolabio.

Steiner, J. (1993). *Psychic retreats: Pathological organizations in psychotic, neurotic and borderline patients*. London: Routledge.

Winnicott, D.W. (1935). The manic defence. In (1958), *Through paediatrics to psycho-analysis*. New-York: Basic Books, 1975.

Winnicott, D.W. (1949). Mind and its relation to the psyche-Soma. In (1958), *Through paediatrics to psycho-analysis*. New-York: Basic Books, 1975.

Winnicott, D.W. (1954). Metapsychological and clinical aspects of regression within the psycho-analytical set-up. In (1958), *Through paediatrics to psycho-analysis*. New-York: Basic Books, 1975.

Winnicott, D.W. (1959). Nothing at the centre. In *Psycho-analytic explorations*. london: routledge, 1989.

Winnicott, D.W. (1965). New light on children's thinking. In *Psychoanalytic explorations*. London: Routledge, 1989.

Winnicott, D.W. (1988). *Human nature*. New York: Routledge.

10

DAYDREAMS AND THEIR EVOLUTIONS[*]

This work discusses the possible evolution of daydreaming towards withdrawal, delusion and hallucination or, on the contrary, towards imagination and more creative functioning in borderline patients and in adolescence. Daydreaming finds its place in a middle ground that can imprison the person or, on the contrary, allow him or her to probe reality even before experiencing it.

In the attempt to fully grasp this complex activity, numerous psychoanalysts and philosophers have noted its difference and similarity to other experiences such as imagination, fantasy, illusion, and dreaming. All authors recognise the ubiquitous nature of the daydreaming activity. According to Freud, daydreaming recomposes the pain/pleasure balance, resolving traumatic anguish and frustration.[1] Although Freud states that daydreams "are the immediate mental precursors of the distressing symptoms" (Freud, 1908, p. 148), he adds that daydream uses "an occasion in the present to construct, on the pattern of the past, a picture of the future" (*Ibid.*). From Freud's latter assertion, we might already glimpse the complex nature and origin of daydreams. On the one hand, they relate to the unconscious, but on the other "according to the topographic theory such attributes are alien to unconscious processes. They are associated with preconscious derivatives that operate according to the laws of the secondary process"[2] (Arlow, 1969, p. 3). Thus, their nature is mixed; while on the one hand,

[*] Re-elaboration of the work presented at the Roman Centre for Psychoanalysis in autumn 2002.

 DOI: 10.4324/9781032663371-13

they are unconscious processes, on the other they are communicated to the self or other consciously. While they refer back to early developmental stages and not only to child sexual theories (*Ibid.*), they also connect with the person's current relationships and interactions, informing us about the patient's representations of the self and object relations.

Finally, Winnicott punctually clarifies the distinction between fantasy and daydreaming, postulating a genetic hypothesis of day-dreaming. He reminds us that in baseline situations the mother offers the child a moment of illusion "which the infant can take as *either* his hallucination *or* a thing belonging to external reality" (Winnicott, 1945, p. 152), that is, the illusion of creating the object that the mother lets him or her find in reality. Maintaining a sustained illusion for as long as necessary by a good enough mother is crucial to the child's mental health, as it is the basis on which a sense of reality and the distinction between me and the not-me are built. When the mother, supporting the child's omnipotence, repeatedly meets the child's "sensory hallucinations" halfway by making them real, she creates what Sechehaye (1956) calls the "symbolic realisation" and Winnicott the paradox of the found/created. "In brief", says Jan Abram, "fantasy – that is, the capacity to fantasise – is linked with having had enough experience of illusion, whereas fantasying – that is, a sort of day-dreaming defence – is a way of dealing with frustrations and psychic pain, because of not having had enough experience of illusion" (Abram, 1996, p. 205).

The multiple functions of daydreams

By observing adult, adolescent, and child patients, we have come to strongly believe that daydreams serve pivotal functions in the inner world of these patients, some of them being in preparation for real life and others as a way of defending themselves against mental pain. Daydreams are, as Freud stated, placed in a middle earth, "certain areas for reservation in their original state" (Freud, 1911, p. 222), and subservient to its author's desires so as to satisfy his or her own archaic desires, without the need to distinguish between reality and fantasy. Freud likens the functioning of daydreaming to that of the dream. Yet while he initially considers the role of the illusion as "evil" because it is an obstacle to the relationship with inner life and personal development, he later revises his position by acknowledging that illusion has a "truth–value" not material, but historical (Freud, 1927, p. 33, 37).

This difference allows for an initial distinction between child fantasies that are based on or related to actual experiences, and child fantasies that conspire in order to avoid the experience (a hallucinatory object of desire) (Britton, 1995).

There is a place in existence for evasion from reality, which has little to do with its defensive elusion. In the case of adolescents, we witness true organisations of fantasies, mental spaces of the imaginary, which hold great usefulness[3] in development, for example, by allowing us to anticipate reality, explore it, and contribute in various ways to the organisation of identity, under specific conditions.

Other times, on the contrary, we may observe ruminative daydreaming that imprisons the person within dangerous withdrawals, which may continue throughout life and segregate personality. Some patients use daydreams for the purpose of coping with a traumatic and frustrating reality.

However, working with severe patients loosens the strictness of our assessment of daydreaming and its vicissitudes. In the most severe patients, the fantasy refuge bounds regressive drives and channels them into a delimited space, the vicissitudes of which we need to observe and study in order to understand whether it will constitute the ultimate prison of the patient's life, or instead foster the integration of dissociated aspects over time.

In other situations, autoerotic fantasy and daydreams play a prosthetic function, namely, that of preventing the anguish related to the sense of emptiness or disintegration that may arise in certain patients.

Therefore, fantasies and daydreaming can constitute psychic withdrawal, yet withdrawing can sometimes be helpful. In withdrawal, the patient might allow himself or herself things that would be felt as terrible or unacceptable in reality. This allows him or her to experiment with them and master them, to then possibly integrate and overcome them.

We must therefore be especially careful in discerning what shores the patient is moving towards. Above all, we must observe whether and how he or she is operating the transformations of these activities. Is daydreaming the only refuge where the patient can derive gratification? Do the gratifications obtained through these reveries increase his or her sense of estrangement, of omnipotence? Does this activity facilitate a relationship with reality, or is it a substitute for it?

Indeed, in some adolescent or young adult patients, fantastic organisations might also evolve and be integrated. Freud gives us an example of this in *Delusion and Dreams in Jensen's "Gradiva"* (1907), where Hanold develops a delusion and presents a world filled with daydreams. Reality testing is virtually absent, and he has negated and split off the memory of Zoe Bertgang from his past, developing a dysperceptive or frankly hallucinatory disorder.

Yet Hanold, at the culmination of this difficult journey, regains contact with reality and transforms the delusion, thanks to Zoe's ability to initially accept the role of Gradiva, a creature buried under the ashes of the volcano, that is, allowing for the reactualisation and revisiting of ancient reality. Zoe/analyst allows Hanold/patient to operate a transference of unconscious fantasies onto a real person, transforming his delusion into a living experience of the present.

What are the relationships between certain daydreams and the products that are instead related to delusion? What is the relationship between massive daydreaming and hallucinations?

The following clinical case might allow us to reflect on these matters.

Santiago is seventeen years old, and despite being a brilliant student, he has decided to stop studying. There are many things he would like to do and he cannot tolerate the idea that choosing one would exclude the others. He calls it the use of "sliding doors", imagining himself in the thousand opportunities or the thousand lives he could have lived. Physically he looks amorphous, dressed in dark clothes. He has never had a girlfriend, never even thinks about it. With friends he says he is "distant, aloof", and can get by as long as they talk about philosophical, intellectual topics. His only passions are music and singing, which help him dream. Santiago was adopted by an Italian couple. When he was in the orphanage, at night in the darkness of the room or in moments of waiting and loneliness, he had often imagined "a mother" holding him. He knew her features, her face, her hair.

When at the age of five he first saw the mother who would adopt him, he felt a strong sense of estrangement: she was not the one he had always imagined!

In Winnicott's words, the child's self-created, "hallucinated" image had not encountered "the object" that could have initiated the process of transformation that is illusion. The use of fantasy that had served a function of comfort and support during difficult times in the institution began to turn into the daydream of sliding doors, as if he had defensively arranged to provide for himself.

On his own initiative, he presented himself for analysis, complaining that he could no longer see the point in going on. With the conclusion of high school, he would find himself at a crossroads and was haunted by the idea of having to make a choice, where taking one path would preclude all others.

In truth, his being in the world was pervaded almost entirely by these doubts, to the point that he sometimes said he "wanted to die". What was the point of living life if it would involve so many renunciations?

He explains that he would rather daydream about a world in which he could be the director of his own story without giving anything up than live real life. He constructs fragments of his autobiography. This activity threatens to undermine all his adolescent investments and infiltrates dream activity, which in the first stage of the analytic process appears limited and static. In his dreams, he sees himself constantly running away from something that is chasing him.

Progressively, what emerged in analysis was that at other times during his growth, the already thin borderland between daydream, perceptual experience, and hallucinatory experience became even thinner, until he was swimming in a fantasy world.

In a foreign city in the company of his parents at the age of eight, in a restaurant he had seen a family photo in which a child was celebrating his birthday, and he felt he could recognise that self of his ideal family. He had retained within himself the memory of this event and, even today, he could not answer his doubts. The picture in the restaurant became the picture of himself and his family. Another of the typical phenomena of these states had thus taken place, namely, when fantasy influences and modifies the perception of reality: was it hallucination or dysperception?

The sliding doors allow him to enter another world, the world of his internal withdrawal, alienating, delusional, but also protective, with which he constructs and reconstructs another of his autobiographical stories. The mother in his story has his skin colour, his own black hair, and is far removed from his real adoptive mother.

Thus begins another peculiar story where he places the few memories of his past, the fragments of the present that he carefully chooses among the myriad of daily events, those images that strike him and that Correale (2013) calls "hypersensorised" (see Chapter 5).

This story in effect alienates him from himself, yet at the same time provides him with internal coherence.

Is there, somewhere in his mind, a self that has had a past with reliable relationships? Santiago made use of a curious mechanism, present for that matter in many borderline or psychotic patients, the grasping from surrounding reality of an element that is disassembled from the context and that he could use in his fantastic construction. He thus used this fragment within a narrative construction.

In so doing, Santiago maintained an illusory sense of continuity of the self that was not fractured by the awareness of the other as separate. He retreated from the relationship with the object that would bring together the scattered fragments of the ego, but which he would also experience as the monster that could swallow him.

And yet, the very metaphor of the sliding doors allows us to reflect on the fact that our adolescent patient stands on a very thin ridge. The doors that may alternate, and that he may pass through, are the doors to omnipotent delusion or the doors to self-reconstruction and acceptance of the mourning consequent to his trauma, of the limit of his story and existence.

However, Santiago makes an effort to represent his internal conflict.

"I had a dream" he says, "a memorable one. The backgrounds are two: a fairy tale forest and a waiting room. The seven dwarfs are chasing the evil queen, but she was beautiful, she didn't look like the witch, I don't know - maybe she was Snow White. I don't know how it is possible because a and not-a cannot live a simultaneous reality. She was on the horse and I was punching her. While I'm doing this the scenery changes: everything becomes small, even the horse becomes a toy. The queen is becoming mechanical. I'm in the waiting room, the horse is intact but it's a toy on the floor. The queen/ Snow White has become a doll and what I have in my hands and have just destroyed is one of my toys, a mini car that turns into a robot. As I say this, I feel it in my body", he comments.

During the associations in session, Santiago, as if anguished by the elaboration he has just produced from the dream and its narration in its representational poignancy, seems to slip, sucked into an undifferentiated and chaotic state, in which a bodily sensory experience prevails. Santiago continues: "I had a flashback doctor ... I was beating the queen/Snow White saying: you killed Snow White, you killed those who cared for us. You killed our mommy. You must die ... ."

In the dream too Santiago seems to be engaged in the struggle against the childhood fantasy of a relationship with a beautiful woman who can also be monstrous (a good and bad mother who also represents the analyst), and who arouses in him both excitement and anger over the trauma he has suffered. Robotisation and de-animation constitute a defence against his destructive rage that threatens to lead him toward psychosis. He rebels in this way against the helplessness that characterised his life in the orphanage and struggles against his white mother, but also against his orphaned Snow White self.

The death anguish of the self and the anger because of the death that his aggression might produce make the situation terrifying, leading him through a further regression to unorganised sensoriality.

Yet the evil and beautiful queen, in the analysis projected in transference onto the analyst, can also be a transformative object, if it resists the patient's efforts to de-animate and roboticise her, and can pave the way out from the enchanted forest of his daydreams.

We see that in dreaming as well as in daydreaming, the sliding doors problem emerges. Two developmental possibilities that open up, one toward frank psychosis, another toward a more objectified world made of emotions and affect, albeit distressing and conflicting. Nonetheless, the sliding doors are also the possibility for his life story to change, and for there to be another story, one in which he remains in contact with his biological parents.

Slipping into psychosis?

In Santiago, the boundaries with the psychotic world are most fragile and uncertain. This is noticeable in several features:

a   The strangeness of communicated contents that are far from the real or libidinal satisfactions typical of his age.
b   The fragility of boundaries with respect to reality. The patient speaks of the sliding doors as a simultaneously coexisting mechanism showing the ease with which he could take one of two paths: toward reality or toward delusion.
c   The loss of the frame that delimits daydream and its spilling over into reality (the dysperception of the photograph).
d   The omnipotent quality of daydreams that might also convey archaic and disorganised experiences of a lack of attunement with the caretaker.
e   Finally, a salient aspect is the fact that the mind now becomes a source of sensory gratification, excluding the body's input and establishing an autocratic and self-sufficient economy. We see an effect of this in Santiago's oniroid state. Sensations are produced in daydream. This aspect is quite different from what occurs in the central masturbatory fantasy where the fantasy triggers the

bodily sensation and is maintained in a reciprocal interaction between body and mind. The one, the fantasy dimension, is related to the other, the bodily dimension.

f Although Santiago presents an oneiric process, we witness a crossing of dream boundaries, and the patient evacuates the anguish connected with the dream by showing a failure to elaborate mental pain.

Daydream and delusion

We know that there is no objective perception of reality, which is always perpetually recreated by our internal world that influences it. Freud points out that the perceived object can be transformed by the encounter with the subject's mental state with the episode of the sandstone figures seen in front of a restaurant in Padua, and found again and again in the form of mysterious figures in his dreams. This appears clear to us by observing children and adolescents, where normal primitive mental states contain omnipotent fantasies that in an adult would be classified as delusions and hallucinations, while in the child and adolescent we can consider them useful for growth. Cowan (1989) calls these phenomena an imaginary perception, which nevertheless roots the subject in a space within the self. An internal space, differentiated from the external one, is thus constituted. We all continuously live with these perceptions, but we can only run the risk even as adults of "relying on the imaginary" if we have achieved the constitution of an inner space and a certain degree of subjectivity allowing us to indulge in this unpredictable experience. Drawing on a paradox, we might say that the experience of having constructed "sense" allows us to lose it. Without this transformation, which has served us well in purifying the burden of reality, we would be overwhelmed by the concreteness of experience.

Forms of psychic evacuation such as hallucinations, excessive projective identifications, manic defences and paranoid delusion, are nothing more than a way to "survive", by establishing a sustainable "economy" for the self. However, at this point, it is necessary to understand the relationship between daydream and delusion.

When Santiago imagines "a mother", he attempts to recreate an essential element of a previous nurturing situation that was lost. The possibility of perceiving himself in this fantasy space prevents him from plunging to the side of hallucination. Yet the daydream that initially took on a developmental declination to protect him from the rawness of his existence, in the lingering absence of a supportive mind (due to the failure in his relationship with his adoptive mother), turns into an imprisoning dimension of fantastic withdrawal.

In withdrawal, the destruction of meaning increasingly distances the person from the possibility of learning from emotional experience, generating a dependence on an omnipotent system that is increasingly based on the psychopathological constructs themselves (De Masi, 2006).

Santiago remains suspended between the dismissal of the reality of his origins, connected with his own birth, and the daydream of a rebirth that has never been constituted, left in a stalemate, "like the movie where the protagonist wakes up and it's always the same day", as he himself says.

In recent years, psychoanalysis has been attempting to broaden its field of research on the topic of these phenomena in which thought seems to collapse, leaving the more or less massive presence of voids in the fabric of the mind uncovered. Several authors since Winnicott (Ferro, 2007; Green, 1990; Levine et al., 2013) have described, with different meanings, borderline or psychotic patients who present disorders in the ability to represent, "a tear in the fabric of the psyche" (Winnicott, 1971a; Levine et al., 2013, p. 5), that results from failures in early relationships. In these patients, the difficulty consists of a defect, frailty or absence of the ability to operate representations, and the difficulty of the transformational processes (*Ibid.*) that are necessary to repair that absence. There are, says Levine, seeming lacerations that can be replaced by omnipotent fantasies.

One wonders whether the production of daydreams, connected with the failure of the capacity to imagine, may not constitute itself as the production of images that remain as "fixed" on the "surface of the mind", even covering the intolerable traumatic dimension. Green speaks of sometimes highly condensed images used as patchwork to cover the internal void, patches to repair a torn internal "narrative" fabric. We believe daydreams to be the derivatives of these highly condensed images that in the course of the subject's life are articulated, depending on the experiences and changes in the context and potentialities of the mind, into organisations of daydreams that repeat the primitive traumatic storyline, although it sometimes presents different forms, with different characters or places. Instead of

184

somatizing, acting on the anguish, or expressing it through a symptom, the person organises it into a core of repetitive daydreams, which sometimes configure a refuge of the mind (Steiner, 1993), and are intermediate formations in the evolution toward the ability to dream the experience or, conversely, discharge them into a delusion or hallucination. Daydreams therefore oscillate between low representational functioning or instead the prelude to frank hallucinations and delusions, belonging to an area of the mind with varying gradients of functioning.

Toward a delusional transformation

Another clinical case might allow us to reflect on the transformation of daydream into delusion. It seems to us that in the latter case, the daydream loses or weakly maintains its connection with the emotions that produced it, and with the traumatic contents of the patient's story. In keeping with this hypothesis, we will be able to differentiate daydreams that originate in a thinking/dreaming capacity that is momentarily blocked but which presents some dynamism and articulation, and daydream structures stemming from an impaired, flattened thinking/dreaming capacity in which symbolic activity is more or less impaired. The former, while not allowing for the development of associative chains, maintain some form of narrativity by containing varyingly extensive fragments of meaning relating to the patient's story. These daydreams, as in the reported cases, treated analytically, may constitute an "oneiric potential". The connection between the daydream contents and the life data that seem connected to it creates and enhances the meaning of the individual's emotional history, promoting the resumption of the work of the unconscious. In the second case, daydream may be the result of the mind's inability to transform, for example, psychic pain brought about by trauma or the appearance of an emotion that conflicts with the remaining part of the personality. Massive emotional avoidance ensues, and the mind may give rise to the creation of an alternative fantasy life, on an evacuative basis, that seemingly maintains no connection with the person's inner life. This type of daydream may border with, even to the point of fully assuming it, the concreteness and rigidity of delusion. Being dominated by the rejection of all those emotions that can connect with the subject's "traumatic historical truth", the latter might remain trapped, "unchanged as split-off pockets (or broad sectors) of psychosis (Bion,

185

1965) or as aspects of the personality in which experience is foreclosed from psychological elaboration" (Ogden, 2004, p. 861).

In short, in cases following a delusional evolution, daydream is built around the original traumatic core, imprisoning it, creating a sort of plaster cast that is apt to maintain it. In this case, the narrative element is secondary, but serves to maintain the hallucinatory core.

In Alfredo, age thirty, whom I present in Chapter 13, the core of day-dream that had built up since adolescence, rooted in the theme of his reincarnation and past lives, precipitates into a psychotic episode in trans-ference. After a summer vacation and the rejection of a woman he had fallen in love with, the patient begins to develop the delusion of being protected by the souls of the dead. He stops going to work and stays at home, in an attempt to heal himself, by drinking his own urine. In session, he himself describes the many times he almost willingly defied death: "in all these situations, the light of the spirits protected me by preventing me from dying – so I went through the metal sheets without getting hurt", he says. Questions around his identity and origin are embedded into these themes. The psychotic episode in transference is also determined by the existence of a secret, unbe-knownst to the patient, that is revealed to the analyst by a colleague, namely, the fact that the patient is the illegitimate son of his mother. Thus, actualised in transference was the repetition of a traumatic relationship that Alfredo had experienced with his parents, who had hidden his true origin from him.

The primitive anguishes experienced in his childhood world and that had generated his omnipotent and salvific fantasies in the past reoccur on occasion of a second trauma. What had formed the core of his daydreams is transformed into some sort of experience that does not come from his inner world, but from the outside, for ex-ample, an encounter with the dead.[4] The last bastion of defence in the face of a renewed traumatic experience is psychosis, which splits the self and evacuates to the outside.

Conclusions

There exists a frailty of boundaries between daydream, imagination, hallucination or delusion. Our experience with patients of different ages and pathologies, who all presented a continuous use of day-dreaming, showed a gradual and continuous oscillation in this activity, alongside a different use of it within the personality. Occasionally, the creation of a cloud of daydream is a method of defence against catastrophe, fragmentation, and breakdown. In

Santiago's case, daydream testifies to the never-acquired, never-lost reality, maintained in suspended animation, allowing the continuity of the patient's self. At other times, however, as in Alfredo's case, these daydreams were the first hint of a brewing delusion. Santiago, in the episode of the restaurant photograph, "enacts a process of depiction halfway between hallucination and the illusory invention of a family more resembling himself and the original family" [tr. by O.M.] (De Vita, 2014). In short, the daydream of finding one's mother and the restaurant dysperception are nonetheless useful: as we have previously mentioned, the one allows one to survive the absence and the second, dysperception, constitutes the sensory object to cling to. To lose everything, to fall into the traumatic void of his primitive experiences, is a far more fearsome event for Santiago, and for any patient, than to resort to the defensive lie that avoids catastrophe. Better, in short, a false representation than nothing at all. However, the opposite can also happen, when the processes of splitting and denegation are so massive that there is no room for dreaming, imagination, or for play. Some individuals will react to this by never leaving factual reality. This will be the psychotic functioning characterised by concreteness, and emptiness of meaning, inhibition in thinking or imagining, yet we can also observe its opposite, namely, escaping from reality by taking refuge in the daydream or lonely, self-reverberating constructions of delusion, which should not be confused with an excess of illusion.

However nuanced and fluctuating the fate of such fantastic defensive organisations may be, it is crucial for the analyst to monitor these comings and goings, especially with adolescent patients, given that awareness of how the functioning of the mind evolves and changes is important to prevent breakdown or the crystallisation of frankly psychotic functioning.

In Santiago's case, we can observe that the patient maintains some mobility in the use of these daydreams. He himself is partially self-critical of these productions and in any case observes their different developmental possibilities (the term sliding doors is his own).

Generally, in adolescent daydreams of a developmental nature, the patient does not cling to them as is the case in delusional situations, where instead the questioning of the delusion often produces deep-rooted anguish, a sense of emptiness.[5] Speaking of phenomena that we consider close, Bion illustrates the functioning of hallucinosis and states that "the concept of hallucinosis needs to be widened to fit a number of configurations which are at present not recognised as being the same" (Bion, 1965, p. 133). He considers hallucinosis an ever-present state, albeit covered by other phenomena that shield it. On the one hand, it is a pathological defence, on the other it is also a background of normal functioning. Bion then adds that a background of hallucinosis preserves the patient's reality intact (*Ibid.,*). We believe he is thus illustrating a containing function, though a crude one, performed by such activity.

We wonder whether daydreams might also be placed in that realm, by displaying the characteristics of that middle ground between unconscious and conscious, between fantasy and delusion, between the primary and the secondary processes, an area that we all navigate more or less consciously in our lives. Daydreaming presents different gradients and directions of functioning; it may retain a potential for transformation into thought and dreaming, or may instead present an evolution into a delusional production, an expression of the outward rejection of internal contents into external territory.

Notes

1 It most easily manifests itself after a present traumatic experience even though it is organised on childhood trauma. The daydreaming we observe in adulthood or adolescence is the reiteration or a defensive distortion of the earlier childhood fantasy. It therefore refers back to an earlier fixation or conflict.

2 Freud asserted that "among the derivatives of the Ucs. instinctual impulses, of the sort we have described, there are some which unite in themselves characters of an opposite kind. On the one hand, they are highly organised, free from self-contradiction, have made use of every acquisition of the system Cs. and would hardly be distinguished in our judgement from the formations of that system. On the other hand, they are unconscious and are incapable of becoming conscious. Thus qualitatively they belong to the system Pcs., but factually to the Ucs" (Freud, 1915, pp. 190).

3 Finally, most adolescent fantasies of a developmental nature, of whatever kind, are an aid to restructuring and reorganising Oedipal vicissitudes. Paradigmatic of these are the masturbatory fantasies long dealt with by Laufers (1984). There are various manifestations of these, such as the family novel, and in some of its forms, autobiographical narrations.

4 The mixed and confusing nature of external and internal is also palpable in the persistence, in these patients who slip into delusion, of alienating

identifications (Cahn, 1991). In fact, the latter compel the subject to relentlessly search for the unattainable origins of their history and identity. Alienating objects continue to be present not only in the past, but in the internal and alas also external world of these patients (their family), and this parasitic and continuous presence prevents the possibility of repressing and indeed determines the slippage into dissociation that had allowed the long persistence of the daydreams.

5 As Lichtenberg and Pao (1974) point out, delusion and daydream serve a different functions given that, at the time of the manifestation of a delusion, the defensive organisation is called upon to restore a basic sense of security comparable to that which the child realises through his or her mother-child duality and which, I would add, the patient has never realised.

References

Abram, J. (1996). *The language of Winnicott: A dictionary of Winnicott's use of words*. London: Routledge, 2007.

Arlow, J.A. (1969). Unconscious fantasy and disturbances of conscious experience. *The Psychoanalytic Quarterly*, *38*, 1–27.

Bion, W.R. (1965). *Transformations*. London: Karnac Books, 1984.

Britton, R. (1995). Reality and unreality in phantasy and fiction. In E.S. Spector Person, P. Fonagy and S.A. Figueira (Eds.), *On Freud's Creative Writers and Day-dreaming*. London: Routledge.

Cahn, R. (1991). *Adolescence et Folie: Les Déliaisons Dangereuses*. Paris: P.U.F.

Correale A. (2013). Allucinatorio e psicosi. *European Journal of Psychoanalysis*.

Cowan, J. (1989). *Mystery of the Dream-Time*. Bridport: Prism.

De Masi, F. (2006). *Vulnerability to psychosis: A psychoanalytic study of the nature and therapy of the psychotic state*. London: Routledge, 2009.

De Vita, C. (2014). Comment to the seminar by Anna Maria Nicolò "Fantasticherie e loro evoluzioni". Scientific Debate at the *Centro Psicoanalitico di Roma*, October 2014.

Ferro, A. (2007). *Avoiding emotions, living emotions*. London: Routledge, 2012.

Freud, S. (1907). Delusions and dreams in Jensen's *Gradiva*. *S.E.* 9: 1–96, London: Hogarth Press.

Freud, S. (1908). Creative writers and day-dreaming. *S.E.* 9: 141–154, London: Hogarth Press.

Freud, S. (1911). Formulations on the two principles of mental functioning. *S.E.*, 12: 213–226, London: Hogarth Press.

Freud, S. (1915). The unconscious. *S.E.*, 14: 159–215, London: Hogarth Press.

Freud, S. (1927). The future of an illusion. *S.E.* 21: 1–56, London: Hogarth Press.

Green, A. (1990). *On private madness*. London: Routledge, 1996.

Laufer, M. and M.E. Laufer (1984). *Adolescence and developmental breakdown: A psychoanalytic view*. London: Routledge, 1995.

Levine, H.B., G.S. Reed, D. Scarfone, Eds. (2013). *Unrepresented states and the construction of meaning: Clinical and theoretical contribution*. London: Routledge.

Lichtenberg, J.D. and P. Pao (1974). Delusion, fantasy and desire. *International Journal of Psychanalysis*, *55*, 273–281.

Ogden, T.H. (2004). This art of psychoanalysis: Dreaming undreamt dreams and interrupted cries. *International Journal of Psychoanalysis*, *85*, 857–877.

Sechehaye, M.A. (1956). The transference in symbolic realization. *International Journal of Psychoanalysis*, *37*, 270–277.

Steiner, J. (1993). *Psychic retreats: Pathological organizations in psychotic, neurotic and borderline patients*. London: Routledge.

Winnicott, D.W. (1945). Primitive emotional development. In (1958), *Through Paediatrics to Psycho-Analysis*. New-York: Basic Books, 1975.

Winnicott, D.W. (1971a). Dreaming, fantasying and living: A case-history describing a primary dissociation. In (1971) *Playing and Reality*. London: Routledge, 2005.

MARTINA

Alienation in the other

In the treatment of adolescents, couples and families, I have observed situations in which the young person, despite an established risk of severe breakdown, was able to compensate for the probable event through a loving relationship that involved him or her totally. Such a relationship was characterised at the beginning by a passionate quality, with a drive to overcome the boundaries of the other to appropriate and merge with them, and this eventually resulted in the overcoming of boundaries of the self, of limits, blockages or bereavements.

The patient developed exaggerated idealisation and massive projective identification in the other, which eventually led to the emptying of the self.

Viederman (1988) speaks, in such cases, of "a euphoric sense of fullness", partly due to the fact that a sense of power of extraordinary exaltation can accompany the attainment of passionate love. I have also seen the extent to which the breakdown of relationships with such characteristics can lead to crises with a psychotic quality, sometimes foreboding the dawn of even serious decompensation.

My work as a psychoanalyst in settings with couples and families has allowed me to observe that the particular quality of certain links is capable of stabilising a personality even throughout life, a personality that otherwise would have engaged in psychotic functioning with limiting symptoms.

I believe the pattern underlying these modes of functioning is a defensive mechanism characterised by externalising into the receiving other, due to their unconscious resonance, unelaborated emotions and experiences. This defence might even be observed in a group as a

DOI: 10.4324/9781032663371-14

whole. As we have seen, the paths to ridding oneself of mental pain are numerous, alongside the normal intrapsychic defence mechanisms. Using the other in the relationship, caring for the other, through the relationship with the other, inducing in some cases suffering or disturbance in the other (Nicolò, 1990), that is, putting the other in the condition in which they express discomfort or suffering in our place, are some of the most common though largely unrecognised ways. The relationship with the other can also be used as compensation for the anguish of annihilation and sense of emptiness, or in situations of severe confusion.

Taken to the excess, this is the mechanism that we observe in sects led by a guru who assumes upon himself the superego role and ideal ego. Indeed, these figures are usually idolised, nullifying doubts and death anxieties. In the face of this externalisation, there is also the fantasy of appropriating characteristics of the other that represent obsolete or dissociated aspects of the self. This operation allows one to regain contact with these split and externalised parts, which may represent unacceptable or prematurely blocked, split or dissociated aspects. It is to be noted, moreover, that the need for fusion and dissolution into the other might underlie these mechanisms as well.

More rarely, such fusional and totalising bonds may allow the maturation of the self because, in a mediated and indirect way through the partner, the patient may contact his or her own split parts and even invest in aspects of the body that the person had previously neglected or split.

In such cases, the appropriation of the other, born on a destructive and de-objectivising matrix, may allow for the realisation of a new identity. To quote Viederman (1988) again, one of the most powerful consequences in passionate relationships is the formation of a new sense of self.

Martina's clinical case seems to me to fittingly illustrate a number of these dynamics.

Martina: compensating with the other

Martina is a woman in her thirties. She comes to treatment urged on by her husband, twenty-nine years her senior, who, however ambivalent, is now tired of his wife's constant demands and need for control.

Martina comes across as contradictory and confused, living in an isolated retreat from which she hardly ever leaves except for grocery shopping. She is afraid of the relationship with the other. She would like a child and complains that her husband feels too old to have one, but her desire is strongly ambivalent.

Martina's relationship with her husband dominates the central scene of therapy in the first few months: the husband who does not want children, the husband who is often away in another city for work, and the husband who only asks for sexual services.

Martina does nothing all week and her life revolves around what her husband says and thinks, who is at times idealised and sometimes felt as persecutor.

The image she elicits is that of a person suspended in space and time, fearful of everything, easily distressed, though she is astonishing for her intelligence, elegance and sensitivity, and above all for the lucidity of her judgments, albeit sectorial.

Martina tells her story: the second child of a very poor family in a small town, she struggles with her father to be able to study and performs brilliantly in school, even though she must provide for her younger siblings.

Her birth results in an early rejection by her mother, who leaves her at the mercy of a loving but somewhat eccentric aunt, who at some point departs, leaving her alone.

With great feelings of inadequacy, Martina associates with wealthier classmates at school and falls hopelessly in love with one, without ever being able to manifest it.

Enroling in a course to obtain a diploma, Martina plans to redeem her family of origin economically and socially.

In the first few months of her work, Martina clings to sessions. She often calls on the phone between sessions only to leave a message on the answering machine.

A sort of anxious depression dominates her, and I reflect upon her passivity and absolute submission to her husband, in fact, in great contrast with the lucidity of her words and rebellion.

After a few months, Martina joins a gym and informs me with panicked anguish that she has been fantasising upon noticing the attention that one of her peers was giving her.

We realise together that her husband plays a very complex role of self-support for her, and thus the story of her encounter with Giovanni emerges fully.

At nineteen, Martina is proudly attending a course in another city and has forgotten all her adolescent loves in order to study, when a seemingly negligible event turns out to be traumatic. Having been asked by a colleague to sign in her place to attend a seminar, Martina slowly begins to develop panic, anguish of being expelled from the course and then followed, controlled, reported, etc. The issue of signing becomes a constant, persecutory idea. She can no longer sign anything, not even an email. Her studies come to a standstill. These paranoid experiences immobilise her, triggering a major regression. The young woman locks herself in the house in panic, in the grip of persecutory ghosts. Martina's family turns to the doctor, who intervenes with medication but sends her to the private school in the town so that the girl can resume some socialisation, perhaps helping with child management given that she had a kindergarten teacher's diploma. At this school, Martina meets Giovanni, the director, who is twenty-nine years her senior. Giovanni is an authority in the town due to his activity in politics and communication skills, always confident about the solutions to adopt. Sure enough, Martina is soon fascinated by him.

The situation falls into place within months, and a few years later Martina marries Giovanni, her mentor.

The episode from when she was twenty seems to have almost disappeared from memory, yet it is an important point.

As the work progresses and the therapeutic relationship grows stronger, Martina develops confidence, and the swiftness of her changes astonishes and worries.

She enrols in a literature course at university, and her husband, whom she sometimes calls daddy, begins to resist paying for therapy. I start to reflect upon how strange and aborted this crisis of Martina's is, immediately recomposed with a marriage to a father figure, as an anticipatory prevention of separation and blockage of evolution, of integration, not only of sexuality, but also of the development of an autonomous thought.

Several sessions appear to confirm this idea: in one of them, the first of the week (of two, because her husband firmly refuses for her to do more), after a year and a half of work, Martina, upon returning from a weekend with her family, tells a dream: "*I was in the garden in the back of a church; a strange monster was chasing me and to escape him, I climbed a wall, thus remaining suspended in mid-air. I couldn't get down for fear of the monster, but neither go forward because of the steepness of the wall, but I knew I would manage to escape him*".

Regarding her associations of this figure with her violent older brother, Martina describes the attempts and suggestions of incestuous abuse on the part of her brother, from whom she had defended herself, but whom she had never been able to report for fear of not being believed.

The following week, back again from her hometown, in session she reports the difficult economic situation of her parents and sister, who is married and has children. Martina says that her husband, who is rich, controls every penny she has, preventing her from helping her family members. She tells me about another dream: *"I am with my sister Anna who recently had a baby. I find myself dressed like I was in eighth grade or ninth grade. My father drives a small bus and runs over the backpack full of books. On a long scrap merchant table (like her working-class grandfather's) I attempt to retrieve my Italian literature from school"*. The dream then changes: *"she looks for photos of herself as a child that confirm she was beautiful. She finds photos of her twelve-thirteen-year-old self, but she/I does not like herself. She/I compares this photo with those of her/my sister at the magnifying glass. Both may be little monsters, but her sister's look was serene and that does it all"*.

She points out that her father disagreed with her enrolling in school because of financial problems, and says that she has no photos from when she was a child, and in the photos as a teenager she was dressed as a nun.

In the interpretation, I highlight her attempt to recover the past and her ability to think about what happened to her. I emphasise the fact that the comparison with her sister, whom she has recently seen again, is difficult for her because not having children is felt as a source of deep pain and limitation to her growth. I mention how this comparison with her sister echoes that with her analyst. Furthermore, I emphasise her difficulty in seeing the positive things she is doing, but also her difficulty in giving herself time to move from being a nun to being a woman and mother.

Gradually, Martina untangles herself from her relationship with her husband who lives far away and developed a sort of double life of which Martina is suspicious. Indeed, as she becomes more autonomous and able to take differentiated initiatives, her relationship with her husband becomes increasingly difficult. Faced with a less passive woman, her husband tightens his grip on the economic aspect, would like to prevent her from meeting family members, and contrasts her burgeoning friendships, which Martina is forced to develop secretly or when he is not there. He has taken to humiliating her, using her as an object of sexual consumption. Beneath the appearance of an elegant, triumphant man, ready for any expense for himself while strategically skimping on everything for his wife, Martina herself detects signs of pressing ageing and masked depressive aspects.

Comment

In my view, certain adolescent cruxes recur, albeit modified in form, and reactivated with respect to other traumatic occasions.

In the first dream, the patient reports being immobilised in a situation of developmental impasse: being in the middle of the wall between releasing incestuous and monstrous drives (and also evidently her monstrous self) and moving towards adulthood. The back of the church perhaps represents a confusing and unprotective maternal space.

In the second session, the patient's description of her situation is extraordinary: beginning with her mirror relationship with her sister Anna-analyst, a double of the self, more fortunate or more serene, who in the mirror relationship can strengthen her in her identity to the point of telling us how the shock of puberty (the period described by the dream in her relationship with an abusive father who overwhelms her) may have hitherto destroyed her capacity for sublimation, thought (books), but also her ambitions for growth and redemption in the future through her study. Today as was then, she experiences her body image as that of a little ungrown monster, thus showing her confusing identification with a mother who rejected her at birth and in her growth as a woman.

We are often confronted with cases that are similar to this one, where patients sometimes come to us driven by indirect motivations.

We might describe it as a developmental rupture, prematurely re-composed, where the subsequent personality organised itself defensively and as compensation. We might then ask: which part of this is residual in Martina's adult personality, inherited from her traumatic story? Or again, what did the total or partial avoidance of adolescence block in the construction of this person? Martina presents:

1   A marriage to a husband-father that interrupted the Oedipal development. On the contrary, to continue her growth, she would have had to free herself from the nostalgic need for fusion with her mother and incestuous fantasies-fears towards her father and brother, towards whom she was also bound by anger and hatred.

2   An inhibition in symbolisation and elaboration that resulted in a momentary block in intellectual growth and in her studies.
3   A difficulty with separation-individuation which, among other things, was re-actualised in the analytic relationship and brought panic whenever she was alone when faced with a decision, with taking responsibility, with expressing herself as a subject.

Of the various parts of Martina's dream, one mainly struck me: when the father, on his bus, runs over his daughter's books. Apart from the obvious reference to the exciting and deadly impact of the pubertal body, this running over of books seems quite relevant to me, as running over the possibilities of sublimation, of invest-ment in cultural objects and thought. The consequence of this is the impossibility of reworking the superego and remaining subservient to parental authority.

Marriage, which had been the cover placed over the volcano of her conflicts and anguishes, went so far as to represent an attempt at developmental transition for Martina, a first shift away from the incestuous parent. Yet this same marriage would have risked blocking her, had it not been for the possibility of growth through psychoanalysis.

Some reflections starting from Searles and Aulagnier

Two authors have been particularly helpful in clarifying these issues for me, and the first is Harold Searles, who in *The Effort to Drive the Other Person Crazy* (1959), a true masterpiece of psychoanalysis, illustrates the motivations in the relationship between people that are capable of generating pathology. One of these, particularly signifi-cant, is the desire to find a soulmate who might relieve an intolerable sense of loneliness (*Ibid.*, p. 8).

This type of dynamic is most common in the relationship between the parent and the sick child, and he also addresses the very strong resistance that the parent enacts to counter the child's drive for autonomy. Searles further shows how the patient comes to intensely idealise the parent by splitting his or her image into two figures, one of which is the personification of evil, the other of protective love. He therefore illustrates (*Ibid.*, p. 9) the all-powerful infantile relationality between the sicker and less mature parts of the parent's personality on the one hand, and the patient's on the other, illustrating the extent to which this represents the greatest obstacle to healing.

The central aspect is the symbiotic mode that characterises the relationship between these people.

Piera Aulagnier devotes many parts of her book *Les Destins du Plaisir: Aliénation, Amour, Passion* (1979) to this very issue. With extreme lucidity, the Franco-Italian psychoanalyst describes the process of alienation and its characteristics, the first of which being the emphasis on the bilateral process, where alienation does not always presuppose a pre-existing pathology. This pattern aims to allow the one being alienated to regain certainty and exclude both doubt and conflict, as we saw happen to Martina after the marriage that had volatilised all her anguish. This is achieved through the alienator's idealisation by the alienated, and Martina, at first, brings a sort of idolisation of her husband, whom she believed to be a great thinker, philosopher, and scholar.

Once such a relationship is established over time, a total disavowal on the part of the alienated person about "the accident that happened to [his or her] thinking" [tr. by O.M.] (*Ibid.*, p. 36) sets in. For this reason, "alienation is a concept thinkable only by an external observer and presupposes an experience that cannot be perceived by the one experiencing it" [tr. by O.M.] (*Ibid.*). This was what happened to Martina, who had never understood the meaning of her developmental rupture; unlike the observer-analyst, who had observed it and pointed it out.

There exists therefore a collusion and complicity between the two participants, yet of this relationship both "the phantasmatic interpretation of this reality, [...] and the possibility of thinking about it" must remain negated [tr. by O.M.] (*Ibid.*, p. 42).

As Aulagnier reiterates, unlike the psychotic, who reconstructs reality by resorting to a delusional theory, the alienated person, in order to preserve their investment, will substitute reality with the alienator's discourse, which is presented as logical and of simple actualisation.

Martina thus handed over to her husband all understanding of reality.

If the advantage for the alienated person is clear, we might miss that for the alienator. We might assume that the one who alienates is defending himself or herself from his or her own madness, killing the thought in the other to avoid contacting his or her own anguish or sinking into severe depression.

This kind of linking therefore allows one to shelter oneself from grief and escape the anguish of death by asserting mastery over the other, and over oneself, through the negation of all weakness and need. Indeed, this is sadly true by observing the behaviours of Martina's husband who negated his ageing and, as Martina became progressively independent and self-confident, multiplied his manic acting out with other women, with unnecessarily wasteful behaviour, with luxury and with split sexual arousal.

Conclusions

We might wonder what would have happened if Martina had been able to heal her adolescent breakdown, becoming aware of her difficulties but also making use of the developmental potential of her crisis. And what would have happened if she had, as she asked, had a child? Perhaps the new emotional balance, resulting from her being a mother and her new bond with her child, would have acted as substitute in offering her further support for a fragile self that could have replaced her husband, who had in turn replaced her mother. Or would this experience of being a mother have perhaps transformed her, given that the grief of not being able to be a mother had led her to therapy?

These questions clearly have no foundation, pertaining as they do to an unverifiable future, and yet, I fail to perceive them as trivial.

In Martina's case, the marriage crisis and the momentary negation of motherhood brought her back to the threshold of that breakdown she had avoided in adolescence, and brought her back to having to relive aspects of that adolescence that should have been experienced as an organising process of subjectivization.

The analysis therefore took on specific meaning by placing the patient anew along her developmental story.

References

Aulagnier, P. (1979). *Les Destins du Plaisir: Aliénation, Amour, Passion.* Paris: P.U.F.

Nicolò, A.M. (1990). Soigner à l'intérieur de l'autre: Notes sur la dynamique entre l'individu et la famille. *Cahiers Critiques de Thérapie Familiale et de Pratique de Réseaux, 12,* 29–51.

Searls, H.F. (1959). The effort to drive the other person crazy - an element in the etiology and psychotherapy of schizophrenia. *British Journal of Medical Psychology, 32,* 1–18.

Viederman, M. (1988). The nature of passionate love. In W. Galin and E. Person (Eds.), *Passionate Attachments: Thinking about Love.* New York: Free Press.

VIOLENCE AS A DEFENCE AGAINST BREAKDOWN[1]

Introduction

In this chapter and the next, I will examine the nature and significance of violent behaviours of adolescents and young people. I wish to propose a number of reflections here on antisocial and violent acting out, some of which I have hypothesised may be a defence against breakdown (Nicolò, 2006).

Adolescence is a violent process of change in which one of the developmental tasks is precisely the integration of aggression. The adolescent must undergo the impetuous intrusion of bodily changes that may be experienced as capable of subjugating him or her with respect to new needs. This integration, provided it is effective, is useful to the adolescent for various purposes, such as asserting himself or herself in his or her new world, negating the frightening dependency, and even managing an adult sexuality in which an aggressive, though not violent, component may exist.

Understanding these aspects requires an accurate distinction between violence and aggression. There are countless discussions around this topic. Among psychoanalysts, for example, there is debate around the extent to which aggression is to be considered instinct or drive, on how far it is permissible to place destructive and constructive aggression under the same term, on its relations to self-destructiveness, to death or to what extent aggression is to be considered a reaction to a traumatic stimulus.

The analyst's specific orientation significantly weighs in these considerations. It changes a great deal whether we consider aggression a primary drive that must be controlled and tamed (Melanie Klein

DOI: 10.4324/9781032663371-15

and Green), or whether we consider it a reaction to frustration, or a reaction of the vulnerable and endangered self (Fonagy & Target, 1997; Mitchell, 1993). In fact, it could be self-defence in times of danger or instead a healthy and useful competitive tool for separation, self-assertion or exploration of the world and interactions with the other.

Following Winnicott (1969a), we might also recall its usefulness to use the object and not just relate to it. In this case, aggression is not organised for the purpose of destruction, and instead provides a sense of being real (Winnicott, 1950).

Clearly, one aspect does not necessarily exclude the other on the clinical level; indeed, in adolescence we often observe the overlapping of these meanings.

Violence and aggression

There exists a profound difference between violence and aggression, in that aggression maintains the link with the object, while violence is de-objectualising and de-subjectualising (Jeammet, 1997). Simply put, we could say that violence renders the other equal to a thing, a concrete object, yet at the same time, the subject implicitly empties itself of its ability to suffer and think.

Campbell (2000) distinguishes two types of violence, sadistic and preservative. The latter finds its goal in the negation of the threat to physical or psychic survival or the maintenance of a sense of identity. This type of functioning may complicate these adolescents' relationship with the peer group, or may result in their passive membership in organised groups such as gangs.

Such groups are characterised by quite particular modes of functioning. In fact, there is often submission to a tyrannical and sadistic leader. The advantage of belonging to them is the nullification of the persecutory superego: there are no perpetrators and victims in them, limits and boundaries are nullified, except for those imposed by the group. Also, there is no mourning, but only omnipotence and thus the rejection of the Oedipus. We could consider the functioning of these groups based on pre-Oedipal, archaic and nonspecific identifications.

A seventeen-year-old boy, treated by me in family sessions for bullying at school against younger boys and behavioural difficulties at home, brings a dream to a session after eight months of treatment: *he was in an unfamiliar house that he knew was his home. Called in, he came for lunch but noticed with amazement that his family members had un-recognisable faces that seemed to be masked inside a kind of nylon stocking that made them all look the same, and this appearance seemed to frighten him.* Prompted by his younger sister, he associates the nylon stocking with episodes from movies and exciting narrations about robberies, muggings and various criminal acts. The parents underestimate the content of the dream, just as they underestimate their son's problems. They take advantage of the sessions to express their anger and disappointment with their son, whom they feel does not obey. In this example, the second skin (Bick, Meltzer), which in the dream is shown metaphorically in the nylons covering the faces of the family members, is an undifferentiating tool, a nullification of identity that is related to the nullification of the sense of responsibility. One cannot recognise who is carrying out an action, everyone has the same face and everyone's identity is misunderstood and misrecognised. The parents treat the boy with great verbal violence and attribute much blame to him, failing to see his frightened and fragile parts and his difficulties in differentiating himself. We might also observe the extent to which baseline aggression can act as detonator if it collides with prior traumatic functioning that may also have characterised certain modes of family functioning of that adolescent. Thus, the precipitation of a double trauma is generated: the boy attempts to rid himself of the traumatic process he is unable to elaborate by attacking a weak child who represents a fragile and shameful aspect of himself. This allows him temporary relief, as well as being helpful in obtaining a negative identity that is built on omnipotence and negation of dependency.

Indeed, Novelletto (2009) asserted that the violent subject attempts to eliminate the traumatic process that he or she is unable to elaborate, as if it were a bomb with a lit fuse to be immediately thrown at the designated enemy before it explodes on the subject himself or herself.

Violence as a defence against breakdown

In the more problematic adolescents, the occurrence of violent acting out must be carefully evaluated because it may constitute, for example, a negation of the depressions and suicidal fantasies that the adolescent carries, and which are then projected onto the other, on whom suffering is inflicted or whose life is threatened.

I believe that, in the case of certain aggressively acting adolescents, we may also be faced with death anxieties related to catastrophically experienced identity reorganisation and phase-specific mourning processes that are expressed in traumatic attitudes towards one's own body or that of others. This behaviour somewhat alleviates psychic suffering. Moreover, such problems of course involve the role of the superego, which clearly cannot be independent of introjections and "parental strictures" and which, as Moses and Eglé Laufer remind us, plays a decisive role in determining the success or failure of the transition from adolescence to the ultimate sexual organisation (Laufer & Laufer, 1984, p. 28).

In more complex cases, however, aggressive acting out is organised as a defence against the fear of a far more severe decompensation, or functions as a powerful negation of passivity or a defence against it. I have had the chance to observe this aspect not only in male adolescents, where this issue is certainly connected with gender identity, but also in girls. In this case, an aggressive stance is a negation of and revolt against the passivisation produced by the alienating intrusions of parental fantasies, or the fear of passivity that is relevant in girls at the onset of puberty.

Self-destructive acting out could be related, according to Ladame (2006) who had analysed cases of suicide attempts, to an interruption of the ability to represent, as well as to an inability to produce thought in images. The psyche presents itself as inert or passive, "the way out may be hallucination, or delusion, or enactment: in fact, both modes reproduce a form of activity" [tr. by O.M.].

The fear of passively enduring age-induced bodily modifications, or the passivity to which such patients who have long been forced to endure parental projections and identity impositions, may stimulate an aggressive revolt as a defence. While this certainly makes their behaviour dangerous, to a certain extent and from the patient's point of view, it also represents an albeit clumsy and unsuccessful attempt to self-organise, rebel and self-assert. Unfortunately, this attempt is often doomed to failure, or to arouse guilt and self-punishment that their sadistic superego does not spare. Yet in itself, this movement should also be valued for its positive characteristics and potential for separation.

A case that I worked on for seven years, from the patient's seventeen years to twenty-three, seems quite paradigmatic in illustrating all the defensive uses that acted out or fantasised aggression served for this patient, but also the antisocial acts as an alternative to a major depressive breakdown, allowing him to somehow handle issues that threatened to be implosive.

A clinical case

Dino was in his second year of high school when he began a treatment that lasted roughly seven years, up to the threshold of graduation.

His father was a very seductive and manipulative man, particularly with Dino who was an only child. He was a rather important man, used to taking great care of his public image and with little time for the family. His mother was very cold and angry about the lack of attention paid to her. She had a less-than-stellar job and, as her son said, was perhaps not particularly intelligent. Certainly, she showed little empathy for her son, devoting all her attention to her husband.

At the beginning of treatment, I saw Dino three times a week, and it was he himself who asked me, apparently out of curiosity, to use the couch. At the beginning of our work, he presented dissocial and violent acting out, used soft drugs massively and cocaine sporadically, dealt drugs for money and frequented fringe groups with delinquent drifts. In this group of outcasts, everyone had a nickname. For example, one of them was called "Sharpener", because he went around armed with a knife. Dino's nickname was "Piece", because he occasionally lost control with furious outbursts, hence, going to "pieces".

In the first session, Dino showed up quite dirty and with a ruined leather jacket full of metal things. Interestingly, he was afraid to place his jacket on a chair, fearing I might get angry at the smell of dirt it emanated. Dino had long hair, dirty and torn clothing, full of metal studs, and frankly aggressive on a superficial level. There was no clear division in his mind between good and bad: for example, he used the same terms or concepts to refer to someone who stole and someone who was robbed (in this regard, he used the verb to "take away"), and he had a very cynical judgment around the police, who prevaricate instead of protecting.

Clearly, his parents were his reference, particularly his father, who seemed formally impeccable.

In the first year of analysis, Dino, physically neglected, falls ill with glomerulonephritis, which he naturally underestimates but can be read as a sign of an impending major depressive aspect. To his mother, who worries about him, Dino responds harshly and sharply by accentuating, in order to hurt her, what could harm him.

His actions sometimes display characteristics of dangerousness, a sort of traumatophilia that testifies to Dino's important anguish.

Around the time of the first vacation, after a quarrel, Dino suddenly escapes from his parents' house, where he feels a persecutory atmosphere, and wanders around Europe with his group of friends, of whom he is the leader, within which he mirrors himself and makes his first reflections on himself and others.

On that journey, he rediscovers the places of his childhood origins and then moves on to distant cities and other nations, alternating between acting out the separation and its opposite.

During this trip, he is arrested by the police because, together with a group of protesters, he has damaged other people's possessions and property (he will later say in session that he had set fire to cars and unpaved the road, throwing stones at the police).

A dream from the first months of analysis seems exemplary in its linearity: *he is in the square in front of the main church in his hometown, a gathering place for many people, but no one notices him. Dino is anguished not to be seen as everyone plays in the snow in the square. Moreover, he is wearing dark glasses and sees poorly. He therefore climbs onto a moped nearby and drives off quickly. The police officers stop him and ask for his ID.*

In his associations, he comments that the police are always attracted to a certain way of dressing, like his. Yet he accentuates this messy, dirty way of dressing; in session, he appears somewhat scattered, and in the first few months of work, he often stands in stunned silence, causing me concern.

Moving, acting in order to be looked at, whilst also escaping the relationship with the other and with himself through acting out (taking the moped and escaping), and defining his identity in a dialectical situation, might be the themes of this dream. From the very beginning, therefore, the motives of his aggressive acting out are outlined: first and foremost, to mark a differentiation from the world of parental objects, keeping at bay the Oedipal objects that are feared as incestuous. The movements connected with being watched and looking (the dark glasses) appear more complex: on the one hand, his anger at never being seen seems evident (his parents are busy with his father's political activity), on the other, the refusal to look might have to do with the refusal to elaborate, to look at himself and his problems as well as at the other, which are basic elements for the elaboration of his identity.

Another of the elements glimpsed in his dream, even more so in his story, is the extent to which aggressive acting out defends him from depression or a more serious breakdown.

Aggression as a defence against depression

Alongside this functioning, Dino highlighted a profound depression that he finally found an opportunity to express in analysis, despite the fear it elicited. In fact, he was terrified of his passive aspects and of his homosexual fantasies, absolutely unconscious, which at first came alongside a difficulty in sexuality. These sexual difficulties and fear of homosexuality amplified and complicated his depressive states.

At the start of relationships with new girls, Dino had premature ejaculation, which, he was nonetheless able to overcome once the relationship was established, at least with certain girls.

Both aspects were projected onto one of his fraternal friends, with whom he went to live at some point, discovering that he had repeatedly attempted suicide and had homosexual fantasies.

Dino used many sessions to discuss the problems of the "other"; at that time, his violent acts greatly diminished, but he was utterly confused and lost. The depression was Marco's, as well as the homosexual fantasies, and even the suicide risk, which also frightened him greatly. These seemed entirely projected onto the friend, although it was possible to see and treat them without his being too frightened by them.

Later, the vicissitudes of a sick puppy who then died, and that his mother had not wanted to take care of, were of great importance in approaching his depressive, deadly aspects and in helping him separate from his parents. Dino followed this dog obsessively, at times tender when he was emotionally able approach it, at times aggressive when he was frightened by his emotions.

The puppy dies, and to Dino's great surprise, he weeps in session over the loss of this first acknowledged bond (girls were emotionally kept at bay). That death, as is often the case with bereavements at this age, marks a significant evolution for Dino, who for the first time rediscovers himself as fragile, and seems to touch upon the possibility of loss. The real experience, external mourning in this case, takes on special importance in that it reverberates an internal mourning process (one of the developmental tasks of adolescence), but precisely because it is real, this mourning is circumscribed and more easily handled.

In that same period, Dino is grappling with his identity-defining anguishes through the reworking of Oedipal themes and incestuous fantasies. These fantasies propel him into a stalemate. Seduced by his father's manipulative and charming ways, he is repelled by his mother, although her regressive aspects frighten him. Also, the fantasy of damaging and killing the woman and her female parts is equally frightening. Interestingly, all this is confirmed by the reality of his sexual difficulties, even though violence reconfirms his gender identity and confers a sense of virility. At this time, Dino tells me a dream that troubled him: *someone is looking at his ears, because his earring has created an infection. He passes in front of his parents' house and a woman draws his attention to something that has happened. Dino hears screaming. Worried that something might have happened, he goes inside and sees a shadow in the stairwell, a strange figure running away that anguishes him, a sort of hairy dwarf with long hair screaming hoarsely. Farther away, a middle-aged woman is injured and battered. Dino approaches, uncertain whether to rescue her or run after the dwarf. He is frightened. He helps her and realizes that she is older than she looks. He feels a sense of pity for the woman, but also for the dwarf, thinking how bad it must be to feel like this. On a wall, many windows of different shapes (which he describes) are set high and open onto a varied panorama, which he is able to see.*

He associates the dwarf with himself.

Indeed, both the session and the dream highlight several interesting aspects.

While on the one hand, the dwarf may represent a monstrous part of his self, I believe he also symbolises, with his stature, hoarse voice and hair, the bodily changes that have frightened Dino, as well as his defensive aggression towards his mother and turmoil as to identity. It seems to me, however, that this dream shows the extent to which a late adolescent can begin to open towards awareness, the varied emotions and their transformation, as represented by the differently shaped windows, by his feeling pity for the old woman and for himself, just when he feels tall enough to look out, by his feeling of embarrassment rather than shame.

Towards the possibility of thinking: the alternative to depressive breakdown

I suppose what allowed our work to continue was, especially in the beginning, the strong albeit unexpressed bond between us. Dino slowly learned to trust. He had a profound need for a welcoming, non-stern adult figure, but above all, he needed to feel there was a place that could contain him with his anguishes, even though he was unable to express them or even think about them. Analytic work, free association, that particular use of the mind that is one of the aims and acquisitions of effective analytic work, were certainly foreign to him, both because of his age and his type of functioning.

At first, of course, he missed many sessions, and when he then began to come, he would remain quiet for a long time. Slowly, Dino learned that he could communicate to me what he was thinking, when he could be aware of it. He thus began to communicate, after a long silence, what seemed like "waking dream flashes" [tr. by O.M.] (Bezoari & Ferro, 1994). He would tell me, for example, about an object he saw in front of him, or he might imagine an actual episode.

Needless to say, these episodes markedly challenged me, defining them diagnostically and finally moving towards overcoming them. During this period, the patient's aggressive acting out had been noticeably contained, which naturally caused an increase in his anxious experiences. Yet, Dino was determined to overcome them and had learned to use analysis, however primitively and concretely, and above all, had learned to trust. His functioning in this trans-formational phase can be seen in this excerpt from a session, after four years of work around the Easter holiday:

> After a long silence, he says: "Well, I imagine a girl asking me 'how old are you?' (he's about to turn twenty-one). Then I'm lying in the gardens of Villa ... and I hear music. Yesterday at Villa ..., there were three young men dressed like the characters of *A Clockwork Orange*. Drugged up as *Droogs*, with a codpiece, bowler hat and cane on the side".
>
> I comment: "I feel like you are telling me about your two souls", and I remind him of other sessions and a dream from a past session.
>
> He replies that a few days before, a friend of his had scolded him for being passive when a car had hit him, punched the driver and said: "Watch how it's done!".
>
> I comment that he is talking about a seemingly passive and perhaps blocked Dino who scares him, but perhaps he is also scared of the Dino – troublemaker and needlessly violent friend – who believes that being active and powerful equals being violent.

209

The patient recalls that today he is less aggressive, and just yesterday he was telling a friend that everyone has at least three or four people in their heads.

End of session.

In my experiences in session, I found the moments in which Dino communicated his daydreams-dreamlike flashes quite delicate, given that he was afraid and ashamed to manifest them.

In this particular session, the theme of his growing up emerges and terrifies him. The girl is a part of him, a girl who asks him to grow up and the analyst who challenges him.

It seems to me that *A Clockwork Orange* and "lying in the sun" are not only moments in his life, but also two personalities he was attempting to reconcile. Over time, it became most evident that he presented alternating moments of regression, which at first frightened him and were felt as helplessness, passivity, lack of thought or torpidity. He would emerge from these states with group-based acting out. With a sometimes vague political overtone, these acts were directed at feeling alive, active, virile and powerful, and counteracting the anguish of death and of not being seen, in relation to which he feared becoming and indeed did sometimes become, passive and torpid.

Whenever these very different aspects of him came into contact, Dino was anguished.

Conclusions

I believe Dino's case fittingly shows the extent to which antisocial acts were used to cope with a depressive breakdown that we very often brushed against in the long silences and deadly atmospheres of some sessions.

For patients like Dino, "acting out is the alternative to despair. Most of the time the patient is hopeless about correcting the original trauma and so lives in a state of relative depression or of dissociations that mask the chaotic state that is always threatening. When, however, the patient starts to make an object relationship, or to cathect a person, then there starts up an antisocial tendency" (Winnicott, 1984, p. 248).

In my clinical practice, I have observed patients for whom this aspect coexists with other, more undifferentiated levels. Such acting out serves to counteract unbearable passivisation and overcome a blockage in thinking, which is another powerful defence they implement. Often, the acting out is accompanied by a sense of omnipotence. According to Ladame (2006), in these situations, a sort of narcissistic invincibility is generated, paving the way for an explosive mixture of masochism and narcissism, and might I add, of more general self-destructiveness.

Both in its origin and in its maintenance, these kinds of symptoms deeply implicate the environment, both the family environment and the subsequent environment, be it treating institutions or psychoanalyst. One or both parents were unempathetic to the patient's needs, who replaced this lack of empathy with something we might subtly describe as false or deceitful, so much so that it sometimes fosters the development of a sort of double identity. The provocations of these patients are aimed at wanting to re-discuss this split at a specific point of rupture, and to stimulate the environment to do likewise, and sometimes these acts are communications of parental aspects that the child carries within without elaboration.

Every so often, we might encounter the repetition of actual trauma scenarios that might have the goal of forcing the original environment into different responses from those originally given.

Dissocial acting out therefore requires careful evaluation on a case-by-case basis to guide our clinical and therapeutic direction.

In my opinion, such defences acted out against depressive breakdown must be fully respected until we are certain, in treatment, that the patient's self is stronger, cohesive and stabilised. In fact, if we oppose such defences, or prematurely attempt to push the patient to criticise or renounce them (e.g., with massive, intrusive, early interpretations), the patient's self may not even withstand the impact of the deep depressive experiences. This can open a very dangerous scenario, ranging from suicide attempt to frank psychotic decompensation.

Too often, as analysts, we underestimate the weight of our interventions on the future evolution of our patients' personalities or even their lives as a whole. Interventions that may appear to be minor can have a major impact, while we should never forget that the symptom is the patient's economically best solution for survival, at least up to then. Such types of symptoms, as those described in Dino's case, should be understood and paradoxically respected at an early stage of the work, until we come to understand the underlying personality organisation, their usefulness at that stage of development, their place in the family environment, and eventually realise what the adolescent is moving towards. They must also be temporarily respected until the experience of being understood and welcomed has been established within the patient, until the adolescent has had the experience of a warm sharing relationship with a significant adult who can survive without retaliation, without being frightened of his or her acting out or even attacks.

Note

1 This paper is a reworking of my chapter "Antisocial acting-out as a defense against breakdown" presented at the international conference *The Psyche-Soma. From Paediatrics to Psychoanalysis. Donald W. Winnicott's Thought* (April 1997) and published in. M. Bertolini, A. Giannakoulas, M. Hernandez (Eds.), *Squiggle & Spaces: Revisiting the Work of D.W. Winnicott*, Vol. 2, Whurr Publishers, London-Philadelphia 2001, pp. 139–144. An Italian version was published in the book edited by myself: *Adolescenza e Violenza* [Adolescence and Violence] (Il Pensiero Scientifico, Rome 2009).

References

Bezoari, M. and A. Ferro (1994). Il posto del sogno all'interno di una teoria del campo. *Rivista di Psicoanalisi, 40,* 251–272.

Campbell, D. (2000). Violence as a defence against breakdown in adolescence. In I. Wise (Ed.), *Adolescence.* London: Routledge.

Fonagy, P. and M. Target (1997). *Attachment and reflective function: Their role in self-organization.* Cambridge University Press.

Jeammet, Ph. (1997). La violence à l'adolescence: Défense identitarie et processus de figuration. *Adolescence, 15,* 2, 1–26.

Ladame, F. (2006). Adolescenza e autodistruzione: Valutazione clinica e note teoriche. *Richard e Piggle, 14,* 2, 191–201.

Laufer, M. and M.E. Laufer (1984). *Adolescence and developmental breakdown: A psychoanalytic view.* London: Routledge, 1995.

Mitchell, S.A. (1993). *Hope and dread in psychoanalysis.* New York: Basic Books.

Nicolò A.M. (2006). I mille volti dell'aggressività in adolescenza [The many faces of aggression in adolescence]. *Richard e Piggle, 14,* 2, 120–131.

Novelletto, A. (2009). *L'Adolescente: Una Prospettiva Psicoanalitica* [The Adolescent: A Psychoanalytical Perspective]. Roma: Astrolabio.

Winnicott, D.W. (1950). Aggression in relation to emotional development. In (1958), *Through Paediatrics to Psycho-Analysis*. New-York: Basic Books, 1975.

Winnicott, D.W. (1969a). On "The use of an object". In *Psycho-Analytic Explorations*. London: Routledge, 1989.

Winnicott, D.W. (1984). *Deprivation and delinquency*. London: Routledge.

13

DELUSION, SECRETS AND RECIPROCITY [1]

It is my conviction that the psychotic symptom lies at the crossroads of issues that affect both the patient's internal world and external interactions, and that madness is never single. Indeed, with sufficient investigation, from the outset, it will appear to be a situation that includes at least one other in interaction with it.

The reflection I made with this patient, whom I called Alfredo, led me to believe that delusion should not fully be considered as a fracture of intersubjectivity, but instead, through it, the patient attempts to recreate a mode of interaction and relationship originally experienced, and which he or she carries as a level of functioning, potentially ever present and activatable. Moreover, through this operation and for communicative purposes, the patient attempts to persuade the other (and the analyst in session) to share the relationship that lies at the origin of the delusion, and to place him or her in this ancient location and particular functioning of his psychotic world.

Delusion, as some authors say, is not narrated in order to be shared; it is a rupture of intersubjectivity and of the dialogic dimension of communication. Clearly, psychoanalysts' views around delusion are markedly contrasting.

Rosenfeld for example, states that these patients live "entirely inside an object [...] suggesting that this hallucinatory world is a representation of the inside of an object, probably the mother" (Meltzer, personal communication, 1963, in Rosenfeld, 1987, p. 168). He goes on to say that "living inside the delusional object seems to be in strong opposition to relating to the outside world, which would imply depending on a real object." (*Ibid.*, p. 169). Of a different opinion are

DOI: 10.4324/9781032663371-16

other authors, with whom I agree, such as Jacobson (1971), who believed that Freud's observation, according to which psychotic patients renounce reality and replace it with a fantasy reality they create, was valid only in those cases in which reality does not lend itself to the patients' purposes and does not offer help in resolving their conflicts. The defensive function of delusion is also recognised (Pao, 1979) when the basic sense of security is threatened.

We know that traumatic situations that increase the state of internal tension to unbearable levels threaten the sense of cohesion of the self, and can result in different forms of regression and different uses of daydream,[2] to the point where the criterion of adaptation to reality is lost, and bizarre or almost frankly delusional content is manifested. However, in every individual, there remains the need, the urge, to make the internal fantasy agree and articulate with reality, and indeed persists insofar as reality permits.

After writing this paper, I read a work by Stolorow, which among others seems quite significant in supporting my position. In fact, he states that the psychotic patient seeks to elicit, through processes of delusional concretisation, "that responsiveness which he needs" [...] and that "to the extent that this archaic, validating intersubjective system is established, the delusions become less necessary and even disappear" (Stolorow et al., 1995, p. 171).

The existence of a core of delusion as pre-existing fantasy that resurfaces at times and as needed is discussed among numerous authors, albeit in somewhat modified form. Freud himself (1907, p. 323; 1937, pp. 551–552) acknowledges delusions' historical core of truth, as well as the existence of a preformed delusional idea, as a state within a state that does not conform to the demands of the real world.

Garcia Badaracco reports in psychotic patients dissociated pathological identifications that "organise as split parts of the mind" or that (even) "become part of a split unconscious" [tr. by O.M.] (Garcia Badaracco, 1989, p. 103). These pathogenic identifications, which some call alienating (Cahn, 1991; Faimberg, 1993), or narcissistic to emphasise the confusion between self and other, cause the psychotic individual to be constituted as a multiple personality that carries and displays in itself the effect of the other. Many authors, even of different orientations, emphasise the multiplicity of aspects or selves in the psychotic patient. Pao (1979), for example, reports temporary shifts from one aspect of self-continuity to another, even in chronic schizophrenics or patients who become physically ill. In the latter

215

situation, there is a shift towards the bodily self with the effect of a temporary period of freedom from psychosis (*Ibid.*, p. 248).

Thus, in the course of the sessions through the material the patient brings us, we might access his or her inner world, but also his or her intrusive and parasitic parental images. These may be perceived as a destructive foreign body, at times exercising absolute dominance over the ego (Jacobson, 1964). Further, we might also access the peculiar emotional and cognitive texture of the family interactions that have comprised the patient and in which he or she has participated, and which tends to be reproduced in the analytic relationship.

We might have an inkling in session of all such contents, through associations, or dreams or general verbal contents. Yet they may present themselves to us through acting out, somatic alterations, attacks or modifications of setting, enactments or our own unexplained counter-transferential, sensory, somatic or emotional experiences.

Because the peculiar emotional and cognitive texture of interactions was organised around a pattern of control, intrusion and submission in the family environment, the patient was deprived of the experience of both reciprocity and the ability to be alone in the presence of the other, experiences that would have allowed the constitution of a more or less stable sense of identity and cohesive self.

When environmental failure or intrusions are so massive to prevent even the constitution of a sector within the internal fantasy and alternative world with a defensive function (Modell, 1990; Rosenfeld, 1988, p. 61), we may witness varying degrees of disintegration and, in certain individuals, the constitution of a delusional secret identity that will bear the mark of these primitive and confusive relationships.[3]

When occasional trauma or unbearable experiences reintroduce the need to resort to such defences, if the patient is contained within a relationship and space that can be trusted, the manifestation of this fantasy world as well as the communication of delusional ideas may be an attempt to draw the analyst into this world, with the implicit possibility of opening to a new reciprocity.

Depending on the evolution of such an experience, the analytic pair has the possibility of transforming all or part of these delusional ideas into a shared or sharable narrative. I believe a case such as Alfredo's to be particularly useful: his story, the material presented and his recurrent crises, allow for more reflection than with other, more regressed or fragmented patients.

216

According to De Masi (2006, p. 285), "the psychotic state stems from damage to the functions, of which the subject is unaware, which are necessary for the maintenance of psychic life and which belong to the *emotional unconscious*. These functions, which are structured with the earliest mother–child relations, are essential to the working of the *dynamic unconscious*". By damaging the emotional unconscious, the use of repression is prevented and the psychotic disorder therefore lies on a different level than the dynamic unconscious, whose exploration is at the origin of neurosis. "As a result, [these patients] are unable to understand their own mental processes, and their dreams appear bizarre and meaningless" (*Ibid.*, p. 285). Further, psychosis itself represents an emotional trauma destined to damage the mental apparatus. When the delusional moment erupts, the delusional part creates a collusive complicity with the healthy part of the patient.

The case of Alfredo

I will focus on only a few aspects of the rather complex psychoanalytic treatment of this patient.

Alfredo comes from a *petit-bourgeois* family. He is prematurely neglected and soon learns to be autonomous partly because his parents are busy with their work and later, in his adolescence, because of the aggressive and destructive behaviours of his twin brother, with whom he was often confused. His mother, always supported by a mystical attitude bordering on delusion, was always cold and distant with an openly sexophobic and hysterically seductive attitude. The indifferent, distant and confused father is experienced by the patient as a liar and cheater. Alfredo suffers precocious abandonment, given that his mother is unable to care for him.

Alfredo's difficulties begin with a breakdown in late adolescence, when he begins entering marginal groups. Following this, therapeutic approaches are attempted, which Alfredo repeatedly discontinues.

Four months into the work, the colleague who sent him to me telephoned and suddenly told me a secret unknown to the patient himself: Alfredo was the child of an illegitimate relationship of his mother, yet, together with his other siblings, he had grown up unaware of this. I was hurt and disturbed by the irruption of the secret into the phone conversation, and into my mind. I merely had time to mumble something, thinking to myself that perhaps sooner or later the relatives would have to tell him, and that I certainly would have preferred not to know.

When he comes to analysis with me, the patient does not show signs of delusion, but he does use heavy drugs occasionally, gets drunk frequently and exhibits disordered and frequent sexual relations with women and men. Moreover, Alfredo often comes to the session with made-up eyes and feminine movements. He has never been in a stable romantic relationship. His job allows him to live in contact with rich and aristocratic people, so Alfredo imagines being able to achieve successful positions, yet these repeatedly founder from the start.

Alfredo reports playing sex games as a teenager and always being manipulated, touched, masturbated by various babysitters, even his father, "all taken by his beauty". Indeed, he is a handsome man with elegant features.

In the first few months of work (apart from testing the analyst's reaction to his oddity), Alfredo tells me about the theory he has constructed since adolescence, with which he attempts to explain himself and his story.

Indeed, he believes in reincarnation and makes assumptions about what other lives he has had in the past: a gambler, a man who committed some serious crime, a woman.

He is also convinced that he was miraculously saved as a child, when he was eight years old, by entities from another life, from a fall that would have caused his death. He believes he might even have overcome the moment of death and come back to life.

We return to this episode several times, given the marked confusion between fantasy and reality. These same themes will return in various ways throughout the analysis and present themselves during recurrent critical episodes of psychotic regression, with a delusional form and organisation. Certainly, there are two accompanying themes: the first is the disordered, confused and eroticised excitement with which, since childhood, he has sought to engage desperately with adults – and which he currently uses to enter into relationship with the other, concealing his anguish of physical and mental impotence; the second is death, with which he seems to be repeatedly playing on the edge with defiance, with cars or frequenting dangerous environments.

In the course of the sessions, Alfredo also broadly reports about a family novel he constructed as a boy, about being the son of another father. While I find the commonality with elements that are present in many adolescent daydreams, these communications disturb me in light of the secret that had been communicated to me.

Repetitive dreams begin to appear that recall a central topic: the construction of an identity.

I will give an example. In the first session of the week, in the third year of work, after informing me that it was his birthday but did not celebrate it, he reports a dream: *he is in the bathroom. His brother wants to kill him. He closed the bathroom door. His father finally informs him, "I will let you go unharmed and free as long as you go to a secret place and with a new identity". A wise old woman enters from a back staircase and shows him a way out through the rooftops to the square.*

He insists on the importance of separating emotionally from his brother, whom, moreover, he has not seen for some time.

In the dream, where I believe we note the hope the patient places in analysis (the old woman from the back staircase showing him the way out through the rooftops), themes about identity, secrecy and the need to construct new aspects of the self return with extraordinary coincidence. The theme of separation, and in general the relationship with his brother, his double, recurs in a dynamic of "who kills whom".

In another of the dreams reported in the session a short time later, for example, he dreams that his brother informed him that they had changed their last name, and with the new last name, they would no longer be able to return to the family home. I report the excerpt from the session.

Alfredo's tone is dull, as has been for some time.

He talks about the weekend he spent with R., a woman, who then left again. He recounts the dream: he was talking to his brother who told him that the two of them had changed their names. He was sorry because he likes his last name and even more his mother's last name. With the new name he would no longer be able to return to the family home because the doorman would not let him pass. He comments that it would be important to remember the last name, maybe it was something like "Vittoria" ["Victory", translator's note]. He talks about the fact that the doorman has been dead for a long time. The house is no longer theirs. The grandparents sold it for financial reasons. He spent a lot of time in that house when he was a child and his parents were away … .

Several meanings might be related to the dream in the session. One of the most noticeable ones, in my opinion, is the extent to which the attainment of a personal identity, corresponding to truer aspects of the self, would have imposed a separation from the familiar world and roots that the patient could not afford at that time.

Comment

Considering the transgenerational dimension, we might observe that these elements also refer to the structuring of the patient's identity from the beginning of his life, and even before the beginning, in the previous generation secret that involved him.

These elements, present yet inactive, reoccur in memory due to the centrality that identity reshaping processes take on in youth.

We know that the need to disidentify from primary objects finds a powerful obstacle in the presence of transgenerational elements, whether conceived as identificatory phantasms or as transgenerational secrets.

The existence of this secret, once again unknown to Alfredo, but present in the constitutive fabric of his identity, functioned by maintaining the primitive link with aspects of his parents, and preventing the constitution of a separate identity.

Even in the analytic process, in Alfredo's case there existed a secret that had arisen outside the setting, in the communication of the colleague. Indeed, this functioned, in countertransference, as an element of seizure of our reciprocity. On it, both I and the patient himself (he, again, unknowingly) were grappling with it, with its characteristics of intrusion, of paralysing surprise.

Through the intrusion of this secret, the relational and affective context that had characterised the global situation, namely, the patient and his family, was being re-actualised in transference in a powerful enactment.

In these years, we witnessed the resurgence of moments of psychotic regression that recurred three times, though progressively modifying themselves. Without fail, real or analytic events confronted the patient with pain or intolerable trauma every time.

In these episodes, the delusional themes that Alfredo carries with him from the beginning resurface, as can be seen in the last two episodes I now report.

Clinical fragment

After the summer holiday, in his fourth year of work, due to a long period of loneliness and after yet another repeated rejection by a woman, Alfredo draws on a cold we both have and informs me that important things must happen these days. On day "X", he must phone C. (a big screen star, beautiful, whom he does not know) because he knows he will have to meet her, as it is written in his destiny. His mother's life has weighed heavily on his. His mother exists in sacrifice and death, and that is where she can be met.

To my simple intervention underlining these reflections of his, Alfred recalls when as a child he ran away into the woods near his home. A voice told him: "You are about to die", he then opened his eyes and saw the precipice. Since then, his life has changed: the souls of the dead whom he is to meet in the house where C., the actress, now lives, protect him.

In the days following the onset of his crisis, Alfredo begins a sort of self-care consisting of urine-therapy: arrogantly, he informs me that he drinks his own urine to purify himself, and is very resistant to the idea of taking psychotropic drugs that may have been recommended by a trusted psychiatrist.

Realising that any interpretation or intervention that he may feel as conflicting with his ideas causes him violent reactions and/or possible acting out, I refrain from offering any, and in a calmer, more welcoming tone, I remain on my concerns about his difficulties, his sense of loneliness and emptiness.

During this period, Alfredo clearly spends his time at home and does not go to work. Progressively, the state of agitation and alarm subsides.

At this stage and in the following sessions, he himself retraces certain aspects of his life: the many times he has almost consciously defied death, motorcycle accidents or unprotected relationships with transsexuals, or the use of syringes that were most likely infected, having been used by prostitutes with AIDS. "In all these situations, the light protected him by preventing him from dying – so he went through the metal sheets without getting hurt" he says.

The spirits have been speaking to him and protecting him since he was a child. They have built for him "a whole way of thinking, they are part of his thinking".

In this, as in other episodes, Alfredo insists on convincing me of the validity of his claims, accusing me of being too rational and scientific if my answers appear to him to disagree, demanding explicit agreement with him.

In the following days, Alfredo is calmer, postponing the opportunity to phone C., the actress, to tell her that their meeting has been predicted since he was a child. He decides that he must become even purer and whiter to be able to talk with the souls of the afterlife in the castle.

From his communications in the various sessions, it was clear to me that the patient wanted to involve me in his delusion, making our relationship a sort of *folie à deux*.

In a certain sense, I sought to work on the crest of the delusion, given it is necessary for the patient, in my view, to feel that the contents of the delusion are accepted and acknowledged, as nuclei of historical truth, with caution against the risk of confusing collusion with the analyst.

I pointed out to him that if, on the one hand, he wants to talk to the spirits of the afterlife, on the other, he is currently talking to me, I am here and interested in his story.

I thus showed interest in both his narrative and the correlation of his narrative with his life and the analytic process. I therefore highlighted that he felt a destiny weighing on him that was beyond him, that in this destiny, his mother's story weighed on his own. Both in his life and in the analysis, he was seeking himself and the other, authentically. I was well aware that for this patient silence itself was experienced as persecutory rejection.

Consequently, in the relationship, it was crucial for Alfredo to feel the dimension of reciprocity, of emotional consonance, which allowed him the possibility to transformatively experience the primitive confusive relationship. This, of course, could accentuate the countertransferential problem, given my unrest around the secret that had been communicated to me. Therefore, my analytic identity was also in question. Moreover, Alfredo made me feel how unreachable other family members, and sometimes even the analyst, seemed to him.

This opened, in my countertransference, a sort of painful wound, in need of soothing, as if he felt I came from a distant and fortunate world, rich in affection and presence, as if he underestimated or did not see the analyst as the product of strenuous experiences as well, the fruit of long discipline.

It seemed to me then that he was relieved by my interpretation of his imagining me as an unreal figure, preventing him from grasping how sometimes, and for some psychoanalysts, the very choice of such a difficult profession could be the expression of arduous and conflicting experiences.

Of course, this attitude of the patient in later periods drifted into the fierce critique of the banality of ordinary life that I represented, especially when the difficulties of life made certain life goals unattainable to him.

In the following months, these contents slumbered. Alfredo seemed to resume his life along the usual regime, both in work and relationships.

At that time, we were able to address the issues related to his precocious need to provide for himself. He also further highlighted his parents' past incestual and confused attitude. Unconscious guilt emerged for his having been well physically, while his mother and other family members had had frequent problems.

This was also made possible by the emergence of an unspecified somatic disorder that drew attention to his body, which he did not take care of, but which allowed for his possible caregiving in the analytic pair.

In this atmosphere, supported by the analytic work, Alfredo continued his search for identity.

Secrets and reciprocity

Alfredo's story illustrates the bizarre and paradoxical entanglement and coagulation of internal issues and environmental reality, of phantasmatic content and affective interactions.

From the very beginning, a double register runs through Alfredo's internal world, the family's phantasmatic life, and the analytical relationship itself. A double register based on splitting and denial, as present in the marital couple, in the parental couple, in the phratry and within the patient himself. Alfredo, as any severe patient with moments of psychotic functioning, coagulates on himself in a paradoxical way two contradictory levels of his own and the family's functioning.

We might see these same contradictory levels recurring in the therapeutic relationship, as shown by the communication of the secret to the analyst who is subjected to in a transgression of the setting, and which functions as a seizure of reciprocity.

It would be erroneous to equate the secret or delusion with a lie, as some do. Lying presupposes a relationship of falsehood and bad faith. A secret, on the contrary, like delusion, refers to a core of historical truth.

Haydée Faimberg has dealt with a particular type of secrets that re-emerge in the psychoanalytic treatment of patients who present specific types of alienating identification, and who condense a transgenerational story, a phenomenon she calls "telescoping" (Faimberg, 1988; 1993).

The work of this psychoanalyst, as that of other French authors on the same topic (De Mijolla, 1981; Kaës et al., 1993), has proved to be enlightening on the theoretical level, particularly with regard to transgenerational transmission.

As Haydée Faimberg (1993, p. 116) illustrates, the countertransference-transference axis is central in patients with these problems. Indeed, the analyst is particularly emotionally implicated. There is, however, a difference between Alfredo's case and cases illustrated by Faimberg. In fact, in the latter, the analyst does not know the patient's secret that manifests through transference, and is brought to light for both patient and analyst with a surprise effect. In these situations, the analyst "must be able to contain […] the anguish of not knowing […] and of not knowing that he does not know" [tr. by O.M.] (*Ibid.*). In Alfredo's case, on the other hand, the analyst knew a secret unknown to the patient. Should she have communicated it to the patient? Would this not have been violence and intrusion? What right did the analyst have to intervene in this way within a person's story, moreover, a fragile person with a loosely cohesive identity?

On the other hand, would not communicating and keeping a secret have altered the analyst's spontaneity, her presence "without memory or desire"?

Indeed, I wondered how I could solve the problem of having become prisoner of a secret that threatened to paralyse, immobilise or deviate the countertransference from its natural evolution, and that reappeared in my eyes whenever, through dreams or associations, the patient, unconsciously aware (allow me this oxymoron) spoke of doubts around his identity or even just his family.

Certain dreams that the patient reported concerning issues of identity also appeared to possibly relate both to issues of the transgenerational secret, and to those of the confusion of self and identity that the patient's pathology presented and the analytic work stimulated.

With respect to all this, I initiated cautious interpretations that highlighted Alfredo's desire to investigate himself, his origin and his birth. Even so, as a response to such interpretations, quite often he would return to focus on current issues, showing himself completely oblivious to anything else, and indeed sometimes irritated by what he experienced as cautious insistence on issues that he felt were confusingly foreign or incomprehensible.

A specific technical problem therefore arose with regard to extra-analytic communication. The latter could have been considered akin to an error of technique, although in some ways unavoidable. But we may ask whether this alleged type of error had any utility. In some ways, a fact that might otherwise have been considered un-elaborable and therefore likely to call into question the analytic work itself, was being reproduced in the transference. On the other hand, this repetition-reedition in the transference was a natural product of Alfredo's own functioning. It placed the analyst in the process on par with the patient in his life and story in a paradoxical position for which any solution would prove impossible, capable of threatening the very identity of the subject.

Yet it is precisely the intrinsic characteristics of this event that laid the groundwork for the transformability of the patient and of his delusional cores.

Slowly, the idea was making its way into the analyst's mind that the relevant event in this situation was not so much the existence of the secret, but the fact that a context, where the seizure of reci-procity was repeated and perpetuated, had come to be recreated in the analytic situation and transference.

We could define this situation as an imposing enactment that the patient had conveyed, and that demanded a resolution by presenting itself anew in the transference situation.

We know today of the importance of using enactment to help the patient who carries unknown or unrepressed traumatic memories.

Secrets and communication

The pathogenicity of secrets must be located within another aspect.

In the 1963 essay *Communicating and not Communicating* Winnicott explicitly puts forward the meaning of secrets as an area of the self. He makes a distinction between simple non-communication as a resting stage and active or reactive non-communication. It is within this process that the possibility of communicating silently and secretly with subjective objects is structured; the latter event which, according to Winnicott, brings a sense of what is real and must periodically reappear to restore balance.

The possibility of structuring a secret dimension of the mind goes hand in hand with the ability to be alone, and is genetically related to the child's experience of reciprocity with the mother. Hence, the paradoxical quality of the self's secret dimension, arising from the possibility of being alone in the presence of another, is defined. Therefore, through the attribution and sharing of meaning with the other, the secrecy of the inner world and fantasy is structured.

Yet, it is of the utmost importance to distinguish the secret space of the self, the protective dimension of secrecy, from the pathological secret.

The relationship between reciprocity and secrecy is crucial in defining the damaging or constructive quality of a secret. As is now well known, we might say that the issue is not so much the content of the secret, nor its presence or absence in the family or individual, given that every family and every individual has psychologically organised a part of the self around a secret. Let us think, for example, of the secret and mysterious space of the primal scene, or the true secret and incommunicable self of each individual. In this regard, it is worth mentioning that there are also certain patients who fabricate false secrets, precisely to compensate for the lack of an internal personal space, and that these false secrets sometimes maintain fragments of the subject's identity, preventing him or her from regressing into a psychotic catastrophe.

Unlike the healthier relationship where the child's experience of reciprocity with the mother goes hand in hand with the ability to be alone and structure a secret dimension of the mind, pathological dimensions are characterised by the creation or perpetuation of a secret, as a dissociated and hidden aspect.

To specify, what is pathological and pathogenic is the sequestering function rather than the object of the secret (Nicolò, 1996b), the taking away of something from a potential space where an elaborative reciprocity can be established between the ego and the other, and between the ego and oneself. In this way, the traumatic repetition of the consequences of the first event is perpetuated, and time stops. One might also witness the establishment of a dual representational register, one of which relates to the secret and the sequestered reality it represents. The continuous parallel coexistence of these two registers within the family and within the subject creates the perpetuation of a state of cleavage that is difficult to overcome. This is due to the fact that an integration would presuppose the possibility for the subject to integrate an alienating and sequestered aspect that does not belong to his or her story, and that he or she has never known personally. To use Alfredo's own words to describe certain states of mind, when he is able to reflect on what is happening to him: "it's like taking a punch from someone without even seeing the punch. Like when a cup falls and breaks, but you can't see anyone dropping it".

Delusion and reciprocity

Delusional ideas therefore define a point and a way of meeting between these two registers given the inability of the patient's mind, but also of family members, to think around those areas that are trans-generationally unthought or unthinkable.

Delusional ideas are – as Alfredo says – "a real alternative way of thinking" that sustains his identity and has functioned in parallel with his other identities from the beginning. As pointed to by urine-therapy (the feeding of his own products albeit of rejection, which according to certain interpretive models could represent a substitute for the milk he did not receive), the emergence of delusional ideas also represents one of the patient's ways of stabilising himself at a time in which his structure is threatened by possible change (many authors mark this function of delusion, such as Giovacchini, 1986). Furthermore, these ideas, or intuitions or constructions, have accompanied Alfredo since childhood, providing him with a subsidiary identity and, moreover, one that is paradoxical in nature; an identity that his family story robbed him of from the start. Clearly, there had always been debate and conflict between these delusional ideas and the healthier part of his personality. Nonetheless, Alfredo was to cope with the imposing anguish produced by the frustrating encounter with the other, or by contextual changes, as in Alfredo's case, when the breaking of the relationship with the girl and the occasional interruption of analysis had precipitated a situation of tension and anguish.

It is likely that the anguished experiences of separation and severance of the link had brought back to the surface in Alfredo's memories of unthinkable traumas, whose traces could be found in that psychotic episode in transference.

In numerous works, but particularly in *The Mother-Infant Experience of Mutuality* (1969), Winnicott emphasises the special features of schizoid or psychotic transference: "these follow traumas in the area in which the baby (for healthy development) must be able to take reliability for granted, the area that is almost covered by an extended use of the term 'holding'" (*Ibid.*, p. 260).

227

In this regard, it is important to point out, given the pervasive use this term has had to the extent that its specific connotations have been lost, that according to Winnicott the term refers not to a benevolent and generic welcoming attitude, but rather to a peculiar experience of emotional resonance between mother and child, and between analyst and patient, which he calls "mutuality". Winnicott defines this mutuality as arising from cross-identifications and with "significance greater than that which is usually called 'object-relating'" (*Ibid.*, p. 256). I believe the term "mutuality" to be analogous to the term 'reciprocity' that I have used throughout this chapter, and very much akin to Stern's "emotional consonance".

I am therefore referring to a complex process, as inferred in Winnicott's work, characterised by intercommunication between patient and analyst, both silently and explicitly, and which allows for the realisation of that capacity for emotional consonance, mutuality, reciprocity that the patient needs, and that was lacking in early traumatic experiences.

I believe that in the reactivation[4] of delusion, the patient attempts to recreate an originally experienced relational model that he or she has always carried as one possible level of functioning. Through this operation and for communicative purposes, he or she attempts to introduce the Other into the psychotic level of functioning of his or her world and to make the analyst relive it with him or her.[5] After all, in Alfredo's case, from the beginning of the analysis, a dynamic of sequestration had also been proposed in transference through the communication of the secret to the analyst. That is, the transference concerned the global situation that had characterised Alfredo since birth, and was peculiar to the phantasmatic functioning of that family.

Faced with the experience of a loss of reciprocity, functioning in the here and now as further trauma, the patient attempts to recover his old "illusion of unity with the other", the original expression of the only relational mode he could experience, which was emotional subjection to the other. This may be experienced by the observer as a retreat into another space or time, yet it always implies a communicative offer, to the observer himself. Indeed, the delusional person always tries to convince the other of the veracity of his or her assertions and to involve him or her in the same *folie à deux* that had characterised the original relationship between the patient and his or her object.

Alfredo thus talks to the dead, pursues the idealised encounter with the actress, as the feminine and mad part of himself, as the mother and as the mad and hidden part of the analyst.

Through this operation, he also keeps the encounter and unity with the mother alive by counteracting fate and actualising her megalomanic fantasies.

In delusion, he therefore becomes the saviour of the mother's family and of the mother herself.

This level of functioning can be reactivated whenever occasional events in real and emotional life jeopardise the cohesion of the Self by opening the way to possible regression, catastrophe and unbearable pain. The hypothesis we might then put forward is that delusion can serve a dual function. On the level of internal economy, the phantasmatic function is diverted under the influence of dissociation, becoming in some ways "a filling activity intended to fill a fundamental void" [tr. by O.M.] (Green, 1977, p. 73), or to compose, as in Alfredo's case, the gap between two internalised registers expressing two paradoxically opposed patterns of functioning. On another level, the delusion represents the patient's attempt to recreate a communicative possibility with the other, specifically with the analyst. On the one hand, this repeats the old relationship, yet on the other, it paves the way to a transformative possibility, a new possibility that arises from experiencing a new relationship of reciprocity, consonance and mutuality, experienced before it is elaborated, never experienced before or experienced in a distorted or unreliable way.

Conclusions in retrospect

Work as psychoanalysts and psychotherapists involves us as individuals who participate with their insights, emotions, feelings and story in the shared construction of a co-created and creative experience. With patients such as Alfredo, the analyst must pay special attention to the languages through which the unrepressed unconscious is expressed, through which buried traumatic memories are conveyed. At times, the work is even more complex and meaningful, given that together with the patient, the analyst must not only discover but even create the emotional unconscious for those patients who have suffered such early trauma that has resulted in ego distortions and changes in the structure of thought (Levine et al., 2013).

229

In the 1949 work, *Mind and its Relation to the Psyche-Soma*, Winnicott distinguishes two types of memories: those that are thinkable in that the child has not suffered excessive interference from the environment, and another type of memories: the unthinkable ones. The latter due to traumatic impingement by the environment when the child is unable or not yet ready to deal with them. These constitute an interference for the continuity of being and are "catalogued" as frozen, waiting for the hope of transformation to open. Winnicott asserts that everything that happens to us is remembered on the emotional and bodily levels.

Thinking back today to my work with Alfredo, and my elaboration written in the 1997 article and reported here with small changes, I might add that the mistake of the colleague who had communicated to me the secret of Alfredo's birth had been an unconscious communication that Alfredo and his environment had unconsciously acted out by relocating me back into the atmosphere of secrecy, of unspoken and of lies that had characterised Alfredo since birth, and that had so largely influenced his identity disorder and delusion.

A curious environmental enactment had been produced. Even Alfredo's dreams, incredibly explicit around the secret of his birth, dreams about changing his last name or being expelled from his father's house, told something that his unrepressed unconscious knew, without knowing. I myself was placed in the position of his parents who knew, but hid the truth. As mentioned, today we know that everything that happens to us is remembered on both the emotional and bodily levels. Klein herself (1952), with her extraordinary intuitive ability, spoke of memories in feelings. With these patients, we are now gradually discovering the importance of emotional consonance, which Stern (1985) describes as attunement. Winnicott holds it is an irreplaceable praesidium in the case of those patients who have been deprived of the experience of creating the world due to the failure of the primary environment, and he also adds that analytic work should allow the discovery, within transference, of early experiences that were missing or distorted in the patient's past. It would be illusory to believe that reciprocity is achieved through a single interpretation, however accurate, relevant and timely. Rather, we are referring to a set of cognitive and emotional interventions of the analyst accompanied, for example, by attitudes and states of mind concerning (as seen here) the analyst's overall emotional experience. In this sense, it rather pertains to the

230

level of what Winnicott calls "'silent communication', namely, communication [that] only becomes noisy when it fails" (Winnicott, 1963c; Winnicott, 1969, p. 259), communication that is respectful of the patient's resources and that does not impose on him or her a maturity beyond his or her strength.

Notes

1 This article was presented at the *Psychosis* Panel of the 40th IPA Congress *Psychoanalysis and Sexuality* (Nicolò, 1997, Barcelona) and was published in this form in the *Revista de Psicoanalysis* de Madrid in 2001 (Delirio, secreto y reciprocidad, *Revista de Psiconalisis*, No. 34, pp. 71–86, Madrid, 2001). I present it here re-elaborated.

2 It is necessary to reconsider the function of delusion in light of that of fantasy and daydreaming. Particularly important is what the Sandlers called "the gyroscopic function of unconscious fantasy", in order to maintain individual balance and promote adaptation (Sandler & Sandler, 1986, pp. 111–124).

3 An Italian psychoanalyst, Ezio Izzo, distinguishes in schizophrenic psychoses a negative and a productive state, pointing out that although "psychotic states are substantiated by a failure of introjective processes [...] productive psychoses with the various types of delusions are instead to be related to an intrusive introjection" [tr. by O.M.] (1994, p. 168).

4 As Pazzagli notes, unlike memories, which are formed in a new way albeit "reorganising material that is already present" [tr. by O.M.] (Pazzagli, 1997, p. 90), delusion draws on an almost unchanged origin and compelled repetition from a sort of archive where, due to the un-elaborability of affects, experiences are stored.

5 In an interesting discussion in the journal *Interazioni*, Racamier argues that delusion is "an attempt to resume the relationship with the object that had previously been lost" and "a channel to think again" [tr. by O.M.] (Racamier, 1994, p. 106).

References

Cahn, R. (1991). *Adolescence et Folie: Les Déliaisons Dangereuses*. Paris: P.U.F.

De Masi, F. (2006). *Vulnerability to psychosis: A psychoanalytic study of the nature and therapy of psychotic state*. London: Routledge, 2009.

De Mijolla, A. (1981). *Les Visiteurs du Moi: Fantasmes d'Identification*. Paris: Les Belles Lettres.

Faimberg, H. (1988). The telescoping of generations: Genealogy of certain identifications. *Contemporary Psychoanalysis*, *24*, 99–117.

Faimberg, H. (1993). À L'écoute du télescopage des générations: pertinence psychanalytique du concept. In R. Kaës *et al.* (Eds.), *Transmission de la Vie Psychique entre Générations*. Paris: Dunod.

Freud, S. (1907). Delusions and dreams in Jensen's *Gradiva*. *S.E.* 9: 1–96, London: Hogarth Press.

Freud, S. (1937). Constructions in analysis. *S.E.*, 23: 255–270, London: Hogarth Press.

García Badaracco, J.E. (1989). *La Comunità Terapeutica Psicoanalitica di Struttura Multifamiliare*. Milano: Franco Angeli.

Giovacchini, P.L. (1986). Structural and therapeutic considerations. In D.B. Feinsilver (Ed.), *Towards a comprehensive model for schizophrenic disorders: Psychoanalytic essays in memory of Ping-Nie Pao*. Hillsdale: Analytic Press.

Green, A. (1977), Il regno appartiene al bambino. In V. Bonaminio and A. Giannakoulas (Eds.), *Il Pensiero di Winnicott*. Roma: Armando, 1982.

Izzo, E.M. (1994). Ruminazione e imitazione: Modelli arcaici dei fenomeni deliranti. In M.L. Mascagni *et al.* (Eds.), *Studi sul Pensiero di Eugenio Gaddini*. Chieti: Métis Editrice.

Jacobson, E. (1964). *The self and the object world*. New York: International University Press.

Jacobson, E. (1971). *Depression: Comparative studies of normal, neurotic, and psychotic conditions*. New York: International University Press.

Kaës, R. *et al.*, Eds. (1993). *Transmission de la Vie Psychique entre Générations*. Paris: Dunod.

Klein, M. (1952). On observing the behaviour of young infants. In (1975) *The Collected Works of Melanie Klein*, Vol. III: *Envy and Gratitude and Other Works*, 1946–1963. London: Routledge, 2007.

Levine, H.B., G.S. Reed, and D. Scarfone, Eds. (2013). *Unrepresented states and the construction of meaning: Clinical and theoretical contribution*. London: Routledge.

Modell, A.H. (1990). *Other times, other realities: Toward a theory of psychoanalytic treatment*. Cambridge, MA: Harvard University Press.

Nicolò, A.M. (1996b). Travail du rêve et secrets de famille. *Groupal, 2*, 123–134.

Nicolò, A.M. (1997). Delirio, secreto y reciprocidad. *Revista de Psicoanálisis de la Asociación Psicoanalítica de Madrid, 2001*, 34, 71–86.

Pao, P.-N. (1979). *Schizophrenic disorders: Theory and treatment from a psychodynamic point of view*. New York: International University Press.

Pazzagli, A. (1997). Deliri, costruzioni e verità. *Psicoanalisi, 1*, 1, 89–100.

Racamier, P.-C. (1994). Lo psicoanalista davanti alle psicosi e alla famiglia. *Interazioni, 1994*, 1, 103–110.

Rosenfeld, D. (1987). *Impasse and interpretation: Therapeutic and nntitherapeutic factors in the psychoanalytic treatment of psychotic, borderline, and neurotic patients*. London: Routledge.

Rosenfeld, D. (1988). *The psychotic: Aspects of the personality*. London: Karnac Books.

Sandler, J. and A.M. Sandler (1986). The Gyroscopic function of unconscious fantasy. In D.B. Feinsilver (Ed.), *Towards a Comprehensive Model for Schizophrenic Disorders: Psychoanalytic Essays in Memory of Ping-Nie Pao*. Hillsdale: Analytic Press.

Stern, D.N. (1985). *The interpersonal world of the infant: A view from psychoanalysis and developmental psychology*. New York: Basic Books.

Stolorow, R.D., B. Brandchaft, and G.E. Atwood (1995). Treatment of psychotic states. In *Psychoanalytic treatment: An intersubjective approach*. New York: Routledge.

Winnicott, D.W. (1949). Mind and its relation to the psyche-soma. In (1958), *Through paediatrics to psycho-analysis*. New-York: Basic Books, 1975.

Winnicott, D.W. (1969). The mother–infant experience of mutuality. In *psychoanalytic explorations*. London: Routledge, 1989.

Winnicott, D.W. (1963c). Communicating and not communicating leading to a study of certain opposites. In (1965) *The maturational processes and the facilitating environment: Studies in the theory of emotional development*. London: Routledge, 1990.

14

THE TRANSGENDER ENIGMA

In my clinical experience, I have observed a number of adolescent patients who defined themselves as transgender or reported a gender choice that was different from the ordinary one: gender queer, gender fluid, a–gender or nonbinary choices, or rejection of sexuality. In these choices was encapsulated the avoidance of an archaic psychotic core, or the escape from the image of an internal monstrous child they hated and wanted to undo. These young people had not lost touch with reality: they went to school or worked, had a social life and sometimes exhibited sensitivity and empathy, however, the reality they dissociated or denied was that of their bodies. In other rare cases, however, these were patients in whom a massive traumatic influence, both individual and environmental, probably so old as to have influenced their growth, was evident. In these cases, one could assume a traumatic influence of such enormous magnitude and at such an early age, as to have had a bearing of some nature on the settlement of the psyche in the body, in short, a storage in their body such as that which recent research has shown us in trauma patients (Leuzinger-Bohleber, 2008).

Solms (2016) pinpoints a disturbance in the prenatal period with respect to the masculinisation or feminisation of the brain. For these patients, I firmly believe there is no other solution but to respect them deeply in their decision, and remain willing to support them throughout a difficult and painful journey. Finally, we cannot disavow the existence of a type of transgender choice around which there is much debate today. In the words of Domenico Di Ceglie, these people have made it possible "to define a new area of human development where the subjective experience of being female or male did not coincide with the physical appearance of the body." (Di Ceglie, 2018, p. 4).

 DOI: 10.4324/9781032663371-17

The PDM itself has declassified the transgender condition from the list of pathologies, and today, many consider nonconforming gender identity as "normal variants of human expression" (Lingiardi, McWilliams, Speranza, 2020).

With the cultural debate that has ensued, with what some have called a transgender emergence (Lev, 2004), they have stimulated the idea that we must distinguish being a woman or a man from the "feminine" or "masculine" characteristics that "are constitutive elements far beyond biological sex" (Sprinz Mondrzak, 2019), though not detached from it.

Winnicott (1971b) was perhaps the first to attempt to distinguish these characteristics by attributing the feminine to being, and the masculine to doing, by establishing an initial undifferentiation between body and world, and by considering gender a psychic component that is distinct from sex and influenced by environment. All such matters, these identities in their multiplicity and multiformity, in their biological but also cultural origins, particularly challenge psychoanalysis, which is fortunately characterised by a wealth of different models and paradigms among them, some of which reveal a great capacity for transformation and growth. In this case, new fields of investigation and research are opened, respecting the great Freudian discovery of psychic bisexuality, which had caused such scandal at the time, also considering that, as Paola Marion (2017) notes, even according to Freud the development of sexual identity is posed *ante litteram* in a constructivist way.

In these phenomena, we find some of the most relevant challenges posed to certain models of psychoanalysis. We ask, for example, how far we can continue to affirm the structuring role of Oedipal identifications, or what is the sense of limit and splitting between male and female in the constitution of the sense of identity. The emergence of these phenomena and the debates they trigger are also connected to an increased cultural acceptance of a polymorphous, multifaceted sexuality that is also a measure of our acceptance of limit, of foreignness, and not only, of our democracy and tolerance. Marc Augé (1994), speaking of the forms of identity dissolution, said that "identity fades as the attitude of tolerating difference disappears" [tr. by O.M.] (*Ibid.*, p. 10).

Nonetheless, it must be very clear to the clinician that these are patients who pose relevant clinical issues and complexities in differential diagnosis.

Some reflections on gender identity

I will now attempt to retrace a number of works, beginning with Freud, that might help us better understand the topic of gender identity. Freud admitted the complexity of the constitution of gender identity: "We are accustomed to say that every human being displays both male and female instinctual impulses, needs and attributes" (1930, p. 53, note 3) and, in 1923, he had also rediscussed his early conception of the Oedipus complex by illustrating the potentiality of a bisexual orientation in all human beings (Freud, 1923a).

Stoller distinguished sex from gender, connoting sex biologically and gender psychologically and culturally. He affirmed that gender identity depends not only on anatomy but is also conditioned by environment: parents, siblings and context (Stoller, 1968, pp. 72–74). As an extension of Stoller's positions, thirty years later, a strong position also emerged among psychoanalysts, especially those most closely associated with the American feminist movement, which states that gender identity is almost exclusively a product of cultural construction (Dimen & Goldner, 2002). In short, gender is acquired prematurely in early family interactions and is assigned, an ongoing assignment and a sort of prescription.

In studying transgender individuals, Saketopoulou goes further and states that gender is "a viable subjective reality" (2014, p. 776). This strong statement implicitly denies the indissoluble soma–psyche integration and contradicts the very Freudian claim according to which the ego is first and foremost a bodily ego. And yet, the many changes we witness today prompt us to revisit certain concepts. Galatzer-Levy, one of the authors who has most extensively studied this issue, states that the assumption that sexual orientation is stable throughout life is a fallacy, reporting numerous cases of crises of orientation in adults or in middle age (Galatzer-Levy & Cohler, 2002). According to this author, it is not only orientation that can change, but also the meaning associated to gender identity. Indeed, this is what the adolescent analyst observes time and again in the adolescent's struggle to achieve this acquisition, also making use of a variety of defences.

Identity is not baggage that we carry intact from the beginning of life to death. It gradually changes based on our encounters and the demands of life, although there is an original core, and we are also active co-constructors of it. Hence, there is a processual component in the constitution of identity, as well as an active participation of the subject in its construction (as a couples analyst, I have seen how shared functioning in the couple may reinforce or instead deny the gender identity of each partner, and may also partially reabsorb homosexual orientations of the couple members).

Furthermore, there exist a number of cultural influences that currently weigh on this process. The impulse to externalise one's inner world, exhibiting one's intimacy or voyeuristically feeding on that of the other, the possibility of overcoming limits that in the past were defined by the biological, by the body, are some of the aspects that characterise the world of adolescents and, indeed, we might say of our entire culture. Above all, sexuality in its various articulations is perhaps the mirror where these themes merge and clash. The idols of the young and not-so-young show us exhibited ambiguous images that capture us, precisely because of their undifferentiation. Prince, Michael Jackson and Harry Styles are some examples.

Today, we are faced with more frequent and massive phenomena of what Freud called the *reactivation of the polymorphous-perverse functioning* that is typical of adolescence, and which also presents itself with the possible presence of bisexual confusions. The use of perverse manoeuvres is one of the usually transient solutions that are present in adolescence and used in the most problematic situations. Confusion around gender identity can result in momentary or definitive choices involving, among others, object choice.

As far as object choice is concerned, to avoid dramatic confusions, it is necessary to distinguish it from gender identity, and to clearly define that there are homosexual choices that are normal, and that the person reaches at the end of adolescence. The World Health Organization has declassified homosexuality from the list of pathologies or paraphilias. However, just as there are apparent heterosexual choices that are a defence or denial of an underlying homosexual functioning, there are also homosexual choices that show immature functioning, or are defensive, and do not arise from an adult object choice. In some cases, I have observed in treatment the homosexual choice as an expression of a primitive bond with the mother, which never evolved. What is called "primary homosexuality" has a decisive weight in this case, and it is not uncommon in the experiments that adolescents make, and indeed it can sometimes even prove helpful along the journey towards self-definition. It might be considered parent to that homoerotic identificatory love that Jessica Benjamin (1995) speaks of, which serves

237

the child in reinforcing the self, yet it stems from the need to narcissistically confirm oneself in one's identity rather than an expression of an object choice towards the other. I have encountered this kind of homosexual choice as the end of a long and torturous struggle that an adolescent or young adult makes in defining his or her identity and avoiding breakdown.

Sexual orientation, sexual identity, gender identity and gender role are different and non-overlapping concepts. Moreover, a psychologically correct approach would suggest the use of the plural: there are numerous homosexualities, just as there are numerous heterosexualities, and also gender identity presents fluid aspects and dissociated parts to be taken into account, even following Freud's (1905) futuristic position that affirmed *the normative abnormality of sexuality*. Having clarified these points, which I believe are essential, I will now return to the topic of this chapter: the transgender enigma.

The blurring of the distinction of gender identity is a theme that is present not only among adolescents, but in society as a whole. From these perspectives, anatomy no longer seems to be destiny. Everyone constructs their own gender idiom for themselves. One can look in the mirror and recognise, or construct oneself, differently from how one was born. Internet sexuality is paradigmatic of these aspects: in it, the real body is excluded, and the adolescent can experience himself or herself in varied and conflicting identity configurations, from being a man or a woman, having a homosexual or heterosexual orientation, to being an adult or an adolescent and so forth.

The importance of accurate diagnosis

It is complex and problematic to be faced with an adolescent who shows, by varied and different communications, that he or she does not recognise himself or herself in his or her own sexed body, or that he or she hates and feels alien to his or her own genitals or to all the gender-related characteristics with which he or she seems to have been born and raised up to that point. The easiest response is to rush the issue by asserting that that adolescent, male or female, is psychotic or has a psychotic core. Unfortunately, this simplistic judgement is dangerous: statistics have testified to a vast increase in these phenomena, and warned us about the frequency of suicide attempts in these patients, before any sex-change surgery if they cannot perform it, but also afterwards if they realise they made a mistake.

Therefore, the challenge for the clinician is imposing: disentangling the various and differing transgender phenomena, distinguishing the transgender who expresses a profound dissociation between sex and gender from those who after careful and prolonged assessment turn out to be compensatory solutions to a possible breakdown, given that clinging to the body represents the deepest anchor and identity issues may often take on the guise of gender confusion.

This is no easy assessment, given that those who argue for a specific transgender identity, even assuming a biological fact, cite the presence of cases with an onset in very early childhood, for example, around the age of three. Yet some statistical studies (Steensma et al., 2013) show that if the onset is early, for example in kindergarten, only 15–25% persist in this choice. In contrast, those who display dysphoria for the first time in adolescence maintain their choice over time.

This distinction is especially crucial for therapeutic purposes, given that, in transgender identity, "mourning the fact that their natal body does not fluidly map onto their gender is a crucial part of the therapeutic process" (Saketopoulou, 2014, p. 781).

There is no doubt, however, that the body represents the core of reality, and misrecognition of the body represents a misrecognition of the first and most foundational reality that characterises us. The consequences of this misrecognition can be at times far-reaching, such as when the body becomes a persecutor, to be hated and killed or negated.

Nevertheless, it is also true that, as Merleau-Ponty (1945) argued, the body is the subject of itself but the object of the other, and the image of the body that comes from the gaze of the other and of ourselves on the self enters into the constitution of this specific internal object. Eglé Laufer (2002) holds that the body is an internalised object that refers to the individual's love relationship with his or her mother, but that it exists in continuity with the body image based on sensory experiences, and the image that others send back to him or her. From the beginning, as in some ways Winnicott asserted, the body we carry within us is also the result of interaction with the other. Alessandra Lemma argues that body image disorders may be "culturally norma-tive and not manifestations of individual pathology" (2010, p. 19; Lemma and Lynch, 2015).

We are thus faced with quite a dilemma that every psycho-therapist must try to solve given that, as Saketopoulou cautions us, there may be a risk of colluding with the patient's unconscious fantasy and the denial it operates of one's sex, but also, on the contrary, there may be the risk of drastically pathologising this choice, calling it a "negation of the biological datum" [tr. by O.M.] (Preta, 2019), even though it is inevitably a "dissociation between the body datum and the psychic representation of one's sex" [tr. by O.M.] (Thanopulos, 2019). In all such cases, we would deny the terrible anguish that accompanies these people, misunderstanding their struggle to exist.

Two questions seem to underlie these issues, as is well illustrated in the volume *Treating Transgender Children and Adolescents: An Interdisciplinary Discussion*, edited by Jack Drescher and William Byne (2013):

- Do transgender children and adolescents suffer from a psychiatric disorder, or can their gender identity and gender role be considered a normal variant of gender expression?
- Should priority be given to intervention to help them accept the body they were born into, or should parents, educational institutions, physicians and psychologists go out of their way to meet their desire for transition?

If we bring these questions back to the topic of this book, namely, developmental ruptures, we must ask: is it the pubertal conflict that produced the gender issue as defence and shell, through which the patient defends himself or herself from decompensation? Or instead, is it a deep gender identity core that produced the pubertal conflict and the hatred of the sexed body, in which the patient does not recognise himself or herself?

From clinical practice

Starting from the examination of two clinical cases, I will attempt to reflect on the differential diagnosis that needs to be made in these cases, as well as emphasise the extent to which the compensatory choice of gender can avoid personality breakdown.

Carolina[1]: avoiding psychotic risk

Carolina begins psychotherapy for cutting at the age of fourteen. She has very irregular periods, and the hated menstruation freezes for up to three months, fuelling her hope that it will never return. Carolina is an only child. Her mother, who comes from a family of intellectuals, has always been strict and unfeminine. Her father, who has humbler origins, is overweight and shows impatience as well as a sense of inferiority towards his wife, although upon closer examination, he appears distant and tyrannical. The parents took much care of school and physical health, rather than of emotional aspects. Carolina feels at the centre of a tug-of-war and does not want to resemble either parent, hating in her body what reminds her of both her father and mother.

From the beginning, she presents herself dressed mostly in black and rock band T-shirts. Her style, she declares, is "between punk and hippy". Of course, she struggles to accept sessions, to which she shows up silent, offended and irritated. She loves music that speaks of alienation from a world in which she does not know whether to feel like a "rejected idiot or a superior being". The adolescent's arduous search for an identity appears from the outset as a critical element, to which Carolina attempts to respond, initially, with membership in a social and political group, by which, however, she will never feel fully accepted. She will then move on to questioning her sexual orientation and then again, her gender identity. Carolina recounts in session: "I have decided to use male pronouns and adjectives to talk about myself ... You have to call me that, too", she tells the analyst (for the past few weeks she has begun to dress in a more masculine way and says she uses breast binders).

She says: "I am gender queer". Gender queer[2] are "those who do not believe in gender binary, but in gender neutral". "For me, the best is when they don't understand whether I am male or female".

"I'm also participating in a blog where there are many others like me [...] when they play the Aladdin's lamp game people say they would like to change just the height or whatever, I say the whole body. I hate everything about my body, especially the most feminine parts, my hips, my breasts, I hate being so female!"

She progressively moves towards terminating treatment, multiplies her acting out, changes her look, has very short hair with a sort of mohawk, which seems to match her personality more and looks very good on her.

At the beginning of this school year (she is now seventeen years old), meeting a group of girls who accept her for who she is and who share homosexual experiences with her has made her feel less alone, yet they are confronting her with her deep and ancient experiences of loneliness (hitherto denied) and rejection (Carolina has experienced bullying episodes that she hid from her parents). Another problem then arises: she has panic attacks, and her body is one of her central problems. She feels she should be "thrown away the way she is, the way she was born, the way she grew up, she is not good in anything, needs to be rebuilt, the body reshaped, the breasts compressed". Her cutting increases, along with a state of deepening confusion and persecution, until she touches on delusional sparks. She will be admitted to a diagnostic and treatment service.

Treated pharmacologically and later in a community, she will show marked improvements after a few years. The most important event, however, is another. In the community, Carolina and a peer guest of her age fall in love, and Carolina has her first tender sexual relations, as she tells her therapist when she visits her spontaneously to say goodbye.

I will now report a clinical fragment from the work with Carolina.

Carolina is a fan of body-modelling, and her ideal is "fitspo" (fitspo is a physique in which muscles are defined, but not exaggeratedly so), and an athletic body. One dream, the only dream a year and a half from the beginning of therapeutic work, seems significant to me: "*I am on a canoe*" she says, "*on a mountain river, at a certain point a lot of other canoes arrive, we go down a drop and arrive where the river becomes formed by people all crowded together, very colourful, talking, feeling good, making a commotion, there is a head … an arm … I pass over it with the canoe and wake up out of anguish*".

The patient associates her trips to the mountains and the canoe she used at the beach, yet she points out that the one in the dream was an all-enclosed kayak, even on top, and sharp. The river of people was the same as the road she travelled with her friends when she had a sort of panic attack because of all those people.

We might wonder whether Carolina, to cope with her panic in the crowd, her social anxiety, turned her body into a phallic container within which to hide, in her omnipotent fantasy. This kayak is like a sharp cocoon that hides her, hides a little girl who lives inside to defend herself from a frightening river of people, a little girl who nevertheless passes omnipotently over people's heads. The primitive maternal aspect and the phallic dimension are contained in this "body-kayak" object that omnipotently fuses the qualities of the masculine and the feminine, albeit remaining split off from Carolina. The omnipotent and confusing bisexual fantasy that rejects sexual differentiation is present in this bizarre object that is split off from her, but also seems to defend her from her panic anxieties about relating to other people.

Comment

In light of all these considerations, we might conclude that in Carolina's case, we are dealing with a pubertal conflict that time and therapeutic work have been able to address.

Carolina hates her female body, showing a childhood terror of merging with her mother and an inability to turn towards a passive and affectless father. The lack of primitive mirroring (Carolina has never been seen, as she herself says), generates a hunger for mirroring in her. Identity is thus achieved, not only by confronting the non-self in order to differentiate oneself, but also in the relationship with the same, with the similar. The other in the group is the double of the self and supports the organisation of a primary identity, which is often lacking in these patients. In asking the analyst to call her by the masculine pronoun and in binding her prominent breasts, she attempts to create a relational fiction where the other, the analyst, is initially forced to pretend to see what is not there, and she attempts to operate a body modification (that too, a pretence). Carolina uses appearance to construct a sort of identity for herself by apparently eluding the complex process of maturation and associated conflicts. Running through the brief case notes, we observe that, at first, Carolina's uncertainty found its organisation in a group of boys and girls with similar issues and, using an internet blog, this uncertainty lost its characteristics of inner struggle and became amplified by the comparisons with other adolescents.

This teenager's exhibited membership in a complex movement that from the United States to Europe is involving many, might appear to us as a still uncertain attempt to belong to a peer group, with the paradoxical goal of differentiating oneself in the undifferentiated.

I believe Carolina's story to be paradigmatic of two significant aspects:

1 The structuring influence of the peer group, known both personally and within chats, in determining gender identity. In this sense, identity is not only the product of an individual process, but in whole or in part, it is a group identity, the result of

the culture and phantasm of a group, be it a family or society or a peer group.

2   Clinging to the body (Carolina begins her journey by expressing anguish through cutting, and over time changes the way she dresses and postures her body, without mentioning the powerful somatization of her menstrual cycle). These patients desperately need to "cling to something", lest they fall into total disorganisation.

Clinging to the body is for Carolina, and for many adolescents today, both an extreme defence and an extreme resource. But the body we have is partly the one defined by our biology and partly the one modified by the gaze of the other, the touch of the other, the word of the other: mother, father, partner, environment, mass media. In Carolina's as in other similar cases, we might note the effort to impress the other, in the sense of arousing the impression in the other, conditioning them in their vision, forcing them to dissociate the real vision of his or her body, which in his or her view, the analyst must see as male, otherwise treatment will be terminated. Carolina's story, as I have already mentioned, ended with her overcoming her anguishes and confusions. Her subsequent experiences with a boy in the community seem to me a significant response to our diagnostic perplexities, if there ever were any.

The transgender solution

However, in a small percentage of patients this is not the case. We are faced with other phenomena that are increasingly frequent to our observation today. Our society, with the undifferentiated, the ambiguous, of rejection of limits, has had one virtue: it has allowed for the emergence of identities that were previously covered to others and even to oneself. We are confronted with specific problems that the PDM has declassified from the realm of pathology, rather emphasising with this term – as Lingiardi et al. (2020) tell us – the painful and anguishing emotional component.

The symbiosis between mother and future transsexual child is mentioned by Stoller as one of the roots of this problem. Stoller deems decisive the quality of the symbiotic relationship created by the mothers of these patients in order to alleviate the deep sense of depressed emptiness that characterises them, and the unconscious connivance of the father figure who does not intervene to prevent, but rather encourages the process of feminisation of the child. He argues that the transexual's identity disorder is not psychotic in nature given that the "delusion" lies within a condition in which reality testing appears intact.

Person and Oversey (1974, 1974a) put forward a position that I consider more accurate and respectful of diversity in clinical practice. These authors consider the possibility of different gradations in the phenomenon by distinguishing, for example, primary and secondary transsexuality, in which they count transvestism, but more importantly, they relate the diversity of pathology to the different sub-stages of the separation–individuation process. They therefore state that children may present differing graduality in their response to the trauma of separation with which they may be forced to grapple prematurely, before the stage of separation between self and object has come to an end. In certain situations, trauma so premature that it carries a threat of fragmentation and annihilation may prompt the child to resort to a fantasy of symbiotic fusion with the mother. Within such a fantasy, the danger of separation is not so much faced or avoided, but rather "nullified", as these authors report, by maintaining an omnipotent fusion with the mother. Agnés Oppenheimer states that the mother of the male transsexual does not confirm her son in his masculinity and uses him for her own narcissism, in the absence of a father who disqualifies him and does not allow being idealised by him as male. Hatred of masculinity ensues, with the construction of a "screen identity" and a neo-reality (Oppenheimer, 1991) consisting of withdrawal from reality and a kind of permanent acting out determined by hatred of masculinity and a denial of homosexuality. Colette Chiland (2005), who has devoted years of work to these patients, speaks instead of the total absence of parental investment in the child's experience of his or her body, disqualifying at length and covertly. Far more accurately, Alessandra Lemma states that, in these cases, "the parent's inability to mirror a child's experience of their body state may contribute to developmental distortions that can manifest clinically as disturbances in sexual development and gender identification" (Lemma, 2015b, p. 98). Following Lemma, it is the process of intersubjective mirroring of body states that is at issue in this field.

In the case of full-blown dysphoria, in addition to the marked body/mind dissociation and the defensive clinging to the symptom, one element seems significant to me: the pursuit of a body that does not exist, which desperately the transgender individual seeks for life, and which is often imagined and idealised. This is not, however, a delusional position embedded in the body, as one might think in patients who use the transgender choice as a defence against breakdown, since "real" transgender individuals do not negate the existence or appearance of their genitalia, or secondary sexual characteristics. Rather, they appear to not bear them and to want to hide them. As mentioned at the beginning of this chapter, hatred and a deep desire to undo the monstrous child body they feel inside are central. It is a dissociation between two identities, the one they feel is apparent, and precisely what we might call "a screen", and the one they feel is deeper. Therefore, in these patients the surgical or medical attempt to intervene with a "transition" then paradoxically configures as an attempt to reduce this dissociation.

This very aspect seems crucial to me, and I have observed it in certain patients of mine with dysphoric disorders, particularly in a transgender male adolescent who wanted to transition. He was a boy of tremendous intelligence and ability who, after the first year in which even for him the defence defined by some as "no entry" had unfolded in all its rigidity, opened himself to a deeper understanding. His mother was a severe borderline who had sequestered him as a child, in fact never capable of any mirroring or recognition of otherness. Giulio says that when they went jogging with his mother, passers-by wondered whether his mother was male or female. His mother had also, shortly before Giulio's birth, undergone a very complicated late-stage abortion that had strongly scarred her, and this traumatic event may have perhaps influenced Giulio, strongly increasing his bond with his mother.

The parents argued frequently and violently.

Giulio had been bullied as a child in a village where he spent his vacations. His first year was marked by long grievances against the violence his parents and brother showed him. He frequently sent me videos of domestic violence, and they ended up in the emergency room for a variety of reasons on a weekly basis.

All of this convinced me to intervene with the family, facilitating separation between the parents, who lived in another city, and the children.

Progressively, Giulio gained confidence and trust in the analysis, and the sessions were enriched with his memories, reflections and numerous dreams. The sessions had become truly intensive work for him, where the experiences of his life emerged. Giulio, although he was curious about it and practised masturbation, would have liked to eliminate sex, which caused him such anguish, and would have liked to postpone it temporally in his imagination to the magical moment when he would become a woman. In his fourth year, when he had decided to take hormones and had feminised his image, he brought his revulsion for male genitalia into a dream. In fact, *he dreamed of masturbating and ejaculating pieces of his genitals. He took these pieces, including his testicles, and laid them aside. They looked like indistinct pieces of flesh to him, but he was happy to expel them.* In his associations, he regretted hating his genitals, a feeling that seemed exaggerated. The rawness and concreteness of this dream are astonishing in a sensitive, educated and intelligent young man, yet parts of it showed the indistinctness that still lingered within him, as well as his feeling of carrying a monstrous and repulsive part within.

Only after surgery, in his opinion, would he finally experience the emotions of sexuality, which he did not feel even in his homosexual initiation, carried out more out of duty of knowledge than out of interest in his partner. At times, he seemed to have an entirely theoretical idea of sex, as if massively negating all desire and drive. For some of these patients, whom I have encountered, sex is an issue they would gladly do without, and sometimes exhibited.

One of the recurring themes, also present in his dreams, was that of the body.

One dream at the end of his first year of psychotherapy is significant: *he was standing in a place full of statues, and for each statue there was a sculptor forging it.* Through subsequent associations, this dream leads us to discuss his desire to forge his body, to have a wonderful body, while he felt ugly and felt his sexual characteristics as unbearable. In fact, Giulio compressed his genitals with bands when he went out. His mother and sister had performed countless cosmetic surgeries, both in a repetitive and compulsive way. Furthermore, at the end of the first year, concealing his intentions from me, he came after having rhinoplasty and facial feminisation. He was in admiration of two singers, a man and a woman, both very ambiguous, whose beauty made him ecstatic. Especially with one of them, he seemed to manifest total identification. In his imagination, at times he and the other were the same person, but he also knew that he was himself. Achieving his identity was a longed-for process and this theme was especially dominant in the beginning, appearing in all its complexity in his dreams that filled the sessions, as Giulio was attached to the analysis and very interested in the work of elaboration.

In a Monday session, sixteen months into treatment, he told a dream: *he was going to a costume party and found himself with the wings of a butterfly.* He associated his wish with a future surgical transformation of his body into a woman as beautiful as a butterfly. Of course, it did little good to tell him that he himself had dreamed of a costume party and that the butterfly wings belonged to a mask. I wondered whether he might, after all, be thinking of the future operation as masquerading himself.

As the work continued, two dissociated aspects became evident: on one hand he continued to develop with active conviction his theory of being transgender, that he had hated his body since he was very small and that he would only be enormously happy when he became a woman. On the other hand, every now and then, beneath the propaganda sold with phrases and concepts drawn from the internet transgender world, which he repeated at the beginning of many sessions, deep anguishes and conflicts would appear, such as the enormous disappointment of being abandoned by a boy he was in love with when he confessed to him that he felt like a woman inside. This event had great traumatic significance for him. He in fact claimed to be a heterosexual woman. The anguish of an underlying identity void seemed to emerge from afar.

This period culminated in a session at a time in which he reported another dream that very eloquently describes the ways in which he was counteracting the void. In the dream, *the singer with whom he massively identified, without any difference, was clinging to a rock suspended in the void and had to hold on with great strength in order not to fall endlessly. He climbed up the rock, but the rock crumbled, and he remained anchored to a fragment that looked like some kind of meteorite left in the void. He desperately spun around.* Giulio recalled how, when approaching puberty around the age of fourteen, the whole world had crumbled. We delved together into the subject of his feeling like the singer clinging to the rock, as he had associated, and Giulio stated that he "didn't exist, wasn't there" unless he totally identified with one of the singers he admired.

I believed the latter to be a significant dream, given that it expressed the patient's loneliness, his clinging to something that perhaps could relate to his body, which, however, was crumbling, spinning in circles, without finding a connection, a solution. Another plausible hypothesis was that he was desperately attached to the mother-rock, both isolated in the world and inextricably bound to survive. Only by using this extreme defence could he exist. In September of his third year of analysis, Giulio separates from his parents and moves to another city where he begins complex training work. He compensates for this commitment with theatre work, which seems to fulfil him. In the new city, he continues to frequently feel persecuted by people, especially the elderly ladies, whom he fears may offend him, and by present and future loneliness, which he inevitably believes people like him may encounter. The deep pain and anguish he carries express themselves through acting out, dreams, or allusions that I can trace in what he tells me. A failed suicide disguised as a car accident was a difficult episode that troubled us both and that he had reported to me carefully. We worked at length on this episode, which he presented as unintentional, whilst acknowledging its bizarre nature. Continuing in clinical work, Giulio, who was living in a rented room with other peers, began oestrogen hormone treatment and strongly accentuated a way of presenting himself that appeared forced and extreme in its feminine appearance. Another person seems to have superimposed himself on him, an invasive mask, yet Giulio claims to be happier. However, he is increasingly able to talk explicitly about his moments of anguish, fears, sense of loneliness and persecution.

At that time (the fourth and a half year of work), a dream appeared in a session at the beginning of the week, showing unspeakable pain: *he realised his mouth was full of pieces of glass, but he had no pain or blood.* No association accompanied this dream, which personally troubled me in signifying how hurt his body could be, how much sharp glass he had had to swallow from a very young age, and how the only way to defend himself was his dissociation.

Comment

I have found these characteristics in other patients with true gender dysphoria. Like Giulio, they presented an inability to recognise themselves in their childhood photos, they particularly accentuated characteristics of aesthetic identity in order to be accepted, they had failed to find objects of identification in their childhood or adolescence, and they felt a great emptiness inside. I believe these dynamics forced them to invent an identity that seems to have been carefully constructed. The idealisation of another body, a body that is not there and the continuous theme of the actor, of someone who, in order to exist, must pretend or put on a mask that conceals an enigmatic figure (as in other dreams of Giulio's), are some types of possible mental functioning I have found in these patients. Giulio then shows us, in the dream of the rock suspended in the void, this powerful mechanism by which it is the other, his idealised actor, that exists. Adolescence, given all the reasons I have extensively discussed in this book, naturally brought these issues to a collision. Some of these patients, like Giulio, would like to stop time. Lemma notes that when these patients succeed in delaying puberty with medication, the effect is to alter time "when the modification is aimed at deleting what the body unconsciously represents for that individual" (Lemma, 2015a, p. 76).

I believe this reflection to be logical and plausible for some, yet I also believe that in others, stopping the time of bodily transformations that progressively increase after puberty is rather lingering in "timelessness", in an infinite stand-by, a no-man's-land where choice is avoided and for some, the deep sense of sexuality avoided.

I argue that in Giulio's case, we are in the presence of such primitive trauma that it has become a constituent part of his bodily self. Moreover, as happens in the most primitive situations, the environmental dynamic is so embedded in shared functioning that to dislodge a cornerstone, if that were ever possible, would bring down the whole edifice.

Our task as analysts will therefore be to accept the limits of our work.

Conclusions

Clinical work with these patients calls into question countless aspects of psychoanalysis, and also of our technique.

It is essential to carry out careful assessment that distinguishes the various forms of the transgender phenomenon, and especially to highlight situations where the gender identity problem is the way through which a potential breakdown manifests itself. For others who claim a "transgender identity", it is necessary to avoid taking normative positions that would only constitute a new and repeated traumatisation that Avgi Saketopoulou (2014) called "massive gender trauma" for people who have not been recognised in their identity since childhood, and especially by their parents.

What the origin of this dysphoria is, whether primary and not secondary to a primitive and severe psychic conflict, is still largely debated. Some hold that there is a biological origin that is articulated around an environmental determinant.

Personally, I have formed the opinion that these individuals have experienced very primitive trauma that has been stored in their bodies. Solms (2016) hypothesises that prenatal trauma could affect gender identity.

All these considerations may change our perspectives of patient therapy while the fact remains certain that gender identity is varied, "a complex, multi-faced experience" (Harris, 2009) and can integrate with the sexed body, or conversely present itself in variously dissociated forms. The position of the caregiver must then seek to comprehend such complexity, and sometimes it would be better to respect the compensatory solutions that a person may use towards their recent or remote traumatic suffering, or towards their being a stranger to self or others, without imposing norms that are sometimes determined by social prejudice that is built into culture and society. In this regard, Juliet Mitchell states that the concept of "sexual difference" – the correct term for the psychoanalytic understanding of masculinity and femininity – implies "reproduction", whereas "gender", used indiscriminately today, shows a shift towards a sexuality that is neither primarily nor predominantly procreative (2004, p. 67). This predominance implies an Oedipal or pre-oedipal organisation, while a non-reproductive sexuality arises from relationships that are not vertical but lateral, which begin with fraternal relationships in a context of peers, or later kindreds (*Ibid.*, p. 75).

With an eye on these new phenomena, certain pillars of psychoanalysis, as well as anthropology, seem to fall in the background, thus perhaps requiring new re-conceptualisations.

Notes

1 Carolina is a patient I treated in supervision.
2 An enormous amount of anthropological and sociological studies, essays and manifestos have proliferated on these topics. Including such studies here would exceed the purpose of this work. Suffice it to say here that the term "queer" is an "umbrella term that encompasses both the vindication of sexual practices that are culturally and socially labeled as marginal", and a series of theoretical elaborations brought

together under the term "queer theory". The queer affirms the transitivity of genders and questions the stability of identity. Sexuality is considered not as an objective reality, but "as a shifting terrain continually redefined by the discourses, representations and self-representations of specific cultural subjects" [tr. by O.M.] (Pustianaz, 2004, p. 441). The queer oppose aligning themselves in any category of identity and seek "to deconstruct any position that asserts a sharp division between sex as a biological datum, gender and sexual desire" [tr. by O.M.] (Demaria, 2007, p. 165).

References

Augé, M. (1994). *Le Sens des Autres: Actualité de l'Anthropologie*. Paris: Fayard.

Benjamin, J. (1995). *Like subjects, love objects: Essays on recognition and sexual difference*. Yale University Press.

Chiland, C. (2005). I genitori dei pazienti transessuali. *Interazioni, 2005*, 1: 35–41.

Demaria, C. (2007). Genere e soggetti sessuati: Le rappresentazioni del femminile. In C. Demaria and S. Nergaard (Eds.), *Studi culturali: Temi e Prospettive a Confronto*. Milano: McGraw-Hill.

Di Ceglie, D. (2018). The use of metaphors in understanding atypical gender identity development and its psychosocial impact. *Journal of Child Psychotherapy, 44*, 1, 5–28.

Dimen, M. and V. Goldner, Eds. (2002). *Gender in psychoanalytic space: between clinic and culture*. New York: Other Press.

Drescher, J. and W. Byne, Eds. (2013). *Treating transgender children and adolescents: An interdisciplinary discussion*. London: Routledge.

Freud, S. (1905). Three essays on the theory of sexuality. *S.E.* 7: 123–146, London: Hogarth Press.

Freud, S. (1923a). The infantile genital organization (An interpolation into the theory of Sexuality). *S.E.* 19: 139–146, London: Hogarth Press.

Freud, S. (1930). Civilization and its discontents. *S.E.* 21: 57–146, London: Hogarth Press.

Galatzer-Levy, R. and B.J. Cohler (2002). Making a gay identity: Coming out, social context, and psychodynamics. *The Annual of Psychoanalysis, 30*, 255–286.

Harris, A. (2009). *Gender as soft assembly*. New York: Routledge.

Laufer, E.M. (2002). Il corpo come oggetto interno. In A.M. Nicolò and I. Ruggiero (Eds.), *La Mente Adolescente e il Corpo Ripudiato*. Milano: Franco Angeli.

Lemma, A. (2010). *Under the skin: A psychoanalytic study of body modification*. London: Routledge.

Lemma, A. (2015a). Present without past: The disruption of temporal integration in case of adolescent transsexuality. In *Minding the Body: The Body in Psychoanalysis and Beyond*. London: Routledge.

Lemma, A. (2015b). The body one has and the body one is: The transsexual's needs to be seen. In *Minding the Body: The Body in Psychoanalysis and Beyond*. London: Routledge.

Lemma, A. and P.E. Lynch (2015). Let's talk about sex or ... maybe not ... In Lemma A. and P.E. Lynch (Eds.), *Sexualities: Contemporary Psychoanalytic Perspectives*. London: Routledge.

Leuzinger-Bohleber, M. (2008). Biographical truths and their clinical consequences: Understanding 'embodied memories' in a third psychoanalysis with a traumatized patient recovered from severe poliomyelitis. *International Journal of Psychoanalysis, 89*, 1165–1187.

Lev, A.I. (2004). *Transgender emergence: Therapeutic guidelines for working with gender-variant people and their families*. Haworth: Haworth Clinical Practice Press.

Lingiardi, V., N. McWilliams, and A.M. Speranza (2020). *PDM-2 0/18: Infanzia e adolescenza*. Milano: Raffaello Cortina.

Marion, P. (2017). Il Disagio del Desiderio: Sessualità e Procreazione nel Tempo delle Biotecnologie. Roma: Donzelli.

Merleau-Ponty, M. (1945), *Phenomenology of perception*. New York: Routledge, 2012.

Mitchell, J. (2004). The difference between gender and sexual difference. In I. Matthis, Eds. (2004), *Dialogues on Sexuality, Gender and Psychoanalysis*. London: Routledge.

Oppenheimer, A. (1991). The wish for a sex change: A challenge to psychoanalysis? *International Journal of Psychoanalysis, 72*, 221–231.

Person, E. and L. Oversey (1974). The transsexual syndrome in the male: I. Primary Transsexualism. *American Journal of Psychotherapy, 28*, 1, 4–20.

Person, E. and L. Oversey (1974a). The transsexual syndrome in the male: II. Secondary transsexualism. *American Journal of Psychotherapy, 28*, 2, 174–193.

Preta, L. (2019). Ragazzi e gender: cosa rischiamo di non capire. *La Repubblica*, June 29th, 2019.

Pustianaz, M. (2004). Studi queer. In M. Cometa, R. Coglitore, and F. Mazzara (Eds.), *Dizionario degli Studi Culturali*. Roma: Meltemi.

Saketopoulou, A. (2014). Mourning the body as bedrock: Developmental considerations in treating transsexual patients analytically. *Journal of the American Psychoanalytic Association, 62*, 5, 733–806.

Solms, M. (2016). The biological foundations of gender: A delicate balance. In G. Schreiber (Ed.), *Transsexualität in Theologie und Neurowissenschaften*. Berlin: De Gruyter.

Sprinz Mondrzak, V. (2019). The feminine, the maternal and the sexual body in adolescence. Talk presented at the panel *The feminine, the Maternal and the Sexual Body in Adolescence*, IPA Congress, London.

Steensma, T.D., J.K. McGuire *et al.* (2013). Factors associated with desistence and persistence of childhood gender dysphoria: A quantitative follow-up study. *Journal of the American Academy of Child and Adolescent Psychiatry*, *52*, 6, 582–590.

Stoller, R.J. (1968). *Sex and gender: The development of masculinity and femininity*. London: Routledge.

Thanopulos, S. (2019). La disforia dell'identità sessuale. *Il Manifesto*, July 13th, 2019.

Winnicott, D.W. (1971b). Creativity and its origins. In (1971) *Playing and Reality*. London: Routledge, 2005.

15

SELF-HARM AND CUTTING

Multiple forms of skin injury have currently taken on epidemic prominence.

Some have always found social and cultural validation, such as with piercings and tattoos, while others are astonishing in their violence and destructiveness, such as burns and cutting and body stitching, which involves embroidery and stitching on the skin. Some piercings seem to reinforce particular sensations, such as those on the genitals; others serve to indelibly mark particular memories of significant events; still others seem to exhibit fantasies to the world about one's identity or how one imagines it, or about one's ideals or manifest covenants of friendship or love or loyalty to the group, to a cause.

However, in order to understand this growing phenomenon, it is necessary to answer a number of questions. For example: what is the relationship between these forms of acting out and the underlying personality? To what extent does adolescence, as a phase-specific type of mental functioning, influence these phenomena? What is the relationship to peer group dynamics? Many other questions crowd our minds, and we wonder, for example, whether it matters how much pain these adolescents inflict on themselves through these practices and what weight the manipulation of the body and the resulting blood loss have. Clinical experience also teaches us that some of these skin wounds are related to self-hatred and self-destructive aspects, to the extent that increasingly severe self-mutilations are sometimes the prodromes of a suicide attempt. In all cases, however, they signal a failure in the process of elaboration and integration of the new, sexed body.

DOI: 10.4324/9781032663371-18

The skin and its meanings

It is doubtless that in this period of life the surface of the skin fulfils, in its role as an erogenous zone, a manifold function in the child's growth (Freud, 1936). The skin, with the sensations it triggers, is internalised as a container (Bick, 1968). But still to be a body, to have a body and to be able to inhabit it (Maiello, 2014) requires that the child and then adolescent have internalised an object with a container function.

Further, as asserted by Freud (1920; 1923; 1925), Bick (1968) and Anzieu (1985), the skin fulfils defensive functions of para-excitation, marking the boundary and border with the outside, but also with the mother or caregiver in general, and can come to represent a "surface of inscription" of all those fantasies, conflicts, and anguishes which – to paraphrase Anzieu (*Ibid.*) – having not found a shell of words, seek in the skin a shell that may somehow signify them. It is also connected with an aspect of identity.

Beneath these phenomena that refer to multiple personal, group, sociological and anthropological meanings (Le Breton, 2004), different dynamics might be concealed. Adolescents themselves ascribe different meanings to them. I would distinguish two categories of marks on the skin, the first more common where the skin functions as a screen for the adolescent's projections, and towards symbolisation.

In this case, tattoos and piercings have a proto-symbolic poignancy: as Catherine Chabert says, they are "attempts at figuration" insofar as they appear to lie halfway between "intentionality, conscious and unconscious", yet also represent "a defence and an elaboration", thus remaining as productions in between the acted out and the symbolised [tr. by O.M.] (Chabert, 1999, p. 60).

In other adolescents, on the other hand, we are faced with more complex situations, such as cutting, which is widespread in a certain group of adolescents, much more than is generally believed. Some of these patients "inflict a real wrapping of suffering on themselves as a way of recreating the function of containing skin function which the mother or the carers have not provided" (Anzieu, 1985, p. 226–227).

The attempt is to self-create that originally severely damaged primitive holding.

In the most extreme situations, the resort to wounding or cutting oneself confers a sense of existence and reality. These latter cases should attract the analyst's attention, given that hatred of the split body is therein manifested, and sometimes prodromes of far more severe attacks on one's own or the other's body, such as suicide attempts.

The skin and self-aggression

Nevertheless, we cannot deny the fact that breaking into the body also refers to a self-aggressive dynamic, for example, turning towards the self an aggression that would otherwise have been directed against the other. In the most severe forms, this dynamic takes on preponderant importance, as we shall see in a case I will report.

In this category of cutting, some adolescents use cutting to evacuate exaggerated tension. When under pressure, they cut themselves, or rather they cut the connection between the thought and awareness, which they feel is too painful, and the act. In these cases, we are speaking of a physical cut that, in producing a sensation of physical pain, casts out and overcomes mental pain. We are therefore talking about a psychic cut of which the physical cut is only the concrete equivalent.

Let us see what happens to Amedeo,[1] twenty-three years old.

Amedeo cuts his chest with a razor blade. The cuts are deep, sharp and regular, leaving deep scars that he feels proud of, and that make him feel more virile. He says the cuts are produced as punishment for the shame he feels after outbursts of great jealousy towards his girlfriend, to whom he constantly attributes thoughts of betrayal and fantasies of desire for strong, Apollonian and virile men.

Amedeo punishes himself for not being sufficiently manly, like the people he imagines his partner is attracted to, and for being unable to contain his jealousy.

He loathes his body. He does not deserve anything, his is a small, ugly, and hideous body. He adds that lately, he has also been trying to purify himself through self-deprivation of food and by drinking eight litres of water a day to cleanse himself: everything that comes in, then goes out. He is also afraid of food in his tummy, of the feeling of fullness, of satiety, perceptions that give him a sense of disgust and revulsion, he feels lazy and inept, while fasting provides him with a sense of purity, purification and elevation. Thus, he begins to impose on himself a rationing of food equal to a quarter of what he would like to eat.

Amedeo is terrified by the image of an unemployed, undershirt-wearing father who sits all day in front of the television in an armchair, railing against the world. He fears that his father's anger and passivity will infect him. He tells about the disgust he feels when he hears him breathe, fearing that the wheezing might enter his nostrils. For a long time, he lives in the house with earplugs in his ears, day and night, to protect himself from what he calls "disgusting penetration".

Amedeo blames his mother for not protecting him from his father and from his hatred, for having always idealised him, Amedeo, too much, considering him a genius, a special boy who should not mix with peers, and for having tormented him with food. Against this food intrusion, as he considers it, Amedeo defends himself by feeling strong enough to resist and eliminate the food he does not want.

In a session during his second year of therapy, he says that his girlfriend got a ring from a friend, and he "lost it". In fact, he took to breaking things, evoking his usual fantasies of "Apollonian" men possessing her and whom he describes as strong and muscular, qualities he acknowledges he does not have. He then says that in the evening he again injured his chest with a razor, taking his usual pleasure in discovering those scars on his chest a few hours later.

He soon speaks of the horror he felt at the account of a friend (a girl) who ended up in the car with a friend of his, with whom she had oral intercourse on that occasion. He was chilled by the girlfriend's amused comments, he indeed speaks his helplessness, his feeling small, different, incapable, in front of men who "fuck" and rape.

"You know", he tells his psychotherapist, "yesterday I decided to tattoo on my chest 'liar' on one side and 'parricide' on the other, I think it's important, it's a sign I want".

Comment

The complex dynamics in which Amedeo struggles appear obvious to all of us.

Behind the fantasy of the idealised male body that he does not possess, unlike other men who therefore have the upper hand over him, there is the ambivalent attraction and disgust in the face of incestual fears for his father, who also represents a passive part of himself that Amedeo abhors. The mother does not help him, drawing him instead towards a primitive and infantilised type of relationship.

Body cuts coagulate numerous meanings in themselves: they reinforce a fragile male identity, punish a body experienced as insignificant, horrid and above all distant from the ideal model he would have liked to represent, a body that also entails the terror of homosexual and passive feelings that frighten him.

The tattoo with the words "liar" and "parricide" seems to explicitly refer on the one hand to Amedeo's need to rid himself of his attraction to the passivity represented by his father. More obscure, however, seems to be the reference to "liar" where, with a paradoxical twist, Amedeo seems to make all his achievements false, but at the same time to assert an identity of his own in the negative. This tattoo with its explicit lettering also seems to express aspects of Amedeo's reflections on his identity and anguishes around his unconscious homosexual fantasies, and is a communication to others and to himself. Yet, the real problem is the very fact that Amedeo confines these statements to an acting out on his skin, placing them again somewhere between the symbolic and the acted out, between thinking and acting, in a sort of suspension that is difficult to resolve. Carving those thoughts on the skin almost seems to petrify them by immobilising them and preventing evolution, although this acting out is certainly a form of communication.

In other situations, such manifestations are so massive and destructive as to be connoted by self- and hetero-destructive dynamics, where the body is definitively split off and treated as an external and foreign object. The latter cases are the most dangerous and should attract the analyst's attention. We must undoubtedly think that, in these latter manifestations, these forms of cutting are prodromes of far more serious attacks on one's own or the other's body, such as suicide attempts.

Laura[2]

Laura's case might allow us to reflect on this, as manifestations of both levels seem to occur in this patient: one where the cut configures as a powerful communication, remaining an attempt at figuration of a conflict or need that cannot yet be expressed in words; and another that performs the function of ensuring cohesion and integration against breakdown, guaranteeing the creation of a shell with the skin.

When the consultation begins, Laura is nineteen years old. She is a highly successful sophomore at an international university and is virtually bilingual. She is a tall girl with simple makeup. She moves stiffly and awkwardly. She never makes eye contact, at least throughout her first year of analysis. She tells her story monotonously and with technical terms, a story that she seems to have "acted" countless times.

Laura started cutting herself roughly three years ago, after two hospitalisations. At first, she saw other girls hospitalised for this reason and thought that she could never do it, that it disgusted her and even scared her. The first few times she tried to cut herself, she felt pain and looked away. Now she no longer feels anything, even if the cuts are deep. After these more striking episodes that required stitches in the hospital, her mother monitors her step by step, never allowing her to close the door to her room. University is the only place where she is left alone. Every event, whether positive or negative, causes her to take refuge in the bathrooms to repeatedly cut her arms or thighs.

Throughout her first year, Laura presents poor and repetitive dialogue, and she herself is mechanical and expressionless. She often recalls the diagnosis of Asperger's that she was given as a child following which, passively, and without conviction, she underwent psychotherapy, speech therapy, and which she uses as a calling card that gives her permission to shut down and be bizarre.

Two events, however, will alter the atmosphere of the analysis: the discovery of an abuse that Laura suffered as a child, and of a later abuse at age fifteen, which the analyst highlights as a traumatic event.

Indeed, Laura communicates the episode of adolescent abuse since the beginning of consultations:

She explains that she never told her mother about it "in order to at least have control over whom to tell or not tell". She also greatly feared her father's reaction, that "he would report everyone and anyone". She briefly recounts the incident, which occurred on a school trip, but mostly points out that the teachers did not take it into proper consideration. Even her classmates had told her, once they were found out, that their manipulating and touching her was a joke. From that moment on, voices arose inside her commanding her to cut herself. The analyst confirms to Laura that the story she tells is of real abuse that must be given credit and attention.

After a subsequent hospitalisation in the clinic due to her cutting, the patient experiences the affectionate presence of the analyst, who maintains the sessions during her hospitalisation.

In the ensuing period of analysis, Laura is gradually able to better contextualise the adolescent abuse episode, but more importantly, she reveals another disturbing episode, which occurred when she was seven years old: her private teacher forced her to kiss her on the mouth and touched her. It is Laura herself who somehow links these episodes with her current symptoms, in a sort of cause/effect relationship.

From a session.

Summarising more recently the different nature of her cuts, Laura says: *Once when the principal had excluded me from something, I don't even remember what from anymore, I carved the word "help" on my leg because I couldn't get out of the experience. It was a way of asking for help. At lunch break I had to be in the car with my father and I wrote a poem about it. It was like I was a tiger in a cage; the more the tiger grows the more the cage shrinks. Another time I carved the word "stupid" because that was how I felt. No scars remained, fortunately, they were superficial cuts. I even told a teacher at the time who had seen me crying, but she just took me to the principal. I make a lot of mistakes when I cry.*

T: *I wonder who these unheard messages were for: the principal just punished you, your parents were all concerned about not seeing you fail the year but not about the cuts, then the school psychologist who you felt betrayed by ... then the psychiatrist who knew your mother who told you that you had to go to the community. You really give me the feeling that no one felt your need for help and that there was a very claustrophobic situation where maybe you lost all hope.*

Laura adds another specification:

L: *It's not that I woke up one morning and said "now I'm going to cut myself for no reason". It's not like I started cutting myself as soon as they started ignoring me. I think it also depends on the things that happened before: the boys throwing themselves at me and touching me, on the field trip when I was fifteen ... so many things happened that no one will ever know! There are certain things that you can't even say. If I told my mother, my family would be completely destroyed.*

Laura becomes evasive, says it is not something you hear every day, and she has never talked to anyone about it.

Slowly, over the following years, the patient will return many times to the memories of her abuse, each time adding a piece to the "puzzle", as Laura calls it. With increasing awareness, she will better recount the episode in which a group of classmates on a school trip had locked her in a room and began touching her, and she will then talk about an earlier episode with a private teacher who touched her as a child.

More recently, Laura says: *I've been thinking about this disturbance I feel when they touch me. It has something to do with Asperger's, but it's not just that. It also has to do with the teacher … On Thursday, the lady who helps us at home, who also helps my grandmother, greeted me, hugged me and did this (rubs a hand on her hip). It bothered me a lot to feel that hand … I scratched myself so much that I still have the marks. I showed them to my mother, I told her: do you understand how much it bothers me? She wanted to disinfect me at all costs. But this has nothing to do with Asperger's, it's about the teacher. When she touched me when I was seven years old and asked me to kiss her* (other times Laura had recounted the episodes). In explaining why she didn't tell her mother, she adds: *Hm … I don't know … I'm afraid that she might tell me that it's not that important … that is, that the teacher thing is not so … that I'm blowing it out of proportion … but now that we're talking about it so much, I think about it, and I understand things.*

Laura recounts how, after the fact, she felt that she was being spied on, teased, that someone was trying to kill her, and she reports visual dysperceptions … *Even today I still think that maybe these things are true, but maybe, I mean I get the doubt …* In the analysis, however, she feels like she is reconstructing a puzzle, each piece falls into place. She sees that it is still incomplete, but she can see that a new picture is being composed before her eyes.

I tell her that she seems to be slipping from her world of delusions that also seemed so true to the world of reality.

Comment

We might speculate that the trauma produced by the two abuses she suffered, the first by her teacher and the second by her classmates, represented a recapitulation of one another, and both of a primal trauma related to her childhood experiences, as at one point emerges in a session that I will narrate below.

The first time, at the age of seven, Laura had reacted with emotional affective anaesthesia, a form of freezing as often happens in such cases. The guilt that causes her to cut herself could well be explained by these repeated episodes.

There was also the element of exhibition to the other and to herself. Laura looks at herself as if she were outside herself; she is the spectator of herself.

At the same time, physical trauma, as Masud Khan (1963) tells us, is always preceded by cumulative relational trauma, and in this case, it would be a recapitulation of an early trauma that had resulted in a disturbance in Laura's sensoriality and sensuality, preventing her from a healthy integration of the genital archaic (Gutton, 2003) with the new sensations of adolescence.

In this case, the real trauma had functioned as an attractor of far deeper themes related to primitive states of the mind.

This will become clearer in subsequent sessions.

The case continues and grows richer

Thanks to Laura's increased participation in the work, we are able to gain access to a panorama that was completely unknown until then.

In a Tuesday session in September, the patient talks about her effort not to hide her arms marred by cuts, and that this aroused astonishment and, she imagines, contempt in one of her friends. This fact prompted her once again to cut and burn herself. The patient claims that her cutting is normal for her, that it does not arouse her pain, unlike the burning that is sometimes painful. Moreover, showing her effort to connect with the other, she reports having talked in the group about losing her privacy because her mother now controls her.

In the next session, the analyst is able to focus with Laura on her passivity and submission to the other, to the things outside and inside her, and also to the disturbing thoughts that reproach her and force her to cut herself.

In a June session of the third year of analysis, the analyst introduces this theme by commenting on her passivity to therapies, and to her mother.

T: (Echoing what Laura said at the beginning of the session) *There is a need for you to be here with me, not only physically, but also with your will, your curiosity, some desire for change.*

L: *I don't believe that so much.*

T: *I can see that. You seem to be expecting therapy, somewhat magically, to put you back on your feet, while you keep repeating the same gestures, the same rituals.*

263

L: But therapy is supposed to help stop doing certain things.

T: Only you can stop, here we can understand why you do them, bring out the emotions you feel, make sense of them, but then it is you who, out of here, can decide how to move in the world. There must be an active part of you that decides to do otherwise.

L: And how does one want that?

T: You entrust others with your will, and you have convinced yourself that getting better or worse depends on others, and you can do nothing but be dragged along.

L: I know that in order to change I have to want it, but I don't ... I want to want it, but I can't. I feel so bad that the cuts help me for a few seconds, and I say to myself, "what do I care, let's do them again!" Sometimes, I try to avoid people who make me want to cut myself.

T: So you try to avoid certain stimuli. In the clinic you would ask for additional medication, or rather they would give it to you, but you often saw that it helped. If you had something to take as needed, even at university, I think you would avoid reaching certain levels of anguish.

L: Hm ... I have to ask mom. Another thing I could do is avoid wearing black, but it's very difficult. If I wear black, it's like I have to cut myself because I can hide it. So coloured clothes make it difficult for me. This has worked a few times.

These themes bring up the first of only two dreams that Laura recounts in the first months of treatment, and about which she makes no association: "*I dreamed that I was angry with my mother because she told me that I could not cut myself, that only she could cut me. I was angry because I wanted to do it myself, like my brother, he was allowed to cut himself*". Aside from expressing some perplexity about the nature of this dream, what is striking is the crux of who has the right to do the cutting/separation in the mother-daughter pair, and the comparison with the brother, who turns out to be autonomous and given the right to individuate himself.

Unravelling the conflict

In an attempt to curb this continuous impulse to cut, the analyst seeks to delve into the seemingly multiple and inexplicable reasons for them. One forcefully emerging element is the severe punishment that the cuts represent.

In a session from the same period:

L: *Ha!* (she smiles), *these days a teacher told me that I shouldn't be so hard on myself. I don't know, I asked her for clarification by email about the layout of the papers to be handed in to her … I didn't want to get a lower grade for something silly.*

T: *The teacher understood how demanding you can be, how strict with yourself.*

L: *Yes … now that the tests are starting, I told myself that if I don't get a certain grade, then I'll cut myself.*

T: *But why do you need to punish yourself for everything? I don't think it's just for a grade, that sounds more like an excuse to me.*

L: *In general because I suck. I have to do it, like it's an obligation. Like if you kill someone, then you have to go to jail.*

T: *You kill yourself. You seem to have a very strict judge inside you that never allows you to be wrong.*

L: *If I do something I have to punish myself; if I don't do it I have to punish myself. If I do it right I have to punish myself, if I do it so I have to punish myself. Even if I do something that is good for others I still have to punish myself. Even if I do one hundred percent I have to punish myself, I immediately think I have to cut myself … I don't know why.*

The analyst proposes not to use the concept of punishment as a synonym of cutting oneself, because one can punish oneself in so many ways. She seems to catch on and adds: *I feel guilty, but I don't know about what, there doesn't necessarily have to be a reason.*

T: *You seem to want to punish yourself just for being alive.* She nods. The analyst reminds her that in a previous session she had said that they had told her mother that there was a risk that she would not be born, and also that she blames her mother for giving birth to her.

L: *In a way, I get angry at my mother for that.*

T: *You seem to say, I shouldn't have been born and so I punish myself for that.* (She nods again.) *The price of all this, however, is your life. And not living is not good, it doesn't give relief, it just isn't, you don't exist.*

L: *That's what I want.*

T: *It seems that you really live trying not to exist, not allowing yourself a normal life. And that you punish both yourself and your mother in this way.*

Pause.

L: Yes, but I don't punish her on purpose. I did say something like that to her once, though … I don't really remember, surely it had something to do with the fact that I was never born, that it was her fault that I'm like this, something about her giving birth to me. She was a little bit hurt by that. I don't know why I came out like that, but it just came to me. I was blaming her, but she didn't do it with bad intentions.

T: Of course not, but maybe it is also right that you can say what you feel, also to differentiate yourself from her, from her thinking. And to relieve, at least of this part, all the hatred you feel, which would then not fall back only and always on yourself, with the consequence of hurting yourself.

L: This is also why I cut or hurt myself, so that I don't think about this. I really did it in all kinds of ways. For the burns I got, I can feel the holes in my skin. If my mother could see it … she's used to the cuts, but not to this.

T: And when you see these holes or feel them by touching yourself, what do you think?

L: That I have to make more, that I deserve them.

T: But you also tell me that it bothers you when you touch yourself to you rub soap on your skin.

L: Yes … but I always think I deserve it, that's the thought that's always there, that leads me to make them. I have to punish myself again and again … I think I only deserve the burns, the cuts, these things.

T: You need to be loved a lot so that you can hate yourself less.

L: I don't think that's possible.

T: I do have this hope, since you told me that you are pleased when Maia (her little dog) runs to you and shows you that she missed you, that she wants to be with you. And so do I, so do your parents care about you, not just Maia.

L: Sometimes Maia is one of the thoughts that stop me … .

T: For now you can only feel her affection, but believe me, people have it for you too.

The next month the analyst notices that the patient is able to look at her and communicate more confidentially, as with her friend, but the analyst feels that "the pain inside" has no words. The cuts she can describe and talk about replace this inner pain, which she feels is far greater and more devastating than the injuries she inflicts upon herself.

In a session the following month, Laura appears more elegant. It was her mother who chose her dress. She talks about her talk with a friend, who asked her if she feels pain from the cuts. She does not actually feel pain. Maybe the burns hurt her, but in truth, she adds, *I found that ... there is the smell ... like ... of burnt. I thought it wouldn't leave marks, like instead maybe getting dirty like when I cut myself, instead ... it smells like burnt flesh.*

T: *Like a body that is tortured, sacrificed, that you seem to have to crush.*
L: *It's not so painful compared to what pain is for me.*
T: *The pain inside? It seems there is huge pain inside, a hatred for yourself and your body, impossible to handle, and that what you show in the cuts, in the burns, on the outside, is just pain that's more tolerable for you.*
L: *That's right. The one inside is a pain that I can't describe in words, I don't know what it is.*
T: *The cuts, burns and everything else, on the other hand, have a name, a meaning for you, and also for those who observe you.*
L: *That's right, the cuts I know, the pain inside I don't ... .*

She goes into a meticulous description of the most recent burns she sometimes inflicts on herself.

Laura repeats that there does not need to be a reason, that she can do it at any time, for something that happens to her, but also for no reason.

She then tells of a compliment she received that she had to undo by cutting herself.

Comment

I particularly wish to focus on the anaesthesia that the patient operates, and on the distinction she makes between the pain from the cuts and from the burns, as well as between physical and mental pain. It seems to me that in this case, as in others, massive dissociation serves to create a defensive shell against suffering, which constitutes a constructed manoeuvre against mental pain. Of great interest to me is the sensory distinction she makes between the pain of the skin and the smell of the burn, a smell that she feels is particularly disturbing.

This sort of diversification of sensations could be likened to the sensory disassembly of which Meltzer spoke (Meltzer et al., 1975) regarding autistic children. The scars that she feels as shameful also serve to hide her, physically and psychologically, from the eye of the other and from her own eye. It is important to note the accurate naming of emotions on the part of the analyst, who puts the patient in touch with her affect and emotional experiences to allow her greater cohesion of the self. Shame, revulsion, fear, awe, pain of the other and pain in herself, all serve her to build a person and a self under the shell.

Tustin spoke of the fact that some autistic children construct sensory shapes with a "calming" function (Tustin, 1986). These are produced by the sensation of bodily movements or substances: for these children, this sensoriality becomes a sort of sensual protection through a form of self-generated encapsulation.

Indeed, Tustin reported some movements that the autistic child makes by, for example, regurgitating food. Self-sensoriality for these children "plays a role of refuge and protection against the catastrophic discovery of an untimely and traumatic separation from the maternal object" [tr. by O.M.] (Gentile, 2017, p. 172).

We may wonder whether Laura uses cutting as a way of calming herself and coping with the catastrophic anguish of a breakdown that would be plausible and possible for a more integrated ego than her own.

In her distinction between the smell of burnt and the pain she does not feel in cutting herself, Laura seems to be captured by partly isolated sensations. In this way, she does not undergo the pain or anguish that would arise from feeling her own body as separate from the mother with whom she is in constant contact.

Didier Anzieu's work on the skin-ego, and especially his observations on the bodies of the severely burned victims, have taught us that such suffering serves to recreate the containing function that was not exerted by the mother or carers (Anzieu, 1985, p. 226–227), thus re-establishing a primitive holding that was lacking or severely damaged in these patients. He also quotes Aulagnier, who observes that "it is through suffering that the body acquires its status as real object" (Aulagnier, 1979, quoted in Anzieu, 1985, p. 227; Aulagnier, 1975). This observation is particularly true in psychotics, where the resort to wounding or cutting oneself confers a sense of existence.

We may thus further delve into the meaning of these cuts that some patients inflict on themselves and which are, in such severe forms, related to a sense of an inconsistent identity, and to a loosely cohesive self that momentarily finds a break to its turbulence and anguishes, precisely thanks to the "wrapping of suffering" that is inflicted. As Anzieu again rightly points out, the investment of the painful body can thus become "narcissistic libido".

We are certainly faced with extreme remedies that nonetheless allow, by cutting the skin, to re-establish precisely some of its primitive psychological functions, such as the sense of body and ego boundaries, as well as the "feeling of being intact and cohesive" (*Ibid.*, p. 22).

Sadly, the use of cutting is becoming increasingly prevalent among adolescents. Certainly, not all those who engage in them present the severity of Laura's case. Nevertheless, certain dynamics we have seen here, albeit more nuanced and less persistent, indeed characterise these other patients.

We might ask why it is precisely in the society of well-being and pleasure that such repeated pain is pursued, with no apparent end except for its self-referral.

In the novel *The Solitude of Prime Numbers* (Giordano, 2008) this phenomenon is described through the protagonist's account of how cutting himself may be the only way to recover the lost sense of skin. The author describes the protagonist, a boy who practised cutting from an early age and who experienced a terrible sense of guilt over the death of his little sister, of which he had been the unintentional cause: "He had learned to set down first his toe and then his heel, keeping his weight towards the outside of the sole to minimise the amount of surface area in contact with the ground. He had perfected this technique years before, when he got up at night and stealthily roamed the house; when the skin of his hands had become so dry that the only way of being aware that they were still his was to pass them over a blade" (*Ibid.*, p. 91).

Notes

1 This case was treated by Dr. Manuela Romagnoli, whom I supervised. My thanks to Dr. Romagnoli.
2 This case was treated by Dr. Laura Penna, whom I supervised. I would like to thank Dr. Penna. It was also re-elaborated in a paper published in

the *Bulletin* (No. 73, pp. 218–226) of the *European Federation of Psychoanalysis* (2019).

References

Anzieu, D. (1985). *The skin-ego.* New York: Routledge, 2018.

Aulagnier, P. (1979). *Les destins du plaisir.* Paris: PUF.

Aulagnier, P. (1975). *The violence of interpretation: From pictogram to statement.* London: Routledge, 2001.

Bick, E. (1968). The experience of the skin in early object-relations. *International Journal of Psychoanalysis, 49,* 484–486.

Chabert, C. (1999). Le passage à l'acte, une tentative de figuration? In International Society for Adolescent Psychiatry, A. Bracconier, Ph. Gutton, and Ph. Jeammet (Eds.), *Troubles de la Personnalité. Troubles des Conduites.* Paris: GREUPP.

Freud, A. (1936). *The ego and the mechanisms of defence.* London: Karnac Books, 1992.

Freud, S. (1920). Beyond the pleasure principle. *S.E.* 18: 1–64, London: Hogarth Press.

Freud, S. (1923). The ego and the id. *S.E.* 19: 3–68, London: Hogarth Press.

Freud, S. (1925). A note upon the 'mystic writing-pad'. *S.E.* 19: 225–232. London: Hogarth Press.

Gentile, A. (2017). Sensorialità: dai dati al senso. *Psiche, 2017,* 1, 157–196.

Giordano, P. (2008). *The solitude of prime numbers.* London: Transworld Publishers, Random House, 2009.

Gutton, Ph. (2003). Esquisse d'une théorie de la génitalité. In *Adolescence, 21,* 2, 217–248.

Khan, M. (1963). The concept of cumulative trauma. In (1974). *The privacy of the self.* London: Routledge, 2019.

Le Breton, D. (2004). La profondeur de la peau. *Adolescence, 22,* 2, 257–271.

Maiello, S. (2014). No-body: Sull'assenza della dimensione corporea negli stati autistici. *Richard e Piggle, 22,* 4, 247–364.

Meltzer, D. et al. (1975). *Explorations in autism: A psychoanalytical study.* London: Karnac Books, 2018.

Tustin, F. (1986). *Autistic barriers in neurotic patients.* London: Routledge.

Sources

Nicolò, A.M. (1997). Delirio, secreto y reciprocidad. *Revista de Psicoanálisis de la Asociación Psicoanalítica de Madrid, 2001,* 34, 71–86.

Nicolò, A.M. (1997a). Antisocial acting-out as a defence against breakdown. In M. Bertolini, A. Giannakoulas, M. Hernandez (Eds.), *Squiggle and Spaces: Revisiting the Work of D.W. Winnicott* (*Vol. 2*). London-Philadelphia: Wurr Publishers, 2001.

Nicolò, A.M. (2000). Le rêve et la construction de l'identité à l'adolescence. *Journal de la psychanalyse de l'enfant*, *28*, 2001, 165–184.

Nicolò, A.M. (2003). Die psychotische Erkrankung in der Adoleszenz [Psychotic illness in adolescence]. *Kinderanalise*, *11*, 4, 395–415.

Nicolò, A.M. (2009b). Breakdown et solutions defensives chez l'adolescent. In S.M. Passone and F. Guignard (Eds.), *Psychanalyse de l'Enfant et de l'Adolescent: États des Lieux et des Perspectives*. Paris: Éditions, In Press.

Nicolò, A.M. (2009c). Introduzione: I mille volti della violenza in adolescenza. In A.M. Nicolò (Ed.), *Adolescenza e Violenza*. Roma: Il Pensiero Scientifico Editore.

Nicolò, A.M. (2009d). Gli agiti antisociali come difesa dal crollo: Riflessioni a partire da un caso clinico. In A.M. Nicolò (Ed.), *Adolescenza e Violenza*. Roma: Il Pensiero Scientifico Editore.

Nicolò, A.M. (2009e). Le radici familiari della violenza nei giovani. In A.M. Nicolò (Ed.), *Adolescenza e Violenza*. Roma: Il Pensiero Scientifico Editore.

Nicolò, A.M. (2015). Modifications to the technique of analysis of BPD adolescents. *Journal of Infant, Child and Adolescent Psychotherapy*, *14*, 70–81.

Nicolò, A.M. (2015a). Psychotic functioning in adolescence: The perverse solution to survive. *International Journal of Psychoanalysis*, *96*, 1335–1353.

Nicolò, A.M. (2016). Il corpo estraneo in adolescenza. In A.M. Nicolò and I. Ruggiero (Eds.), *La Mente Adolescente e il Corpo Ripudiato*. Milano: Franco Angeli.

Nicolò, A.M. (2016a). Le nuove sessualità in adolescenza e non solo. In A.M. Nicolò and I. Ruggiero (Eds.), *La Mente Adolescente e il Corpo Ripudiato*. Milano: Franco Angeli.

Nicolò, A.M. (2016b). La paura del crollo e oltre. In C. Busato Barbaglio, A. Macchia, A.M. Nicolò (Eds.), *Winnicott e la Psicoanalisi del Futuro*. Roma: Alpes Italia.

Nicolò, A.M. (2017). Ennui et adolescence: Entre défense et attente. *Revue française de Psychanalyse*, *81*, 4, 973–983.

Nicolò, A.M. (2019). Self-cutting in adolescence. *Bulletin EPF*, *73*, 218–227.

For Product Safety Concerns and Information please contact our EU
representative GPSR@taylorandfrancis.com
Taylor & Francis Verlag GmbH, Kaufingerstraße 24, 80331 München, Germany

www.ingramcontent.com/pod-product-compliance
Lightning Source LLC
Chambersburg PA
CBHW050339270326
41926CB00016B/3519